FAME
BECAME
OF HIM

FAME BECAME OF HIM

HEMINGWAY
as Public Writer

John Raeburn

Indiana University Press • *Bloomington*

Library of Congress Cataloging in Publication Data

Raeburn, John.
　　Fame became of him.

　　Includes index.
　　1. Hemingway, Ernest, 1899–1961—Appreciation.
I. Title.
PS3515.E37Z7543　1984　　　813'.52　　　83-48831
ISBN 0-253-12690-8
1 2 3 4 5 88 87 86 85 84

For
Gordon M. Raeburn
and
Katherine Calwell Raeburn

. . . the lad in the Rue Notre Dame des Champs
At the carpenter's loft on the left-hand side going down—
The lad with the supple look like a sleepy panther—
And what became of him? Fame became of him.
Veteran out of the wars before he was twenty:
Famous at twenty-five: thirty a master—
Whittled a style for his time from a walnut stick
In a carpenter's loft in a street of that April city.

—Archibald MacLeish,
"Years of the Dog"

And all the legends that he started in his life
Live on and prosper,
Unhampered now by his existence.

—Ernest Hemingway,
"T. Roosevelt"

CONTENTS

ACKNOWLEDGMENTS

Three chapters of this book first appeared in substantially different form elsewhere: Chapter 1 in the *Journal of Popular Culture;* Chapter 2 in the *Rocky Mountain Review;* and Chapter 4 in the *Fitzgerald/Hemingway Annual.* I am grateful to the editors of these publications for giving me a forum to try out some of my early ideas.

The University of Iowa awarded me an Old Gold Fellowship and a developmental leave which provided time and leisure for writing. The Graduate College of the university also granted funds for preparing the manuscript.

Eunice Prosser, who skillfully typed the manuscript, provided a number of helpful editorial suggestions.

I have had the support and unselfish assistance of a number of friends and colleagues, whom it is now a pleasure to thank formally: John Cawelti; Harry and Evelyn Dawson; Lincoln Faller; Franklin Fisher; Ed Folsom; Larry Goldstein; Kathleen Kamerick; Chris and Pam Lohmann; Joe Mullin; Lyall Powers; Bob Sayre; Bob Stilwell; Al Stone; Steve Weiland; and Jan Youga.

My largest debts of gratitude are to the following four persons, each of whom contributed substantially to the writing of this book. Bob Lucid first suggested the idea for it and provided intelligent counsel, especially when I was in the difficult early stages of writing. Jim Gindin read many of the chapters, always with a sympathetic but critical eye. In less tangible but even more important ways, he also gave much-appreciated help and encouragement. Gillian Kimble supported me in ways too numerous to list, and I shall always be grateful for and fondly remember her aid and comfort. Paul Baender gave unstintingly of his time and editorial skill when the manuscript was in its final stages. His advice immeasurably improved the clarity of its argument and its prose.

LIST OF ABBREVIATIONS

AMF   *A Moveable Feast*
DIA   *Death in the Afternoon*
EH   Ernest Hemingway
GHOA   *Green Hills of Africa*
TDS   "The Dangerous Summer"

FAME
BECAME
OF HIM

1

The Public Writer

As one of its "Photoquiz" features in the mid-1950s, *Look* magazine challenged readers to identify celebrities from photographs of each person's publicly identifying characteristic, his trademark. In one photograph, a battered military cap with "scrambled eggs" on the visor implied General Douglas MacArthur; in another, a bulbous nose suggested W. C. Fields. With a single exception all fifteen photographs were of political or show business personalities presumably familiar to *Look* readers. The exception was Ernest Hemingway, whose trademark was a curly white beard.[1] It is difficult to imagine any contemporary American writer other than Hemingway in *Look*'s photoquiz; he alone of his generation enjoyed the double distinction of being a respected novelist and a celebrity. His fame was so large that *Look* editors could legitimately place him beside Charlie Chaplin, Cary Grant, President Eisenhower, Marlon Brando, and other luminaries from the worlds of politics and entertainment. Hemingway was a "star"; he was a culture hero to millions of his countrymen, not all of them intellectuals or even readers of books.

How this novelist—one of the most significant in modern American literature—became a celebrity is the subject of this book. Hemingway's literary achievement is tangential to understanding that public fame. The clarity of his prose style in his short stories, the deft characterizations of Jake Barnes and his friends in *The Sun Also Rises*, the economy and precision in the narrative of the retreat from Caporetto in *A Farewell to Arms*, his thematic ambition in *For Whom the Bell Tolls*, none of these things which readers have honored in Hemingway's work was of crucial importance in the development of his public reputation. Many readers recognized his literary genius, but they did not make up the bulk of the audience which gave him his standing as a culture hero. That audience was composed of the millions of readers of *Life* and *Esquire*, of *Time* and *Newsweek*, and its members were not so much interested in Hemingway the craftsman and anatomist of postwar malaise as they were in Hemingway the galvanic man of action.

American cultural history provides several precedents for this kind of relationship between writer and audience. The tradition of the public writer is an old one in America, dating from the beginnings of our national literature. The public writer is one who, having first established his preeminence as an artist, becomes honored by many more people than those who ordinarily read books; his audience is a national one which cuts across divisions marked by class, social position, and education. Washington Irving was America's first public writer, his career capped by his nationally hailed appointment as United States minister to Spain. Until his crustiness alienated much of his public, James Fenimore Cooper vied with Irving as the public writer of his age. At mid-century the New England Sages—Emerson, Longfellow, Holmes, Lowell, and Whittier—assumed a national prominence they were to maintain for over a generation. They were succeeded by Mark Twain, who very nearly achieved his ambition to be the "most conspicuous person on the planet."[2] All of these writers, so different in their attitudes and so unequal in their talents, shared one thing: what they wrote, what they said, and how they comported themselves were of greater interest to their countrymen than the activities of other writers of their time. In the first quarter of the twentieth century there was no public writer comparable in national stature to the New England Sages or to Mark Twain. But Hemingway was soon to become the most public of American writers, surpassing in extent of fame all those earlier figures. His career spanned a generation, and during those years his tenure as *the* public writer of his time was virtually undisputed. (His closest competitor, Robert Frost, was never really a serious challenger.) But Hemingway differed from his predecessors in an important respect—he was a celebrity as well as a public writer.

As Daniel Boorstin points out, the celebrity, as our age understands the term, is a twentieth-century phenomenon.[3] The scope of fame in previous eras was limited by primitive systems of mass communication. The average man could not know much about famous persons' private lives because few institutions were devoted largely to disseminating intimate information about them. Only with the multiplication of the mass media and the microscopic specialization of their concerns did the famous person become the celebrity. The mass media create the celebrity not so much by extolling his accomplishments but by revealing, defining, and advertising his personality, for they are aware that his personality attracts the public to him. The mass media and the celebrity have a symbiotic relationship: in return for the fame they bestow upon him, the celebrity allows his private life to become a commodity for a mass audience.

The public writers of the nineteenth century were not celebrities. We should call them personages, men whose achievements were well known but whose private lives remained unknown or comparatively obscure. William Dean Howells once told about a visit he made in the late 1860s to the Ohio home of Congressman James A. Garfield, and this incident illustrates the reverence felt toward the New England Sages by their contemporaries. He had begun to tell Garfield about a recent trip to Boston, where he had met the city's great literary figures, when the future President asked him to wait a moment and, dashing into his yard, began to summon his neighbors, who were enjoying the warm evening on their porches. "'Come over here,' he shouted, 'he's telling about Holmes and Longfellow and Lowell and Whittier!'" and, as Howells relates it, at Garfield's bidding "dim forms began to mount the fences and follow him up to his veranda."[4] Edward Bok also testified to the homage paid by ordinary people to the New England Sages. As a boy Bok visited Oliver Wendell Holmes in Cambridge. At their parting the Doctor put him on a bus back to Boston; when Bok tried to give the conductor his fare, the man refused it. "That's all right," he said. "Doctor Holmes paid me your fare, and I'm going to keep that nickel if I lose my job for it."[5]

Garfield and the bus conductor were responding not to any particular feature in the literary achievement of the New England Sages but to a widely shared belief in the sacerdotal function of the man of letters. In this view, the writer was a public figure who represented the highest ideality, not only in his works but in himself as a public man. His social role was to be an emblem of the good and the true, and in this role he ministered to the imperfections of his countrymen. Josiah G. Holland, the editor of *Scribner's Monthly*, understood what the New England Sages represented when, on the occasion of the Whittier birthday dinner in 1877, he said, "The influence which these beloved and venerated poets exercise upon the public mind and character, simply by being lovely and venerable, is, in the highest and sweetest degree, salutary and salvatory."[6]

The New England Sages used institutional and quasi-institutional structures to reach a larger audience and to demonstrate their ideal characters: some of them gave popular lectures in the Lyceums and elsewhere; others participated in ceremonial public occasions like the dedication of the monument commemorating the battles of Lexington and Concord; all took part in a number of celebrated semi-public affairs, of which the Whittier birthday dinner was only the most famous; all, except Holmes, were more or less associated with antislavery agitation; and one, Lowell, even assumed important political posts, as minister to Spain and to England.

The nineteenth-century American literary world had been largely dominated by four magazines, *Harper's*, the *Century*, the *Atlantic*, and *Scribner's*, which together measured the tone of American cultural life. While they were not so hostile to new literary tendencies as has sometimes been alleged, they supported the idealist view of the artist and advocated the New England Sages as models younger artists should emulate. For these magazines, inquiry into the private lives of the hallowed artists would have been presumptuous; they were obviously noble men whose public performances were a warrant of their goodness, and to descend to anecdote about their private lives—to discuss, for example, the tragic death of Longfellow's wife in a fire, or to describe in detail how Emerson spent his day—would have been a invasion of privacy and an unthinkable concession to vulgarity.

But by 1920 the cultural authority of these magazines had diminished: all of them, save the *Atlantic*, were losing circulation, and the standards of taste they endorsed in the nineteenth century had even become objects of ridicule. More important, a revolution had occurred in American journalism. The number of magazines in circulation had increased from two hundred in 1860 to over one thousand eight hundred at the turn of the century, and scores of new ones were appearing every year. Newspapers were expanding in numbers and size; like the magazines, they had 'profited from such technological advances as the halftone photographic process and the Mergenthaler linotype machine. Most magazines and all newspapers were considerably less expensive than the nineteenth-century literary magazines had been, and they tried to secure a larger and for the most part different kind of audience than *Harper's*, *Scribner's*, the *Atlantic*, and the *Century* had addressed. The new magazines were less literary than their predecessors, but many made sallies into the world of literature, partly out of a sense of editorial responsibility, partly because they wanted a mixture of subjects to attract the largest possible audience. Hence articles of literary interest might be published along with photographic features on current debutantes or previews of Paris fashions. Newspapers also paid more attention to literary matters. Edward Bok's syndicated column of literary gossip first appeared in the 1880s, and in 1896 the New York *Times* instituted its regular literary supplement. With this expansion of the mass media and the diffusion of literary authority came a different way of looking at the artist. To the public he was no longer the secular priest of ideality whose private life was inviolable; rather, he was a skilled entertainer whose personal activities and opinions were of interest as complements to his writing.

The reasons for this shift from the impersonal to the personal are several. First, serious writers were not often defenders of traditional cultivation and ideality. Theodore Dreiser, Sherwood Anderson, Sinclair Lewis, F. Scott Fitzgerald, and others either disregarded or openly attacked canons of nineteenth-century taste. They had found contemporary life wanting in intellectual, emotional, and spiritual nourishment, and their readers were interested in how they managed their own lives. Second, literature had become more intensely a business. Aggressive publishers were entering the market and challenging the older conservative houses; and they were competing for the attention of a reading public larger than ever before, thanks in part to the greater numbers of Americans finishing high school and college. In this competitive atmosphere the publishing houses' advertising and publicity departments were assuming more and more importance, performing functions other than the traditional one of a dignified announcement of the publication of a book. Hoping to create interest in their books, publicists supplied personal data about their authors to the news media. Third, the growth of the media created its own imperatives; there were more pages in periodicals to be filled with news and features than ever before. In their efforts to fill these pages and enlarge their audience, editors turned more to "soft" news about personalities in high society, film, drama, sports, and literature. Books were still newsworthy but so were the lives of their creators. Fourth, what the newspaper and magazine audience expected in literary journalism had changed since the nineteenth century. The readers of the nineteenth-century magazines had been satisfied with the literature and with sober discussions of ideas. The twentieth-century audience wanted more: it wanted—in the words of Malcolm Cowley and Henry Seidel Canby, both practitioners of twentieth-century literary journalism—"more personality and more human interest."[7] Newspaper columns such as those written by F.P.A. and Christopher Morley helped satisfy this craving for the personal, as did newspaper and magazine features on the literary world and human interest pieces on particular authors.

The greater interest in personality was an essential circumstance wherein Hemingway could become a celebrity. Versions of his private life were public property during most of his career. The appetite for information about him was unquenchable: periodicals aimed at every level of readership regularly reported his opinions and personal activities; the saga of his life was recounted in magazines ranging from the *New Yorker* to *Life* to *True;* newspaper columnists as dissimilar as Joseph Alsop and Leonard Lyons often discussed him in their columns. In the eight years after his death he was the subject of no less than seven book-length biographies. His fame was not, as with most serious writers, limited to a literary elite, nor was it even primarily an artistic fame. Of course he was recognized as a distinguished novelist, but the mass media which lionized him and were ultimately responsible for his reputation as *the* American writer had a keener interest in his personality. They purveyed Hemingway the warrior, Hemingway the sportsman, Hemingway the *bon vivant*, and all the other public Hemingways; the master of modern prose was of secondary interest.

Far from being either the unwitting or the unwilling recipient of this personal attention as he liked to intimate he was, Hemingway was the architect of his public reputation. Early in his career, he began to shape a public personality which quickly became one of his most famous creations, during his lifetime perhaps the most famous one. For the rest of his career he advertised his public personality in his considerable body of nonfiction, for whatever his nominal subject, his real subject was himself. These periodic "situation reports," as he called one of his self-dramatizing essays, kept his public abreast of his current exploits and presented a version of his personality which for the most part the mass media adopted in their appreciations of him.

Some basic distinctions are necessary. A writer's public reputation measures something different from what his literary reputation measures and is not based upon a qualitative assessment of his artistic achievement; it is not his literary reputation extended into a larger arena. The detective novelist Mickey Spillane has a public reputation, and a large one; if he has a literary reputation, it is a sort of antireputation. The sales of Spillane's novels did not guarantee him a public reputation, but they created the conditions whereby he could secure one. What gave him his public reputation was a general conviction that he had much in common with his fictional hero, Mike Hammer, and the reinforcement of that conviction in articles and through his frequent appearances on television. Eventually he went so far as to have his wife pose nude for the dust jacket of one of his novels. Spillane achieved his public reputation because he parlayed his commercial success as a novelist into a personal fame; he became his own hero. As this suggests, a writer creates his public reputation by displaying his personality before a large audience, and in doing so, he is abetted by the information brokers of the mass media more than by literary critics.

Neither of the two standard measures of a writer's success, large sales and critical recognition, is an adequate predictor of public reputation. The romance writer Frank Yerby, whose books have

sold more copies than those of any other modern American novelist, has no public reputation whatsoever, while William Faulkner,
critically acclaimed as the most significant American novelist of his
time, had only a slightly larger one than Yerby. Public reputation is
a quantitative measurement rather than a qualitative: it is gauged
by how nearly media coverage of a writer's activities approaches the
saturation point, and the important factor in it is not variety, but
repetition. Its fundamental form is the anecdote; the more frequently the same anecdotes about the writer's personality are repeated in the mass media, the more likely his public reputation will
be large. Public reputation is also present tense, since it is predi-
cated on the artist's personality; once he dies, his public reputation
disappears at least within a generation. But while he lives, if his
public reputation is large enough—if he has exploited the mass
media successfully—even the most casual peruser of newspapers,
magazines, and the electronic media will have a sense of who and
what he is.

The audience which gives a writer literary reputation is an elite;
the audience which gives him public reputation is larger and more
heterogeneous. The intellectual elite in America is more fluid and
less restrictive than its counterparts in France or England, but it is
an elite nonetheless. It is made up of persons we variously but
confidently call literate and educated general readers; it may also be
defined as the readership of those periodicals which cater to it. In
the nineteenth century an elite sustained the *Atlantic*, *Harper's*,
Scribner's, and the *Century*, and it took its literary cues from them;
the periodical range of the twentieth-century elite is less easy to
identify, but the modern elite supports, among others, the *New
York Review of Books*, *Partisan Review*, the *New Republic*, the *Nation*,
and to some extent the rejuvenated *Atlantic* and *Harper's*. Literary
discussion by professional critics is a staple in these periodicals, and
if the standards of criticism have changed since the nineteenth
century, the tone has not: it is still sober, reflective, and judicious,
and it is interested in the qualities of a writer's work. The audience
which gives the writer his public reputation does not support these
periodicals. It is not completely indifferent to questions of literary
value, but it demands above all attention to the writer's personality.

Writers ordinarily attract scant attention from newspapers and
magazines beyond notices in book-review sections; their profes-

sional and private lives, unlike those of politicians, sports figures, and actors, are not often purveyed in feature articles, interviews, news stories, gossip columns, photographic essays, and the like. It is not difficult to understand this neglect. The mass media attempt to appeal to the widest possible audience, and that undifferentiated audience is not much interested in high culture or the people who produce it. Leo Lowenthal, who studied social values in magazine biographies, did not discover one profile of a serious writer among the 125 biographies in his sample. Not surprisingly, he found that Americans were interested in reading about the private lives of show business personalities and sports heroes, with political leaders running a distant third.[8]

Most novelists accept their social obscurity and content themselves with being private writers. Some doubtless harbor a yearning for a large public reputation, but few are willing to behave themselves in such a way as to get it, and fewer still possess the requisite charisma to make it a possibility. Instead they write to and for an elite and succor themselves with the reasonable hope that their work will continue to affect the consciousness of posterity. Wallace Stevens, a very private writer indeed, expressed the private writer's assumptions when he remarked that "time and time again it has been said that [the poet] may not address himself to an elite. I think he may. There is not a poet whom we prize living today that does not address himself to an elite. The poet will continue to do this. . . . And that elite, if it responds . . . will thereafter do for the poet what he cannot do for himself, that is to say, receive his poetry."[9] Like the poet, the serious modern novelist addresses himself primarily to an elite and pins his hopes for recognition on its response. To Stevens's observation about the artist's audience might be added Flaubert's remark about the writer's public reception. "If your work of art is good," he said, "if it is *right*, it will evoke its response, it will find its place, in six months time, in six years or when you are dead. What does it matter?"[10]

For Hemingway it mattered very much when and from what quarters recognition came. Although he occasionally spoke of being willing to wait for the judgment of history, his actions belied his words. He wanted immediate public recognition and approbation and he labored to get them. He groused to Ford Madox Ford in 1924 that it took years for a writer to become known,[11] but for him

it was only a few years before he was more famous in his own era
than any writer had ever been in a previous one.

He took special pride from the beginning of his career in the
appeal of his works to a larger audience than the usual public for
books. He told his editor at Boni and Liveright, publishers of *In
Our Time*, his first book to appear in America, that the advantage of
his fiction was that it could be read by both highbrows and low-
brows.[12] He still felt the same way nearly thirty years later when he
published *The Old Man and the Sea*, the last of his books to appear in
his lifetime. He wrote an editor at *Life*, in which the novel was to be
printed in one issue, that he was pleased because so many people
who could not afford to buy a bound copy would be able to read it.
That, he said, made him happier than having a Nobel Prize.[13] His
candor here was questionable, but his judgment about the appeal of
his work was not.[14] But recognizing the genuineness as well as the
appeal of his literary art, we must not forget that Hemingway also
gave his talent and energy to the invention and promulgation of a
public personality; and even if it was of a lesser order of creation, its
success was important to him, perhaps as important as the success
of his art. He published during his career seven novels, over fifty
short stories, and a play; he also wrote two published books of
nonfiction, another which was virtually finished at his death, yet
another which was complete but had only been published in part,
and enough essays and reportage to fill a couple of substantial
volumes. In nearly all of this nonfictional material he was shaping
his public personality, and because he did this with such skillful
repetition, he was able to make himself the darling of the mass
media. He amply satisfied the requirements of journalists: he was a
vigorous and colorful character who, as Morley Callaghan remarked, "made men want to talk about him,"[15] and he was willing
to make public his private life, thus providing a ready-made personality to be turned to account. His public reputation, then, was
created by a dynamic relationship between his advertisements of
his personality and the mass media's exploitation of it. Once this
relationship was established—and it materialized early in his
career—he was on his way toward becoming both the public writer
of his time and a celebrity of the first magnitude.

As Randall Jarrell once remarked, in the twentieth century celebrities "*are* our fictional characters";[16] they give us our cues about the

good and satisfying life, and they provide us with a vicarious enjoyment of rich and dramatic personal experience. Hemingway, as a public writer and a celebrity, was one of his most vivid and memorable characters, one who left his personal imprint on his times to a degree never before realized by any American writer. He occasionally felt uncomfortable with his role as public writer—in 1954, for example, he told Bernard Berenson that it was bad for a writer to have too much adulation, and that he wanted to have no more publicity, only the opportunity to write great books[17]—but despite his disclaimers, he was unrelenting in his efforts to maintain his public image and fame. If Mark Twain was the Lincoln of American literature, as Howells said he was, then Hemingway was the Theodore Roosevelt: "Teddy" and "Papa" (and the famous nicknames were testimony to the public affection they commanded) each joined in one forceful individual the man of thought with the man of action, the distinctive public personality with the genius for making news, and those volatile combinations rendered them irresistible to their contemporaries, who loved them more for the legend of their lives than for their objective achievements.

2

"The Artist's Reward"

1924–1929

I

The rapidity of Hemingway's rise to literary fame and honor was extraordinary. In 1924 a young and obscure former newspaperman living in a garret, he became by 1930 the most famous and respected novelist of his generation. Literary critics hailed him at the beginning of his career as the brightest star in American fiction and its best hope for the future. His fellow writers were equally taken with him, and many showed their admiration by imitating him. By the end of the decade, just five years after the appearance of *In Our Time* (1925), it was already possible to speak of Hemingway's influence on contemporary American fiction as greater than that of any other writer, living or dead.

He published five books between 1925 and 1930, and all save *The Torrents of Spring* (1926) received enthusiastic notices. (Even that—his most insignificant work—was not treated really unkindly.) A sampling of the reviews of *In Our Time*, *The Sun Also Rises* (1926), *Men Without Women* (1927), and *A Farewell to Arms* (1929) turns up phrases which illustrate the nearly unqualified admiration his work received: "his very prose seems to have an organic being of its own"; "among the first men writing today"; "if there is better dialogue being written today I do not know where to find it"; "magnificent writing"; "a truly magnificent work"; "a real occasion for patriotic rejoicing"; "will match up as narrative prose with anything that's been written since there was any English language."[1]

By the age of thirty, Hemingway was already spoken of as a modern master; he was, in Jimmy Durante's phrase, "the toast of the intellectuals."

This meteoric rise to literary eminence was accompanied by a different kind of fame—personal fame—which at first was subordinate to his literary renown, rather soon vied with it on equal terms, and eventually surpassed it to make Hemingway not simply the best-known writer but one of the most famous men of his time. Enthusiasm among the intellectual elite, which nearly canonized him in the 1920s, waxed and waned after 1930, but the enthusiasm of the public, the guarantor of his personal fame, never wavered once it took him up as its champion. This disparity between his literary reputation and his public reputation, indeed the fact that he had a public reputation, was one of the most arresting aspects of Hemingway's career, and not only in a sociological sense. His own acute awareness of the public response to his personality, and his sense of what this response meant, affected what he chose to write about and what he said when he did write. Nearly everything he published after 1930 reflected this awareness.

Even as a very young man he showed a special talent for making news. As a friend later remarked, "he couldn't walk down the street and stub his toe without having a newsman who happened to be walking with him magnify the little accident into a near fatality."[2] Stepping off the troop ship from Italy, where he had been wounded in battle, the eighteen-year-old veteran was corralled by a New York *Sun* reporter for an interview, the first of many dockside press conferences he would thereafter hold. Afterward the reporter filed a story insisting that Hemingway had been more battered than any other man who fought against the Central Powers.[3] About the same time the Chicago *American* stated that Hemingway was "the worst shot-up man in the U.S."[4] Both assertions exaggerated—he had been seriously injured though not so badly as many others—but they were characteristic of the exaggeration that always occurred when Hemingway's exploits were reported. There was something galvanic about his bearing and personality which provoked such fascination that even newsmen, supposedly cynical and skeptical, could not resist. When he began to publish fiction in the early 1920s, achieving first a limited literary reputation among American expatriates in Paris and soon a larger one among intellectuals in

America, he also began to acquire a personal fame which, if not yet independent of his literary fame, was discrete from it.

What he thought of his personal celebrity at this early date is not clear, although in later years he certainly encouraged and enjoyed it. In a letter of late 1924 to Edmund Wilson praising the critic's review of *Three Stories and Ten Poems* (1923) and *in our time* (1924), both issued in limited editions by small expatriate publishers, Hemingway professed to be disgusted by public mention of his private life. Wilson had found Hemingway's prose "of the first distinction" and said nothing in his review about the young writer himself. For this Hemingway was grateful: "It was cool and clear minded and decent and impersonal and sympathetic. Christ how I hate this terrible personal stuff. Do you remember my writing from Toronto wanting some reviews and publicity? and then got some and it turned me sick."[5] There is mystery as to which reviews made him ill; Wilson's was only the third to appear anywhere, and the first in America. The other two had been published in *transatlantic review*, were favorable, and contained nothing personal. But his comment to Wilson seems to show that at that time he wanted to be treated as a private artist—in the way writers were traditionally treated, as an invisible presence.

If he sincerely believed this in 1924, he did not know his own mind, because when he wrote Wilson he had already begun formulating the public personality which would eventually be the spur to his personal fame. In these early years, while he was busy establishing his literary reputation, it was only imperfectly developed; it would not emerge as full imago until the 1930s, when he would expend much energy on refining and publicizing it.

That personality appeared germinally in 1924 in *transatlantic review*, a Paris-based little magazine of the 1920s. During the thirteen-month life of *transatlantic review* Hemingway made seven contributions and served for a time as its editor. In it he published three of his best short stories, "Indian Camp," "The Doctor and the Doctor's Wife," and "Cross-Country Snow," as well as three "letters" and an appreciation of Joseph Conrad. This roughly equal proportion of fiction to nonfiction was to remain constant; he spoke in his own voice more often than other fiction writers of his generation. And the tone as well as the quantity of his nonfiction suggest that he intended more through it than earning extra money or doing preliminary sketches for later stories.

Almost all his nonfiction, starting with the pieces in *transatlantic review*, is vividly personal; very little can be described as reportage, although that is often its putative purpose. The strongest impression evoked by these pieces is of the writer's personality—his attitudes, biases, character, and behavior. Whether he is describing a bullfight, discussing literature, or analyzing a political event, Hemingway is always center stage, overpowering the nominal subject. These works were sketches toward an autobiography; they bear the relation to formal autobiography that the Nick Adams stories do to a novel: the fragments as a group present a rounded view of a personality. In both the stories and the nonfiction what is important is not what happens but rather the attitudes of the central characters and the way they behave in critical situations. If we regard the nonfiction as sketches toward an autobiography, however, we must remember that this is a public autobiography. Whether these public revelations squared with the "real" personality of Hemingway is a fascinating question, but the answer must remain problematical because of the difficulty of determining the "real" Hemingway.

II

While he had published over a hundred articles in the Toronto *Star Weekly* and the Toronto *Daily Star* between 1920 and 1924, his articles for *transatlantic review* were his first for an audience which would be nearly as interested in the author as in the articles. Unlike most of his pieces for the Toronto papers, what he published in the magazine was written with the knowledge that he already possessed a small but significant literary reputation. These early pieces, therefore, are the departure point for understanding his shaping of his public personality. They have slight literary value, but they indicate some of the more salient aspects of the public image that was to become the hallmark of Hemingway as a public writer.

His first nonfiction contribution to *transatlantic review* was a chatty letter dated "The Quarter: Early Spring." For the most part a potpourri of gossipy items about Montparnasse locals, it also included a gratuitous blast at literary critics, whom he characterized as "the eunuchs of literature."[6] There could not have been any personal animus in this derogation, since the first review of his work had appeared only one month before (in *transatlantic review*) and it had been favorable. He was interested in having his work reviewed; he had written Edmund Wilson a few months earlier asking how to place his books before reviewers. Despite his lifelong antipathy for critics and the breezy contempt he affected toward their cavils, there is evidence that he read them with great attention; often he was so disturbed by their comments that he counterattacked, ridiculing their attitudes, maligning them personally, and even brawling with one of them. Damning his critics was more than a crotchet; it was a manifestation of his public personality—he often abandoned measured response for vituperation, and shifted the focus of disagreement from ideas to personalities. His and his critics' *ad hominem* arguments had the effect of confusing his literary with his personal reputation, a confusion that became more apparent with each passing year. The public, if the mass media are any indication, loved him for his contentiousness; his critics did not.

Hemingway indulged in some literary criticism of his own in his eulogy for Joseph Conrad in the September 1924 number of the magazine. Ford Madox Ford, the editor, had been Conrad's friend and collaborator and it was natural that *transatlantic review* do a special supplement in his memory. For his part Hemingway chose to discuss literary politics, particularly the fashion of dismissing Conrad as insignificant and praising T. S. Eliot as the current great writer:

> It is agreed by most of the people I know that Conrad is a bad writer, just as it is agreed that T. S. Eliot is a good writer. If I knew that by grinding Mr. Eliot into a fine dry powder and sprinkling that powder over Mr. Conrad's grave Mr. Conrad would shortly appear, looking very annoyed at the forced return, and commence writing, I would leave for London early tomorrow morning with a sausage grinder.[7]

Overtly Hemingway was jesting at Eliot's rebirth theme in "The Waste Land," but the grotesque image was surely hostile. The Conrad essay provoked an angry response from Eliot, and Ford printed an apology in a subsequent issue. Offended by what he considered Ford's excessive timidity, Hemingway resigned from the magazine and stopped speaking to him, though they both continued to go to the same places to meet the same people night after night.

His Conrad tribute hinted at several traits he exhibited thereafter that helped enlarge his public reputation: outspokenness, aggressiveness, and contentiousness. There is also competitiveness, a trait which would become famous. Conrad was dead, and not of Hemingway's generation anyway, but Eliot was very much alive, only ten years older than Hemingway, and, along with Joyce, one of the best-known and widely admired literary artists among the avant-garde. On the other hand, as early as 1925, Hemingway was beginning to be mentioned as a "modern master": Edmund Wilson had said in the *Dial* that *In Our Time* had "more artistic dignity than anything else about the period of the war that [had] as yet been written by an American,"[8] and Ford had publicly praised Hemingway as "the best writer in America at this moment, . . . the most conscientious, the most master of his craft, the most consummate."[9] Hemingway himself, even at this early date, believed that he was destined to be a great writer.[10] The attack on Eliot was an effort to demote the poet from the championship ranks, opening the way for a challenger to assume the title. The boxing metaphor, which Hemingway later used to define his own eminence, allowed for only one champion.

His interest in sports expressed his competitive drive. He went to his first bullfight in 1923, and it became a special passion. One of his letters in *transatlantic review* mentioned the Pamplona bullfight fiesta, later to be a setting in *The Sun Also Rises*. He was reluctant to write much about the fiesta itself. An essay about it, he wrote, would only be journalism and the sole reason for writing journalism was money. He suggested that "once you have put a thing into words, unless you do it 'on your knees' you kill it. If you do write it 'on your knees' . . . the thirty francs a page is only a supplementary reward."[11] His insistence that he was an artist committed to his work contrasted with many of his other public stances. Particularly after 1930 he often comported himself and even wrote about himself as an unliterary sportsman, drinker, and hail-fellow-well-met. Nevertheless, for the rest of his life he insisted his one true calling was literature and little else was of much importance. Increasingly there was something plaintive about these assertions, as if he felt that by publicly affirming his preeminent devotion to art it would become a reality. They revealed his disquietude about becoming a public writer, a disquietude, however, never strong enough to make him cease exploiting the image he had created. Paradoxically, these advertisements of artistic integrity were themselves bound up in this image: they suggested that there was something heroic about him as a writer, and hinted that he had made great psychic sacrifices and had taken large risks in order to practice his art.

His "Pamplona Letter" concluded with yet another reason for not wanting to write about the fiesta. "The less publicity it has, the better," he said, because almost everyone "who deserved to be at Pamplona" had been there, and "the more people that think it is a terrible, brutal, degrading relic of etc. the better."[12] The implication that he was a member of a select fraternity of initiates became familiar to readers of his fiction, and it was important as well in his public personality. He often assumed the role of taste-arbiter, expressing contempt for "outsiders" or "tourists," anyone who did not share his preferences in food, drink, locales, literature, and sports.

The *transatlantic review* articles are trivial in terms of Hemingway's literary career, but they are significant in terms of his career as public writer. They reveal that his public personality was incipient at the outset of his professional life, and that he was willing to use it for self-aggrandizement. They were a preview of the self-advertisements that would spread his fame in the next decade beyond the limited audience provided by an intellectual elite; and they foreshadowed that in his nonfiction his great subject was to be himself. Eight years later, when he returned to advertising his personality in his nonfiction, he was addressing a larger readership than that of the *transatlantic review*, and he had a more comprehensive sense of what kind of personality he wished to circulate. In the meantime there were others eager to increase his fame as writer and man, and in the last half of the 1920s they helped that fame spread to an extent that even he probably thought unlikely.

What made Hemingway's fame in the 1920s different from later years was its locus—at that time it was largely confined to the intellectual elite and based mainly on his artistic skill. Critics and journalists commented on his personality but usually as an afterthought; their interest was in his literary achievements. But during the 1920s he was winning several kinds of personal fame, and even so early this fame made him different from other serious writers.

III

The first of the many Hemingways to receive extensive public attention was Hemingway the young expatriate. Expatriation fascinated the American press in the 1920s. Essays excoriating or pitying expatriates appeared frequently in such magazines as *Harper's* and the *Saturday Evening Post;* these condemnations, in turn, spurred other essays defending the expatriates and explaining why young Americans lived abroad. The controversy is suggestive of the quarrels in American newspapers and magazines over the "beatniks" of the 1950s and the "hippies" of the 1960s; the censure was similarly shrill and mindless, the defense equally superficial and facile.

Hemingway was one of the most prominent figures in the American colony in Paris. Malcolm Cowley remembered going to a New York speakeasy in the winter of 1925–1926 and finding it filled with recently returned expatriate writers and their wives. All of them, according to Cowley, were telling stories about Hemingway and talking in a "tough, matter-of-fact and confidential" way that he later recognized as the Hemingway manner. Then, "in the middle of the evening one of them rose, took off his jacket and used it to show how he would dominate a bull."[13] This scene took place before the publication of *The Sun Also Rises* (although after *In Our Time* and "The Undefeated"), so these admirers were likely responding as much to Hemingway's personality as to anything he had written. Having achieved celebrity in the expatriate community, he naturally became a newsworthy figure to journalists interested in the ways of Americans in Paris.

Robert Forrest Wilson's essay, "Paris for Young Art," in the *Bookman* of June 1925 was typical of journalistic reports on expatriate writers. Mixing evaluation with biographical tidbits, Wilson focused on Hemingway as one of the most arresting and successful of the young Americans in Paris. He predicted that he would not long remain in the 300-copy echelon of writers (*Three Stories and Ten Poems* had been published in an edition of 300). Hemingway, wrote Wilson, "is a young man of vigorous health and physique who has been a soldier and war correspondent, who now represents a Toronto newspaper in Paris, is versed in European politics, and is occasionally assigned by one or another of the New York newspapers to report some peace conference or League of Nations meeting; and who when not writing in his quarters on the Rue Notre-Dame-des-Champs mingles democratically with the artist-writer crowd at the Café du Dôme."[14] Although some of Wilson's information was incorrect—Hemingway was no longer a correspondent for the Toronto *Star*, nor was he on assignment for any New York paper—it was not so inaccurate as some of the fantastic stories about his life that appeared later.

By lauding Hemingway's work and emphasizing his association with the "artist-writer crowd at the Café du Dôme," Wilson was appealing to two usually discrete attitudes toward expatriates. The first, the positive, characterized the expatriate as a dedicated artist who lived in Europe because it was less expensive than America, or more congenial to creativity, or lent itself more easily to the formation of an artistic community, or had more intellectual vitality. Most important was the belief that the expatriate artist disciplined himself, worked diligently, and produced important and enduring works of art. By valuing Hemingway's work, Wilson seemed to be linking him with this tradition. The other conception, the negative, saw the expatriates as malcontents who had turned their backs on their native land for specious and neurotic reasons. In *The Sun Also Rises* Bill Gorton ironically catalogues the assumptions that underlay this view: "You're an expatriate. You've lost touch with the soil. You get precious. Fake European standards have ruined you. You drink yourself to death. You become obsessed by sex. You spend all your time talking, not working. You're an expatriate, see? You hang around cafes."[15] By associating Hemingway with those Americans who frequented the Dôme, Wilson, perhaps innocently, suggested that his residence in Paris was not entirely admirable. But Wilson's essay was sympathetic, and, in its admiration for the artist and the man, was representative of the favorable journalistic exposure Hemingway early commanded.

In a review of *In Our Time*, Burton Rascoe, in the 1920s one of the leading American literary journalists, addressed himself more explicitly than Wilson had to identifying Hemingway as expatriate. He made it a special point to assure his readers that Hemingway did not conform to the conventional (that is, the negative) image of the expatriate. He had met him in the company of Tristan Tzara, Ford Madox Ford, and E. E. Cummings at a *bal musette* near the Pantheon, and he supposed that Hemingway had done his share of sitting around the Dôme and the Rotonde discussing literature and art: "And he is, therefore, by all accounts, supposed to be very precious and esoteric, and against America and disgruntled and neurotic and a failure." But, he went on to say, Hemingway was not any of these things:

> He lives in Paris, he told me, for at least three reasons: he finds it cheaper to live there; he can get a change of scene and environment such as would be impossible in America at small expense; and he likes a bit of wine with his meals. He is a robust, hulking sort of chap, with a clear skin and a healthy, ruddy color, who is probably the slouchiest dresser in the Montparnasse quarter. There is nothing decadent, precious, arty, superior, or anti-American about him.[16]

Rascoe's characterization of Hemingway as the epitome of the "good expatriate" struck a note that reviewers and critics would repeat often in the late 1920s, when several singled him out as an artist who remained manly and unaffected even after the first flush of critical and popular success.

His fame as an expatriate increased after the publication of *The Sun Also Rises* in October 1926. Much of the novel's initial notoriety stemmed from its being known as a *roman à clef;* one wag even suggested it should have been titled *Six Characters in Search of an Author—With Guns.* Several reviewers, including "Genet" in the *New Yorker*, Rascoe in the New York *Sun*, and an anonymous critic in the *Dial*, emphasized its factual basis. Another who noted the connection between Hemingway's own experience and the fictional action was Cleveland B. Chase in the *Saturday Review of Literature*. Chase said that anyone familiar with the American colony in Paris should be able to recognize immediately almost all the characters in *The Sun Also Rises;* even the fishing trip to Burguete, he added, took place in the spring of 1924.[17] Robert Littell called the novel a "*succès de scandale* of a *roman à clef* floated on *vin ordinaire*." Littell, whose sympathetic assessment in the *New Republic* was the first general

essay on Hemingway's work to appear anywhere, felt the autobiographical basis of his fiction was one of its most significant aspects.
He applauded Hemingway's ability to transform his experience
through "selective reporting" into successful works of art.[18] The
effect of these correlations between fiction and reality was to make
people believe Hemingway "lived it up to write it down." This
belief was partially true even then, but it was to become altogether
true in the next decade when he returned to nonfiction. But even in
the 1920s, before he began to advertise himself deliberately, he was
already gaining a reputation for adventurous and colorful exploits.

The social effect of *The Sun Also Rises* was enormous. Malcolm
Cowley recalled that Smith College girls in New York modeled
themselves after Lady Brett Ashley and that "hundreds of bright
young men from the Middle West were trying to be Hemingway
heroes, talking in tough understatements from the sides of their
mouths. . . ."[19] Richmond Barrett noted that young people regarded
the novel as their bible, "learned it by heart and, deserting their
families and running away from college, immediately took ship to
Paris to be the disciples of the new faith under the awnings of the
Dôme and the Rotonde and the other sidewalk cafes."[20] *The Sun Also
Rises* made Hemingway a spokesman for his generation, like
F. Scott Fitzgerald in the early 1920s and Jack Kerouac in the late
1950s, so that what he did and said now became even more newsworthy.

Most but not all reviews of *The Sun Also Rises* were favorable.
Unlike critics who praised the novel for its rendering of Parisian
expatriate life, the reviewer for *Time* implied that Hemingway had
failed to live up to the promise of *In Our Time* because he had taken
on the affectations of the conventional expatriate: "his interests,"
Time said, "appear to have grown soggy with much sitting around
sloppy cafe tables in the so-called Latin (it should be called American) quarter of Paris."[21] This disparagement was almost unique in
the history of *Time*'s response to Hemingway. Once he became a
celebrity the magazine took him up as its favorite American writer,
praising his works and extolling his personality. In its review of
Men Without Women the next year, *Time* praised the book and, in an
unabashed reversal, said of *The Sun Also Rises* that it "made critics
realize that at least one of the Americans who live in Paris can do
something more important than sit about in restaurants."[22]

Several reviews and appreciations of *The Sun Also Rises* spread inaccurate and improbable stories about Hemingway which persisted for years despite his occasional attempts to set the record straight. The distortions in the *Bookman* for May 1927 suggest how far Hemingway's commentators could stray. The author of this article on "rising stars in American fiction" wrote that Hemingway was born in Illinois but spent his boyhood in Michigan (he spent only his boyhood summers there); that he was an amateur boxer of "some distinction," unlike Robert Cohn (in *The Sun Also Rises*, Cohn was middleweight boxing champion of Princeton; Hemingway, although reportedly a competent boxer, was never a tournament fighter, as the *Bookman* implied he was); that he joined the ambulance corps and went abroad before the United States entered the war (he made the Atlantic crossing in May 1918, thirteen months after the declaration of war); that he enlisted in the crack Italian combat corps, the *Arditi* (he did not); and that he was wounded in action three times (he was wounded only once, although seriously).[23] Most of these untruths reappeared in various guises for years; the swashbuckling story about his enlistment in the *Arditi* was perhaps the most tenacious: even Malcolm Cowley repeated it in his introduction to the *Portable Hemingway*, published in 1944.[24] Because so many untruths commonly permeated talk about Hemingway's life, distinguishing fact from fiction became nearly impossible. A kind of Gresham's Law operated: the more improbable the tale, the greater currency it had, and the fabrications tended to eclipse the truth.

IV

In the early years Hemingway attempted to correct some of these farfetched stories. In 1927 he tried to establish the truth to the author of a literary gossip column in the *New York Herald Tribune Books*. Contrary to rumor, he said, he was not a football star in high school or a boxing instructor in college, nor did he have two children. The Italian decorations he received in the war were not for distinguished service, but had been awarded merely as a compliment to an American serving with the Italian army.[25] But it was fruitless to expose these legends; they were good stories and apparently consistent with his character, and once in circulation they became entrenched. Hemingway himself probably started some of them. In his biography of the novelist, Carlos Baker establishes Hemingway's propensity for inventing fabulous stories about his exploits. On one occasion he bragged to friends that he had learned the art of knife-throwing from members of the *Arditi*, who offered him an Austrian prisoner to practice on.[26] Years later he would tell A. E. Hotchner that one of his sexual conquests during World War I was the famous spy Mata Hari.[27] Mata Hari was executed the year before he arrived in Europe.

Time's review of *Men Without Women*, six months after his disclaimer to the *Herald Tribune*, demonstrated the tenacity of the legends:

> His father was a doctor in Oak Park, Ill. Author Hemingway was a football star and boxer at school. In the War he was severely wounded serving with the Italian Arditi, of whom he was almost the youngest member. Since the Armistice he has lived . . . in Paris. Every spring he goes down to Pamplona to watch the bullfights; on an occasion when he entered the arena himself, several of his ribs got broken by a bull. He expects soon to return to the U.S., perhaps to stay. With him he will bring his second and a small bullfight cinema film which he made himself.[28]

Time embroidered on the factual frame of boyhood in Illinois, service as an ambulance driver on the Italian front, and expatriation in Paris. Some of these elaborations were familiar, some were new. *Time*'s "second" implied that Hemingway was fighting professionally—there is no evidence that he ever did. The bullfight film, like the second, was somebody's figment.

Hemingway's interest in bullfighting was an important feature of his public reputation even in the 1920s. The obvious reason for the awareness of his *afición* was his use of the bullfight in his fiction. Of his work before 1928 six of the miniatures of *In Our Time*, the last half of *The Sun Also Rises*, and one short story, "The Undefeated," were concerned with the sport. Journalists, moreover, frequently noted his exploits in the ring. As early as 1924 the Chicago *Tribune* reported in a front-page story his narrow escape from death when he was gored rescuing Donald Ogden Stewart from a mauling.[29] The *Herald Tribune*'s literary columnist alluded to his interest in bullfighting several times in the mid-1920s, once noting that he had suffered three broken ribs from "an annoyed toro."[30] Burton Rascoe recounted for his readers what Hemingway had told him about "what you have to learn to be a good bullfighter. He had palled around a bit with a famous bullfighter in Seville and then gone in for bullfighting himself for the experience and fun of it."[31] A few years later Rascoe passed along a Ford Madox Ford anecdote about Hemingway saving John Dos Passos from a goring at Pamplona. According to Ford, Dos Passos was tossed by the bull, but Hemingway grabbed it by the neck before it could impale his friend, and both escaped with only bruises.[32]

These anecdotes reinforced the notion that Hemingway was a man of great physical courage, an impression already well established by the story of his enlistment in the *Arditi*. Fearlessness and capacity for confronting danger were important qualities in his public reputation; and they were qualities that in his later nonfiction he often claimed. There was something anomalous about a writer who fought bulls, but this kind of anomaly would make him famous. No writer has ever been so public a sportsman as Hemingway; he became at least as celebrated for his sporting prowess as for his literary achievements. Even in these early years newspapers and magazines frequently emphasized his athletic skills; a columnist in the *Bookman*, apropos of nothing, reported that Hemingway was "an amateur toreador, a semi-professional prizefighter, and an expert at skiing."[33] The novelty of a major writer who was also an accomplished sportsman accounted for much of the public attention, but novelty alone was not the entire reason. There was also a factor of cultural conditioning.

As social commentators have noted, public distrust of artists and intellectuals has long been common in American culture; this suspicion has produced a stereotype of the artist and intellectual as, in Richard Hofstadter's words, "pretentious, conceited, effeminate, and snobbish; and very likely immoral, dangerous, and subversive."[34] American popular culture is replete with portraits of foppish, affected artists and intellectuals; popular expressions as dissimilar as Horatio Alger's novel *Adrift in New York* and Frank Capra's film *Mr. Deeds Goes to Town* share this view. In *Anti-Intellectualism in American Life* Richard Hofstader explains the antagonism professional politicians in the late nineteenth century felt toward men of culture. "Invoking a well-established preconception of the American male," Hofstader writes, "the politicans argued that culture is impractical and men of culture are ineffectual, that culture is feminine and cultivated men tend to be effeminate."[35]

With such attitudes in mind, one can understand the amount of attention paid Hemingway the sportsman. He joined what were commonly held to be opposites; for an artist to pursue sports in an expert way violated the logic of a deep prejudice about culture and masculinity. Because he reconciled them he was newsworthy; because he did so in such dramatic fashion—boxing and bullfighting were among the sports most demanding of strength, skill, and courage—he was potentially heroic. All that was necessary to fulfill this potential was proper public exposure, and that was not long in coming.

The frequent appearance of Hemingway's picture in newspapers and magazines fostered the impression of his virility. Photographs and drawings emphasized his rugged handsomeness, and many portrayed him engaged in sport. *Bookman* reported that a female artist it had commissioned to draw him feared she would not produce a good caricature because he was "too good-looking."[36] Dorothy Parker testified to the effect of his photograph:

> Young women, in especial, are all of a quiver for information. (Sometimes I think that the wide publication of that smiling photograph, the one with the slanted cap and the shirt flung open above the dark sweater, was perhaps a mistake.)
>   "Ooh," they say, "do you know Ernest Hemingway? Ooh, I'd just *love* to meet him! Ooh, tell me what he's *like!*"[37]

This kind of homage is usually reserved for movie stars, and the comparison is not inappropriate. Hemingway's photograph appeared so frequently in the mass media over the years that his face became as familiar as that of any Hollywood leading man.

V

The publication of *A Farewell to Arms* in 1929 irrevocably established Hemingway as a major literary figure. It was a critical and popular success, leading most of the best-seller lists six weeks after publication. Apparently many readers chose to regard it as autobiographical, for in the second printing, at Hemingway's request, a disclaimer was added to the copyright page stating that the book was solely fiction. He also had his publisher make a similar statement to the press. Three years later, when the film version of the book was released, Hemingway again protested against "the romantic and false military and personal career" which was being attributed to him.[38] The similarity of his own and his hero's experience on the Italian front made irresistible a belief that he was Frederic Henry. Twenty years later *Coronet* magazine would call Hemingway's description of the Caporetto retreat "a vivid fragment of memory."[39] He had not participated in the retreat at all.

Along with the acclaim for *A Farewell to Arms* came another honor, one of the premier accolades accorded a celebrity: a profile in the *New Yorker*. Unlike the more famous profile by Lillian Ross twenty-one years later, this one, by Dorothy Parker, was unambiguously sympathetic to him as man and artist. He was, said Parker, "far and away the first American artist." This was the longest appreciation to date and the first instance of a large-circulation magazine featuring his personality; it also marked the close of the first stage of Hemingway's rise to public fame. It codified prevalent attitudes held by literary critics and the intellectual elite during the 1920s. These attitudes would change during the next decade, and because of this change Parker's profile assumes a developmental importance beyond its intrinsic value.

Parker wanted to describe the "real" Hemingway, not the Hemingway of the newspapers and magazines. "Of no other living man," she said, "has so much tripe been penned and spoken." She catalogued stories of the previous half-dozen years: Hemingway was illiterate; he was an incurable womanizer; he hated sports but liked to show off; he hung around the Cafe Select at all hours drinking absinthe; he hated America; he had been a stockyard worker, a safecracker, and a tramp. None of this was true, but "people so much wanted him to be a figure out of a saga that they went to the length of providing the saga themselves." Parker, however, was not averse to a little saga-making herself. She began the profile by equating her awe of Hemingway with a tourist's reverence at a spectacular Grand Canyon sunset, and from this majestic comparison moved on to describe the "real" Hemingway, adding her own distortions. He left home at an early age, she said, to become a prizefighter, but instead became a foreign correspondent, giving up journalism at the beginning of the war to join the Italian army. At the front he suffered seven major wounds and would wear an aluminum kneecap for the rest of his life. In truth he had been wounded only once, did not have an aluminum kneecap, was neither overseas nor a reporter when the United States entered the war, did not join the Italian army (he was in the Red Cross), and did not leave home to become a prizefighter. By making his early life so dramatic Parker was doing what others had done. There was something compelling in Hemingway's personality that encouraged myth-making and defeated even scrupulous efforts to tell the truth, and by the time of Parker's profile one could hardly disentangle the truth from the hyperbolic fantasies. The trait in Hemingway's personality which made him seem larger than life was his charisma, a notoriously indefinable quality. The Greeks, who coined the word, probably came as close as possible to making sense of it when they called it a divine gift, easily recognized but ineffable.

Although she exaggerated his colorful past, Parker wanted to portray Hemingway as preeminently a serious artist with an almost religious devotion to his craft. Her subtitle, "The Artist's Reward," was taken from a letter to Scott Fitzgerald in which Hemingway described a writer's torment after he has gone over his work so often he can no longer tell if it is good. Admiringly she told how he rewrote the conclusion of A Farewell to Arms seventy times, hoping only to come nearer his meaning. Creation was painful for him: "He works like hell and through it. Nothing comes easily to him; he struggles, sets down a word, scratches it out, and begins all over. He regards his art as hard and dirty work, with no hope of better conditions." His artistic integrity was of a piece with his personal courage:

> He has the most profound bravery that it has ever been my privilege to see. . . . He has had pain, ill-health, and the kind of poverty that you don't believe—the kind of which actual hunger is the attendant; he has had about eight times the normal allotment of responsibilities. And he has never compromised. He has never turned off on an easier path than the one he staked himself. It takes courage.[40]

Her assertion that Hemingway was the model of the uncorrupted artist, that his life met his definition of courage as "grace under pressure," stressed what critics had been implying since In Our Time and The Sun Also Rises. As William Troy later remarked,

Hemingway was in the 1920s the supreme representative for his generation of the "pure artist" who resisted any temptation to be deflected from his art.[41] Whatever the public attention to nonliterary aspects of his private life—and it was considerable—his standing as an artist was paramount. Some people would later argue that he was still an uncorrupted artist, but opinion would never again be so close to unanimous as it was in 1929. Rather, beginning in the early 1930s and continuing thereafter, many critics argued that he was faltering because he diverted his attention from art to establish and perpetuate his celebrity. In the next decade he would indeed exchange the literary reputation he had earned with the intellectual elite for a public reputation which made him independent of that elite; and to do this he needed to exploit his public personality more self-consciously than he had in the 1920s.

The week that Dorothy Parker's profile appeared on the newsstands, a small item in a New York newspaper reported a fight Hemingway had had in Paris with another writer, Morley Callaghan. The full story of that fight and its aftermath, not to be completely told for over thirty years, revealed how concerned Hemingway was with his public reputation even at this early date; and it foreshadowed the attention he would give after 1929 to preserving and enlarging his personal fame.

According to the New York *Herald Tribune*, Hemingway was holding forth at the Dôme one evening about how Callaghan's ignorance of prizefighting was reflected in his short stories on boxing, whereupon Callaghan challenged him. They arranged for a place to fight, invited a large audience, squared off, and Callaghan knocked Hemingway out. The timekeeper became so excited that he forgot to count Hemingway out, and he "had to stagger up and finish the round."[42] This anecdote portrayed Hemingway as a braggart and bully who got what he deserved, and it debunked his boxing prowess. When Callaghan read the account in the *Herald Tribune*, he later said, he knew that it might destroy "a legend very important to Hemingway," and so he asked the newspaper for a retraction.[43] In his letter, most of which the *Herald Tribune* printed, he denied that he had challenged Hemingway or knocked him out; he added that the few times they had boxed they had merely been trying to develop a beer thirst.[44]

That was the end of the matter until Callaghan made the event the central incident in his memoir of the 1920s, *That Summer in Paris*, written after Hemingway's death. According to Callaghan's memoir, the truth bore little relation either to the *Herald Tribune* version or his correction. In one of the friendly matches they fought in the summer of 1929, Callaghan did knock Hemingway down, but not out, and the timekeeper, F. Scott Fitzgerald, did allow the round to continue an extra minute or so. But after Hemingway's brief angry flare at Fitzgerald, the match ended and the three men for the moment remained friends. The fictitious version some months later in the *Herald Tribune*, however, led to reactions in Hemingway's later manner. After Callaghan had written his denial, but before his letter was published, he received a cable from Fitzgerald demanding a public retraction. The implication that he was the source of the erroneous story so enraged Callaghan that he wrote an insulting letter back to Fitzgerald. Several weeks later a letter to Callaghan from Hemingway revealed that he had insisted Fitzgerald send the cable. Hemingway said that since he and not Fitzgerald was the guilty party, he would be happy to have Callaghan transfer to him the epithets he had directed at Fitzgerald; he added that he was coming back to the United States and would be happy to meet Callaghan to resolve their dispute in a direct and manly fashion. What the dispute entailed at this juncture is not clear, for Hemingway admitted in his letter that he knew Callaghan was not the source of the *Herald Tribune*'s story. Callaghan replied that although he regretted the affair he was still angry at Hemingway for insisting that Fitzgerald send the cable; he said that he would try to work up a fresh set of epithets. Over a month later the affair took another bizarre turn. Hemingway wrote Callaghan to say that his earlier letter had been written in an irrational fit of anger and that he had never meant it to be mailed, but that his wife had posted it by mistake. He had been justifiably angry, he said, at the newspaper story, but now he had nothing but friendly feelings. Nevertheless, he added, he was sure he could knock Callaghan out in a maximum of five two-minute rounds if he wanted to. Callaghan replied that he could hardly agree; why not just forget and disarm? Whatever Hemingway further thought Callaghan never discovered; the two never saw one another or communicated again. The misunderstandings also destroyed the friendship of Fitzgerald and Callaghan, who likewise never met again.[45]

Callaghan's account acknowledges that he and Hemingway shared the blame for the fiasco; the greatest fault, nevertheless, was obviously Hemingway's. Had he not been so protective of his public reputation and demanded that Fitzgerald send the cable, the affair would have blown over with Callaghan's retraction. But obviously he was concerned, and profoundly; moreover, his boast that he could knock Callaghan out demonstrated how seriously he regarded his boxing skill. The public implication that he might be anything less than a very good fighter was painful to him. He reportedly told Josephine Herbst shortly after the Callaghan affair that his writing was nothing and his boxing everything.[46]

As the Dorothy Parker profile closed the first phase of Hemingway's career as a public writer, so the Callaghan affair opened the second. Since 1925 he had earned considerable renown as an expatriate, a war hero, and a sportsman, but his fame as an artist had overshadowed his personal fame. After his first tentative attempt to develop a public personality in his essays for *transatlantic review*, he concentrated on writing the fiction which would establish his literary reputation, and did not actively work at a public reputation. Following the success of *A Farewell to Arms*, his priorities changed. Having been acclaimed by the intellectual elite as the most promising young writer of his time he set out to broaden the base of his support by advertising his public personality in a series of books and articles featuring himself. He began to publicize himself as someone more than a writer—indeed, it often seemed, as someone only incidentally a writer. It was a strange thing to do, especially for a writer at the pinnacle of literary success, and it seemed irrational to many of his former admirers, who viewed his new direction first with alarm and then with disgust. This new direction was not, however, so eccentric and senseless as it first appeared; once the tangle of Hemingway's motives is unraveled, his behavior in the 1930s possesses its own kind of coherence and logic.

3

"A Public with a Clear Recognition of One's Size"

The year 1929 saw the publication not only of *A Farewell to Arms*, but also of *The Sound and the Fury*, *Look Homeward Angel*, and *Dodsworth*. But it was Hemingway's novel that was usually acclaimed the best of the year, and it was Hemingway who was usually singled out as the genius of the age. *Time*'s response was typical. *A Farewell to Arms*, their reviewer wrote, "fulfills the prophecies that his most excited admirers have made about Ernest Hemingway."[1] The novel also sold well, appearing high on the best-seller lists. Hemingway felt pride that he had remained true to his own lights and still achieved critical and commercial success.[2] Indeed by 1930 he was widely regarded as peerless: Fitzgerald had not published a novel in five years, and seemed only to be writing trashy stories for the *Saturday Evening Post*; Lewis's limitations had become apparent since *Main Street*; Faulkner's new novel struck most reviewers as opaque; Anderson's work had fallen off since *Winesburg, Ohio*; Dos Passos's most interesting fiction was still in the future; and Wolfe's first novel, while promising, was flawed by lack of discipline.

Hemingway virtually had the field to himself, and at only thirty years of age; his future could not have seemed brighter. Why was it, then, that at this moment he began to promote a public personality so at odds with his standing as an uncorruptible artist? Why, when his stature as a major novelist seemed secure, did he insist on publicizing his personal heroism and asserting his authority on matters irrelevant to his calling? Why, in short, did he in the early 1930s begin to cultivate a large public reputation?

Easy answers to these questions will not take us far in explaining Hemingway's ambition to become the public writer of his time. The simplest explanation is that by becoming a public writer he could make more money. The author who has a large public is inevitably going to sell more than the writer whose appeal is only to the intellectual elite. And there is no doubt that Hemingway, whose style of life became opulent during the 1930s, welcomed additional money—his expenses included a new home in Key West, from which he shuttled to Europe, Wyoming, Africa, Havana, and Bimini; a two-month African safari estimated to have cost over $20,000; and a seaworthy fishing cruiser, the *Pilar*. Living in this grand style required a grand income, and although the second Mrs. Hemingway's uncle provided much of the money for the house and the safari, the long-range financial rewards of being a public writer must have been a temptation to make himself into one. But a desire for money is not a wholly satisfactory explanation for the turn in his career after *A Farewell to Arms*. If money alone were the reason, he could have cashed in by turning to screenwriting and by producing glossy stories of the *Saturday Evening Post* variety, two possibilities he stoutly resisted.

Earning big money was a sign of something else, though: his standing as the major novelist of his time. Intensely competitive, Hemingway was greatly concerned with his place in the rankings for the literary heavyweight championship. In a famous interview in 1950 with Lillian Ross of the *New Yorker*, he said that he had won the title in the 1920s, had defended it in the 1930s and 1940s, and was still prepared to defend it against all comers.[3] This competitiveness (itself an important aspect of his public personality) demanded recognition of his championship, and one measure of recognition was money.

Hemingway's reactions to adverse criticism in the early years also help explain his cultivation of a public image. In her 1929 profile Dorothy Parker noted that he was "outrageously sensitive to criticism," and that he brooded over what even the most insignificant critic said about his work.[4] Hemingway's response to Robert Herrick's review of *A Farewell to Arms* in the *Bookman*

confirms Parker's observation. Herrick argued that Hemingway
was a "dirty" writer and *A Farewell to Arms* little more than a
salacious book. It was a silly criticism, but Hemingway's response
was sillier. He wrote an open letter in which he threatened the
Bookman editor with a spanking for publishing Herrick's review.[5]
He had earlier taken offense at reviews of *Men Without Women*.
Virginia Woolf, who in her review of that book called him "courageous," "candid," and "highly skilled," also suggested that he was
too "self-consciously virile" and that his talent was showing signs of
shrinkage.[6] Hemingway's reaction, in a letter to Maxwell Perkins,
was to assert that the Bloomsbury writers were in league to keep
down young challengers.[7] His response to mildly disparaging reviews by Joseph Wood Krutch and Lee Wilson Dodd was more
splenetic. He composed a poem, "Valentine," dedicated it to
Dodd, and published it in *Little Review*. It began, "Sing a song of
critics / pockets full of lye / four and twenty critics /hope that you
will die / hope that you will peter out / hope that you will fail," and
then concluded by quoting a number of phrases from the offending
reviews.[8] His sensitivity surfaced again in *Death in the Afternoon*,
notably in "A Natural History of the Dead." In this "short story"
he attacked the New Humanists, a group of conservative critics
calling for a return to moral values and for decorum in literature.
The specific stimulus for this attack was the Herrick review of *A
Farewell to Arms*, for the *Bookman* was aligned with the New
Humanists. Herrick was not a Humanist, but his moralistic tone of
disapproval, his publication in the *Bookman*, and subsequent de-
fenses of his review by the editor, Seward Collins, were enough for
Hemingway. His response was characteristic: the New Humanists
were naive and stupid to demand that literature be decorous, and
their insularity disqualified them from judging literature. His own
qualifications were impeccable because he knew the rough and
tumble of life, and to prove it he listed indecorous and grotesque
scenes he had witnessed: the mutilation of women munitions work-
ers killed in an explosion; the agonies of a soldier whose skull was
smashed; and the death of a Spanish influenza victim who drowns
in his own mucus and then "shits the bed full." "So now," he
wrote, "I want to see the death of any self-called Humanist . . . to
see the actual death of members of this literary sect and watch the
noble exits that they make. . . . I hope to see the finish of a few, and

speculate how worms will try that long preserved sterility; with all their quaint pamphlets gone to bust and into foot-notes all their lust."[9]

The heat of Hemingway's counterattacks in this period of general critical good will toward his work demonstrates the thinness of his skin. If he had not striven so to become a public writer, his belligerence might be merely an amusing footnote to his career, but because he did work so hard at it, his intemperate responses are more significant.

His distrust of critics, his longstanding suspicion—to become a conviction—that they were out to get him, was consistent with his seeking a public esteem independent of the literary establishment. This general audience would not be so susceptible as the intellectuals to critical opinion, and thus it could insulate the writer's reputation from critical disfavor. His stature as a champion would be confirmed not by a few critics but by a large heterogeneous audience which felt a personal loyalty to him. Critical disfavor counts less when the writer, in Norman Mailer's words, has used his personality to create "a public with a clear recognition of one's size."[10] This is what Hemingway did with his public personality, and his heated reactions to the few hostile reviews of the 1920s show partly why he did it. The critics had made him champion with their early enthusiasm, and by creating a public personality and thereby enlarging his reputation, he was trying to make certain that what the critics had done they could not easily undo.

His public personality offered self-protection in another, more intimate way. The public Hemingway, as developed in the 1930s, was rugged, virile, and self-confident. He seemed to be in absolute control of himself, capable of the appropriate response in any situation. Implicit in all that Hemingway said publicly about his life was the conviction that it was satisfactory in every way. Perhaps it was, but if so, it shared little with his fictional protagonists of the previous decade. For Nick Adams, Jake Barnes, and Frederic Henry, day-to-day existence held real terrors; they often seemed nearly overwhelmed by life. Nick Adams fishing the Big Two-Hearted River and trying not to think, Jake Barnes crying in front of his mirror, Frederic Henry walking away in the rain after Catherine's death, these are among the most vivid images in Hemingway's early fiction. His characters, in Wyndham Lewis's phrase, are

"those to whom things happen."[11] In their fragility and their tenuous grip on themselves they are the antithesis of the heroic figure of
Hemingway's later self-portraits. The self-confident, assertive
public personality might convince his audience, and perhaps not
incidentally himself, that he was not like those earlier protagonists,
that he had come through and had mastered the terrors which kept
Nick Adams, Jake Barnes, and Frederic Henry awake in the night.

While still a correspondent for the Toronto *Star* in 1923,
Hemingway composed a sketch of a colleague which foreshadows
his own later behavior: "[He] is very romantic. But I can never
understand all the way inside of him because he is romantic. I am
romantic too and that is the trouble. You cannot dismiss him or
classify him because he is always acting and you cannot tell how
much of it is acting. He also acts inside himself. He is an officer and
a gentleman. It is better that way."[12] This little sketch is somewhat
enigmatic, but Hemingway clearly believed that acting, in the
sense of romantic posing, might baffle classification and dismissal.
Acting was a disguise, or a series of disguises, that hid from public
view the essential inner self. If we assume that the "real" Hemingway was similar to those early fictional figures—and there is much
biographical evidence to support this, for example, his insomnia,
his melancholia, the psychological centrality of the war wound—
then the public personality might keep that similarity private.

His public personality served in still another way. The early
fiction did not moralize. Hemingway's art was one of implication,
and rarely did the authorial voice announce a judgment or deliver a
homily. This austerity gave his fiction the spareness and objectivity
which made it prized, but removing himself from his narrative
thwarted that part of him which delighted in being a teacher and
pundit. (He did allow pedagogy to Count Mippipopolous and
Count Greffi, two of his "tutor" figures.) Leicester Hemingway
remarked that his older brother "was never very content in life
unless he had a spiritual kid brother nearby. He needed someone he
could show off to as well as teach. He needed uncritical admiration.
If the kid brother could show a little worshipful awe, that was a
distinct aid in the relationship."[13] There were several spiritual kid
brothers through the years, among them Arnold Gingrich, John
Groth, and A. E. Hotchner, as well as Leicester Hemingway, but
the most important one was collective, the public itself, which

assumed that role because of the way Hemingway designed and promoted his public personality. His nonfiction gave him license to be pedagogical whereas his fiction did not. In *Death in the Afternoon*, his essays for *Esquire*, *Green Hills of Africa*, and his dispatches from Spain during the civil war, he could assert his likes and dislikes, recount his travels, instruct in the proper way of doing things, predict the course of international politics, dramatize his exploits, and brag about his savvy and skill. These displays of knowledge and competence, besides satisfying a need to teach, made his readers his spectators and solicited their admiration.

When John Peale Bishop remarked in 1936 that the author of *In Our Time* and *The Sun Also Rises* had been transformed into the "legendary Hemingway," a public figure whose personal fame equalled or even outstripped his literary renown,[14] he was reiterating what other commentators had noticed in the preceding two or three years. There had been a Hemingway legend in the 1920s, but it was subordinate; by the middle of the next decade his fame was more than literary, and it came from a large, heterogeneous audience. By 1936 he was truly a celebrity—a public figure more renowned for his personality than for his accomplishments, however substantial those might be.

4

"A Public Character"

DEATH IN THE AFTERNOON

Between 1930 and 1936 Hemingway wrote nearly a score of short stories, among them "A Clean Well-Lighted Place," "Fathers and Sons," "The Snows of Kilimanjaro," and "The Short Happy Life of Francis Macomber"—but he produced even more nonfiction, including two books, *Death in the Afternoon* and *Green Hills of Africa*, twenty-five "letters" for *Esquire*, and a scattering of essays and letters for other periodicals. All the nonfiction he published in the 1930s was important to his personal fame, but *Death in the Afternoon* (1932) was the most important. It signalled the shift in his relationship with his audience, and, more comprehensively than anything else he wrote, it formulated his public personality. He said that he wrote the book because nothing in Spanish or English provided an introduction to modern bullfighting,[1] and as a beginner's guide it is still unsurpassed, at least in English. But, more than a manual, it was a portrait of the author as he wished to appear.

Hemingway is less obviously a hero in *Death in the Afternoon* than he was to become in his *Esquire* letters (1933–1936), *Green Hills of Africa* (1935), or *A Moveable Feast* (1963); here he is a spectator, and so the possibilities for self-dramatization do not include action in a conventional sense. But he is the hero because his personality so dominates the book. As one reviewer wrote, "the quality of its author's character is imprinted in the ink of the type on every page."[2] The self-portrait in *Death in the Afternoon* is of a man worldly, knowledgeable, hardened, a bit cynical, yet charged with enormous gusto.

This self-portrait is a mosaic composed of interpolated sketches, each highlighting a distinctive aspect of the author's personality. They involve nine roles, and these nine roles are the foundation of his public personality. Each recurs again and again in Hemingway's later self-advertisements, and journalists were to discuss him largely in terms of them.

The first and most obvious role was the sportsman. Any reader of *The Sun Also Rises* would know of Hemingway's interest in bullfighting, but *Death in the Afternoon* afforded wider scope than the fiction could to demonstrate expertise. The quality of information is impressive. Every aspect of the sport, from where the best bulls are bred to the disposition of the dead beast after the *corrida*, is explained. Evaluations of matadors, contemporary and past, are extensive and detailed. His wide experience was the warrant of his authority. Not only had he attended hundreds of fights, he had taken on calves and cows in village *capeas*, amateur events which, if not dangerous, simulated *corrida* conditions. He was also an intimate of great bullfighters and thus privy to inside information. He had watched them in the ring, drunk with them in cafes, conversed with them in their dressing rooms, and seen them as their wounds were treated.

Closely related to the sportsman role was the role of the manly man, tough and virile. To many non-Spaniards bullfighting was a cruel sport. For an American writer to make it a favorite subject raised questions about the writer. As one reviewer of *Death in the Afternoon* said, the important thing was "not only whether the book [was] good but whether Mr. Hemingway himself [was] good."[3] The subject matter allowed Hemingway to flaunt his hard-boiled view of life and death, and suggested a perhaps inordinate fascination with courage. For Hemingway squeamishness was opposed to manliness. He railed against a recent law which made protective quilts obligatory for picadors' horses; this innovation, he said, deprived people of the fun of seeing horses drag their entrails after they had been gored (*DIA*, 7–8). He also cited the "spiritual enjoyment" of killing, calling it "one of the greatest enjoyments of a part of the human race" (*DIA*, 232). Because killing and death were central in bullfighting, he argued that it was manlier than Anglo-American games, which concerned abstract winning (*DIA*, 22). The manly man was militantly virile, and in *Death in the Afternoon* Hemingway spoke contemptuously of several actual or suspected homosexual writers: Jean Cocteau, Raymond Radiguet, Oscar Wilde, Walt Whitman, and André Gide, categorizing them as "the mincing gentry" (*DIA*, 205, 71). The manly man also hated the inhibitive and masturbatory, and so Hemingway called Waldo Frank's pseudomystical style in *Virgin Spain* "erectile writing." The remedy was heterosexual action: "I wonder what such a book as *Virgin Spain* would have been like if written after a few good pieces of that sovereign specific for making a man see clearly. . . . It seems as though, had the brain been cleared sufficiently, by a few good pieces, there might have been no book at all" (*DIA*, 54). The master of straightforward prose, on the other hand, evidently well used that "sovereign specific."

The third role was that of exposer of sham. Danger and death had taught Hemingway that life was tenuous, and in this knowledge he perceived the essential and true more accurately than people less experienced. *Death in the Afternoon* contains numerous jeering attacks on people he thought phony, hypocritical, or witless. The matador Nino de Palma (the model for Pedro Romero in *The Sun Also Rises*) demonstrated "cowardice in its least attractive form; its fat-rumped, prematurely bald from using hair fixatives, prematurely senile form" (*DIA*, 88). The New Humanists—critics who disapproved of his work—were ignorant and foolish, products of "decorous cohabitation" despite the fact that "the position prescribed for procreation is indecorous, highly indecorous" (*DIA*, 139). Waldo Frank's book on Spain was a fake not only because of Frank's sex life but because, lacking even a minimal understanding of the country, he relied on a flatulent and abstract mysticism (*DIA*, 53–54). Abstractness or "any over-metaphysical tendency" was "horseshit" (*DIA*, 95). Years later his theorem ran: "The most essential gift for a good writer is a built-in, shock-proof, shit detector."[4]

The fourth role was that of arbiter of taste. *Death in the Afternoon* characteristically has asides on painting, wine, literature, and food. Near the beginning, for one example among the many too familiar to list, Hemingway makes an extended comparison between enjoying bullfights and enjoying wine, from which he goes on:

> In wine, most people at the start prefer sweet vintages, Sauternes, Graves, Barsac, and sparkling wines, such as not too dry champagne and sparkling Burgundy because of their picturesque quality while later they would trade all these for a light but full and fine example of the Grand crus of Medoc though it may be in a plain bottle without label, dust, or cobwebs, with nothing picturesque, but only its honesty and delicacy and the light body of it on your tongue, cool in your mouth and warm when you have drunk it. (*DIA*, 10–11)

Hemingway's self-promotion as a connoisseur is a dominant motif in the book and of his public image generally.

The fifth role, closely related to the arbiter of taste, was that of world traveler. *Death in the Afternoon* is as much a travel book as a treatise on bullfighting. Hemingway put into it knowledge he had acquired on trips to Spain since the early 1920s; one critic calls it "a cross between Baedecker and Duncan Hines."[5] The discussions of cities and regions are full and detailed; Hemingway even tells his readers what to order at various cafes: "On hot nights [in Madrid] you can go to the Bombilla to sit and drink cider and dance and it is always cool when you stop dancing there in the leafyness of the long plantings of trees where the mist rises from the small river. On cold nights you can drink sherry brandy and go to bed" (*DIA*, 48). He also instructs readers about Spanish etiquette. How to ogle women at the bullring: it is bad taste to use field glasses in the ring before the fight, but a compliment to use them in the *barrera*, the first row of seats (*DIA*, 40–42). As a guidebook to the pleasures of Spain, *Death in the Afternoon* is prescriptive; the visitor could do no better than to follow the author's instructions. In similar ways Hemingway would treat Spain again—also France, Africa, Cuba, Bimini, Italy, Switzerland, Austria, Turkey, Key West, and the Rocky Mountains. Acknowledging his reputation as a globetrotter, in 1934 *Vanity Fair* dubbed Hemingway and his wife "America's Favorite Gypsy Couple."[6]

His preferences in wine and food, his descriptions of *ferias* and bullfights, and his directions for enjoying life in Spain suggest the sixth role, that of *bon vivant*. According to *Death in the Afternoon* Hemingway's life was glamorous, exciting, and, as he once said of

bullfighters, lived "all the way up." As a *cognoscente* he could mar-
shal his experiences, none of them ordinary or banal, to yield a full
measure of enjoyment. That he was a master of the art of living was
a perennial characteristic of Hemingway's nonfiction and the public
personality; he implied he was in perfect control of his life and
would not trade it for any other imaginable one.

The seventh role was that of insider. Enjoyment of bullfighting
was enhanced by friendship with *toreros*, and Hemingway could
write with authority about Spain in general because he claimed to
see it like a native. Madrid, he says, "has none of the look you
expect of Spain. It is modern rather than picturesque, no costumes,
practically no Cordoban hats, except on the heads of phonies, no
castanets, and no disgusting fakes like the gypsy caves at Granada.
There is not one local-colored place for tourists in the town. Yet
when you get to know it, it is the most Spanish of all cities, the best to
live in, the finest people, month in and month out the finest climate
. . ." (*DIA*, 51, italics added). Most often Hemingway represented
himself as an insider of in-groups—a double distinction—whether
bullfighters, soldiers, or white hunters. The line between outsiders
and inner circles was as strict in his nonfiction as in his fiction. He
never failed to make clear where he belonged.

The eighth role was that of stoic and battle-scarred veteran.
Being such a veteran gave one the right to be an insider, to eat and
drink well, for one knew the rigor of life from violent and shattering
experiences. *Death in the Afternoon* concerns the killing of men as
well as animals, deaths the author has witnessed. Death, he says,
"is the unescapable reality, the one thing any man may be sure of;
the only security; . . . it transcends all modern comforts and . . .
with it you do not need a bathtub in every American home, nor,
when you have it, do you need the radio" (*DIA*, 266). Besides the
deaths of bullfighters, he describes killings he saw in Italy during
the war. He tells what putrefying bodies look and smell like, and
recounts his grisly experience burying victims of a munitions-
factory explosion near Milan (*DIA*, 133–134). Like those of his
fictional heroes who had been given philosophic knowledge in their
awareness of death, he spoke with the authority derived from experience.

The final role, the most important in Hemingway's public reputation, was the heroic artist. The artist, he says, pays a high price for the knowledge he transmutes into art.

> There are some things which cannot be learned quickly and time, which is all we have, must be paid heavily for the acquiring. They are the very simplest things and because it takes a man's life to know them the little new that each man gets from life is very costly and the only heritage he has to leave. Every novel which is truly written contributes to the total knowledge which is there at the disposal of the next writer who comes, but the next writer must pay, always, a certain nominal percentage in experience to be able to understand and assimilate what is available as his birthright and what he must, in turn, take his departure from. (*DIA*, 192)

The artist is heroic because he suffers pain and loss for the sake of his art. He is a sacrificial figure: he must experience more intensely than other persons (and for Hemingway consciousness was usually equated with pain) in order to add to human knowledge. With this romantic view of the artist, Hemingway inevitably focused attention on his personality. This formulation stressed experience as basic to craft, and suggested that an understanding of the artist's life would enrich understanding of his art.

Bullfighting was Hemingway's metaphor or model for the artist's way. He was first attracted to the bullfight because only there, after the war, could he observe violent death, one of the "simplest things" and therefore one of the most important for a writer to study (*DIA*, 2). The sport gave him a standard of heroism which emphasized the importance of physical courage, self-control, and stoicism. The great bullfighters had "cojones." They took chances with their lives, relying upon skill and dexterity so that spectators might vicariously triumph over death (*DIA*, 213). The bullfighter was an artist, and the bullfight an artistic performance that paralleled classical tragedy (*DIA*, 20–21, 99).

By celebrating the bullfighter as an heroic artist, he suggested his own conception of how the artist should behave and what his social function should be. The artist's obligation was to seek out danger and test himself against it; if he was not a bullfighter he ought to find other spheres of comparable risk, sending back reports of what he had learned. Unlike the bullfighter, the writer had no opportunity to enact his encounters with danger before his audience. His novels presumably contained the distillation of the knowledge he had won, but they were not the experiences themselves. Readers might make inferences about the writer from his work, but they would necessarily remain guesses. But this gap between the writer's experience and the audience's perception could be considerably narrowed by first-person accounts of events in the writer's life. If these were not the actual events, they described real experiences without compelling the writer to don a fictional mask. Writing about his own experiences, Hemingway could simulate the immediacy of the bullfight and solicit his audience's evaluation of his courage and of his standing as a heroic artist. Much of his nonfiction writing after 1932 dramatized how well he himself met the standards of performance which he borrowed from the bullfight.

These, then, were the nine roles in *Death in the Afternoon*—sportsman, manly man, exposer of sham, arbiter of taste, world traveler, *bon vivant*, insider, stoic and battle-scarred veteran, and heroic artist. All of them might be inferred from Hemingway's previous fiction, but in *Death in the Afternoon* he was clearly writing about himself. He knew that to publicize his life made him vulnerable. While he was writing *Death in the Afternoon* he was invited to contribute a foreword to a bibliography of his works, but he refused because, he said, it might deflect attention to his personality; he wanted his fiction to be evaluated on its merits without reference to anything he personally said or did.[7] Later he publicly replied to a reviewer who had taken exception to his comments about Jean Cocteau. Cocteau, Hemingway said, was a "public character" and therefore not exempt from personal criticism.[8] Hemingway recognized that the artist who became a "public character" might have his work judged in terms of his personality or have his work disregarded and his personality judged instead. Nevertheless, Hemingway's desire for heroic celebrity overrode his misgivings. In *Death in the Afternoon* he created a personal character so successful and so memorable that it bulked larger than his fiction in the public mind. Hemingway's "rich and roaring life," as one mass-circulation magazine later characterized it, "was his own best story."[9] *Death in the Afternoon* helped stimulate a continuing thirst for details about Hemingway's private life, and the author and the media were to supply them copiously thereafter.

5

"A Cross Between D'Artagnan and Don Juan"

1930–1935

I

Two months after *Death in the Afternoon* was published, the editors of *Apparel Arts*, a menswear trade journal, began planning a new general circulation magazine they hoped would have the appeal for men *Vogue* had for women. The magazine was to combine features of masculine interest with current men's fashions, to be sold in a glossy format at fifty cents, ten times the price of *The Saturday Evening Post*, *Liberty*, and *Collier's*, the leading magazines of the day. The editors hoped to justify the price by publishing only the best material by well-known authorities, and they drew up a list of desirable contributors and subjects that included Bobby Jones on golf, Rudy Vallee on show business, Gene Tunney on boxing, and Hemingway on fishing.[1]

Hemingway became a regular contributor to *Esquire*, as the magazine was named; by August 1936 his byline had appeared in twenty-eight of the first thirty-three numbers. Arnold Gingrich, *Esquire*'s editor-in-chief, had landed him by promising to pay double the standard rate: $200 per contribution in the early days, $500 by 1936. Hemingway insisted on these special rates as part of his general policy; top prices, he told Gingrich, made magazines realize what a splendid writer he was.[2] Gingrich assured him that he could write about anything, and that no unauthorized editing would be done on his material.

Hemingway published three short stories in *Esquire* between 1933 and mid-1936, but his contributions were mostly personal essays, or "letters," each about a topic on his mind at the moment. As in much of his nonfiction, the nominal subjects were often subordinate to displays of his character and personality. In *Death in the Afternoon* the bulk and comprehensiveness of information gave the book an identity beyond the author's; in the *Esquire* letters he was freer to indulge himself. Also, he could legitimately assume that his *Esquire* readers wanted to know more about him.

Publishing in *Esquire* meant that Hemingway was reaching a larger and more heterogeneous audience than ever before. Originally a quarterly, the magazine was an instant success upon its appearance in the autumn of 1933. The first number, with a print run of 105,000 copies, quickly sold out, and the editors were persuaded to publish monthly, beginning with the second issue. By the end of the first year circulation nearly doubled; by the end of 1936 it was selling some 550,000 copies a month, more than any other magazine of comparable cost.[3] Since a magazine is usually read by several persons, these figures meant that Hemingway's potential readership in *Esquire* was probably never less than a quarter of a million, and by 1936 he may have reached one and a half to two million. And he was addressing this readership nearly every month for over two and a half years. While the effect of the *Esquire* letters on his public reputation is incalculable, one can surely say that no major American novelist before Hemingway ever had so large an audience for such a sustained period, and that none ever had like opportunity to talk about himself and to expect admiration in return.

In a promotional booklet sent to prospective advertisers Gingrich outlined *Esquire*'s coverage. It was to be "a new kind of magazine— one that will answer the question of What to do? What to eat, what to drink, what to wear, how to play, what to read—in short a magazine dedicated to the improvement of the new leisure."[4] Hemingway's contributions dovetailed nicely with these aims. Most of them told how he spent his non-working hours, always implying that his readers should follow or at least admire his example as a consumer of leisure time. He was proud that his letters were practical,[5] that they could teach readers how to catch a marlin, what to look for in a bullfight, how to stalk a lion, where to buy good champagne in Paris, what brand of beer to drink on a fishing cruise.

In the *Esquire* letters, Hemingway fleshed out all his roles in *Death in the Afternoon*. In "Marlin off the Morro," his first letter, he wrote about fishing in the Gulf Stream near Havana. He bragged a little about his catch and instructed readers how to fish for marlin and how to enjoy their own expeditions, addressing readers as "you," in a familiar and pedagogical tone. After waking up in your room on the northeast corner of the Ambos Mundos Hotel in Havana, "you take a shower, pull on an old pair of khaki pants and a shirt, take the pair of moccasins that are dry, put the other pair in the window so they will be dry next night, walk to the elevator, ride down, get a paper at the desk, walk across the corner to the cafe and have breakfast." He told readers what they should order for breakfast and what brand of beer to take along on the boat, and suggested a delicious lunch of iced alligator pears, with french dressing and little mustard.[6] Once again he was demonstrating his intimate knowledge of a foreign locale and his ability to discriminate among drinks and foods, and emphasizing as well that he was a man successful enough to take off and fish for three uninterrupted months.

In subsequent letters he took readers along on more fishing expeditions out of Key West and Havana, as well as on his travels to France, Spain, Africa, the American West, and Bimini. He seemed to spend more time in leisure than at work, and his implication was that there was no better guide to the "new leisure" than he. Not many readers could live on his scale. Frequent trips to glamorous places, fishing the Gulf Stream for months, hunting lions in Africa and elk in Montana, dining on woodcock "flambé with armagnac cooked in his own juice and butter, a little mustard added to make a sauce, with two strips of bacon and pommes soufflé and Corton, Pommard Beaune, or Chambertin to drink"[7]—all these pleasures in the *Esquire* letters were beyond ordinary reach. Often individuals become celebrities because their lives seem inimitably glamorous and exciting. But readers could also maintain a kinship with Hemingway: the man casting his line for bass, or sighting along the gun barrel at a duck, or taking a tramp in the woods, or even mixing a drink or choosing a bottle of wine, could feel he too was part of the world described so vividly in *Esquire*. John W. Aldridge remembers that as a young man he and his friends took hikes in the country "when we carried along with us the big loaf of hard bread, the wedge of sour cheese, and the dry red wine of those magnificent moments at Caporetto, the Swiss ski lodge, and the fishing stream in Spain." Hemingway's gift to the generation which followed his own, Aldridge thought, was "a way of looking at life, perhaps, and of ordering and giving meaning to our experience."[8] That way of looking at life had first found expression in his fiction, but during the 1930s it underwent a sea change: the pleasures of leisure became in his nonfiction ends in themselves and were no longer compensations connected with the deprivations of Nick Adams, Jake Barnes, and Frederic Henry.

Social analysts, among them C. Wright Mills, have argued that the gospel of work, central among American values throughout the nineteenth century, was supplanted in the twentieth century by a gospel of leisure. Mills suggests that "the new middle class," made up mainly of managers, technocrats, bureaucrats, and other salaried professionals, sees work as an activity tolerable only because it can "buy" leisure. This new middle class turns to the mass media for cues on how to spend leisure time. Leisure, and what Mills calls the "machinery of amusement," have become "the center of character-forming influences, of identification models," and public attention has shifted from producers to those persons "who are significant, not in terms of what they have achieved, but in terms of having money and time to spend."[9] Mills's analysis helps explain the popularity of Hemingway's public personality. His use of leisure time suited the social code *Esquire* proposed to serve. Hemingway was making himself into an "identification model," in Mills's phrase. After 1936 he wrote less often about how he spent his free time, but by then the mass media would take up where he left off.

During his three-year stint for *Esquire* newspapers and magazines were only beginning to publicize Hemingway's glamorous life. *Vogue* singled him out as one of five "bright people, gay people" who needed to get away from "a diet of city life and organized resort life" in order to save "their wit, their health, their backchat." The other four were Emily Post, Katherine Cornell, Maurice Fatio (an architect who had designed much of Palm Beach), and Cyrus McCormick. Hemingway escaped "the steady grind," according to

Vogue, by spending much of his time in Key West, where food and wine were cheap, swimming and fishing year-round activities, and life in general simple and unsophisticated.[10] O. O. McIntyre, a nationally syndicated columnist, noted that Hemingway's Key West residence had "the most beautiful house and grounds in town," and that his study was "strewn with skins of lions and tigers [sic] shot in Africa." The novelist's routine for entertaining his many guests, McIntyre wrote, was to take them fishing on the *Pilar* in the morning, and then to treat them to a lunch of fresh fish prepared by the boat's cook and served on board, a meal "replete with Spanish wines and liqueurs." McIntyre thought Hemingway was "leading the life of the fabulous Riley."[11]

Notable, too, was *Vanity Fair*'s nomination in July 1934 of Hemingway and his wife as "America's Favorite Gypsy Couple," supplanting Douglas Fairbanks and Mary Pickford. The magazine reported that the Hemingways were deep-sea fishing in Key West at the moment, "but soon, no doubt, they will be off to Montana, on the trail of the lonely moose; or to Spain, where charges the tragic bull, as described in *Death in the Afternoon;* or to Africa, where there must be a couple of lions who haven't yet met up with Mr. Hemingway." A three-quarter-page photograph of the novelist and his wife on the S.S. *Paris* documented the Hemingways' gypsy ways.[12] As a traveling celebrity he was a magnet to reporters. Dockside in 1934, he told several of them that he had returned from Africa only to make enough money for another safari the next winter.[13] Gossip columnists also began to take notice. While he was in New York to see the Joe Louis–Max Baer fight, one columnist mentioned him as the reigning figure at the Stork Club; another noted that he was being entertained by the socialite polo player Winston Guest.[14]

These few references in the mass media to his leisure pursuits were nothing like the microscopic scrutiny his private life would receive in later years, but they indicated that his public personality was having its effect on journalists, who were a receptive audience for several of his roles in *Death in the Afternoon.* But much of Hemingway's appeal as a celebrity stemmed from his reconciliation of the gospels of work and leisure, for the gospel of work survived in America, if only out of nostalgia for Victorian values. He often indicated that his leisure activities inspired his fiction, and that he deserved them because otherwise he labored conscientiously at his craft. By 1936 he had published eight books in eleven years as well as the letters for *Esquire*—undeniable evidence of his industry. In his letter for May 1935 he apologized for the lack of action in preceding contributions. He had been finishing a book and it had taken all his energy. "There is no quieter and less eventful life than that of a writer when he is working hard," he said; "if he is working as hard as he should everything goes into the writing." But now the work was finished, he added, and he was looking forward to four months of fishing off Bimini, Havana, and Key West.[15]

His public reputation was the beneficiary of a shift to the gospel of leisure, but his appeal was greatly magnified by his fulfillment of the requirements of the gospels of both work and leisure. He advertised himself frequently as a champion competitor at work and play, and implied that he had achieved in his life a balance between the two that his readers would be wise to emulate. Hemingway enjoyed fulfilling leisure and fulfilling work, a way of life attractive to countrymen confused by the decline of an old ethic and the rise of a new one.

II

In the *Esquire* letters Hemingway emphasized his sportsman role. Nineteen out of the twenty-five featured his sporting opinions, his triumphs at fishing and hunting, and his advice on techniques for enjoying sports. In nearly all the sporting letters he was active; he had moved from the *barrera* into the arena. The bullfighter was the primary hero in *Death in the Afternoon;* in *Esquire* the author took his place.

More than half of the sporting letters discussed catching marlin and other deep-sea fish. Still using the instructional "you," he informed readers that when you hook a marlin "you feel their speed, their force and their savage power as intimately as if you were riding a bucking horse. For half an hour, an hour, or five hours, you are fastened to the fish as much as he is fastened to you and you tame him and break him the way a wild horse is broken and finally lead him to the boat."[16] His successes confirmed his strength and stamina: the number and size of his catches were always impressive.[17] In one letter he told how he brought in a 420-pound marlin, and gave an inventory, including brand names, of the equipment he used.[18] In another he talked about fishing at Bimini, where a marlin his friend Henry Strater caught was half-eaten by sharks; this account led to a discussion of the best way to catch large fish, emphasizing particularly a proper leader.[19] In still another, he discussed the adjustments of tactics necessary in fighting various types of fish.[20] Cumulatively the fishing letters suggested that he was a star fisherman. He was certainly one of the most quoted: by 1935 the fishing letters were cited by writers in such sporting magazines as *Field and Stream* and *Outdoor Life*, adding another dimension to public awareness of him as more than "merely" an author of fiction.

In its "Sport" section for July 24, 1933, *Time* announced that Hemingway, fortified by his "usual wicker demi-john of wine," had two weeks earlier hooked and boated the largest marlin ever captured off the Cuban coast, a giant fish weighing 468 pounds and measuring over twelve feet. This was especially significant because he "had fought the bucking sea bronco alone and *without harness*." To give readers some idea of the magnitude of his achievement, the magazine reproduced a photograph of Hemingway posed beside the marlin as it hung from the customs house scales.[21] A few years later *Outdoor Life* reported that he had caught a 786-pound mako shark, only twelve pounds shy of the world record.[22] A number of his catches, including one near Bimini of the first unmutilated tuna ever taken south of New York, were celebrated in a 1936 *Yachting* piece reviewing fishing in the previous year.[23] *Scribner's Magazine*, while serializing *Green Hills of Africa*, touted Hemingway as a world-class fisherman and repeated the story of the unmutilated tuna. "The hard part of catching them [in Bimini]," the magazine added, "is to bring them up fast when they sound before the sharks can hit them. When the water is from 400 to 700 fathoms it's not easy."[24] A literary gossip column in the New York *World-Telegram* recounted a titanic six-hour fifty-minute battle between Hemingway and a 514-pound tuna; the boating of the tuna, the column reported, provoked such antics on board that part of the deck collapsed.[25] In *Pleasure* (an imitator of *Esquire*), S. Kip Farrington, Jr., ranked Hemingway as one of the best marlin fishermen along the Atlantic coast.[26] Farrington revised his estimate of Hemingway's fishing skill upward in a book, *Atlantic Game Fishing*, which included several anecdotes about Hemingway's expertise: now he

became one of the two greatest fishermen in the world.[27] In 1936
Esquire printed a cartoon in which a mother fish assures her young
ones that "we can all relax now, children—Mr. Hemingway has
gone north."[28]

For a writer to be a fisherman was not unusual, but for him to be
touted as one of the world's greatest fishermen was something else.
Hemingway's *Esquire* letters did much to establish this reputation,
which was obviously dear to him. He wanted very much to be
known as a champion sportsman, and this desire suggested yet
another reason for cultivating his public reputation so assiduously,
one imbedded in his childhood. In the Hemingway family his
mother was the devoted disciple of culture and his father the lover
of the outdoors, particularly of hunting and fishing; his feelings
toward his father were ambivalent, but those toward his mother
were not. More than one acquaintance remarked that he truly and
absolutely hated her. Without being unduly psychological, then, it
is reasonable to see his love of sport as an attempt to dissociate
himself in some degree from the realm that his mother presided
over in family life in favor of the one that his father represented. In
any case, a distrust of culture would not be unusual in a man born
around the turn of the century; as we have seen, high culture in
America has traditionally been regarded as a feminine preserve in
which a truly manly man was not much interested. This would
only have been exacerbated for Hemingway because of his antipathy for his culture-loving mother. Hence his love of sport had its
psychological roots at least in part in his family situation. But why
the need to make his sporting prowess so public, to be known as a
champion? He was famed as an artist, perhaps the most important
American novelist of his age—he was his mother's son and excelled
in her sphere, in spite of his feelings about her—and, with the
dichotomy between art and masculinity firmly impressed upon him
in childhood, he needed to exorcise in a public manner some of the
onus attached to culture. And the way to achieve that was to excel
in some indisputably masculine activity and to be famed for that
excellence.

Hemingway's fame as a sportsman in the 1930s rested mainly on
his special competence in bullfighting, deep-sea fishing, and hunting. (Boxing, by this time, was of less importance.) He traveled to
Africa in the winter of 1933–1934 to hunt big game, and out of that

safari came three letters for *Esquire* and a nonfiction book (as well as two fine short stories) based upon his experiences. Nothing he did until the outbreak of the Spanish civil war was to have so great or so enduring effect on his public reputation as the African trip. The novelist who had dramatized grace under pressure in fiction could now demonstrate that virtue in himself, and the nonfiction about the trip became a public record of his meeting the challenges he sought. His self-portrayal as the stalwart hunter of lion, kudu, rhinoceros, buffalo, and other big game remained one of the most vivid and dramatic elements of his personal fame although he returned to Africa only once thereafter, twenty years later. Africa offered the same moral advantage as bullfighting, but here he rather than the bullfighter took the chances and administered the deaths. He admitted that he was too old and too heavy to be a successful bullfighter, but his condition was no obstacle to becoming a great hunter.

His first African letter in *Esquire* found him in Nairobi recovering from an attack of amoebic dysentery. The disease, he explained, was easily cured once diagnosed, and he expected to be back in camp south of Ngocongoro in three days. His medication had made him somewhat incoherent, and he apologized for the poor letter and promised to atone with "a lot of facts" in his next. He praised the country as the finest he had ever seen and listed his party's trophies, archly prefacing the list "if anyone is interested," as he knew everyone would be. This letter also printed a photograph Hemingway had taken of a live black-maned lion from only twelve feet away. His caption said that the Lonsdale Library described the black-maned lion as "a difficult beast to photograph dead or alive"— testament to the photographer's courage and skill as a stalker.[29]

His next letter, two months later, discussed the methods and ethics of lion hunting. He distinguished between "tourists," who kill lions in unethical ways ("shootism"), and "sportsmen," who properly hunt on foot and in daylight. He was a sportsman, and to prove it he told about his first lion, dispatched with a single shot from one hundred yards. Being a sportsman, he emphasized, was perilous. The odds are about ten to one that the hunter will not be in serious danger if he can shoot accurately and knows where to aim (as Hemingway showed he did), but if he only wounds the lion and has to stalk him, the probability of a maiming increases to about one in two. "So do not let anyone tell you that lion shooting . . . is no longer a sporting show. The only way the danger can be removed or mitigated is by your own ability to shoot, and that is as it should be."[30] If Hemingway's *Esquire* readers had read *Death in the Afternoon*, they could spot the resemblance between the lion hunter's code and the bullfighter's, for the matador gave true emotion to his spectators only if he adhered to exact rules which maximized his personal danger. With the African hunter it was essentially the same.

The discourse on lion hunting was complemented by a photograph of Hemingway in full safari regalia, posed with the black-maned lion he described killing. The importance of photographs to his public reputation cannot be overemphasized. By his death in 1961, according to the *International Celebrity Register*, his face was "as familiar to millions as the countenance of Clark Gable or Ted Williams."[31] Hemingway's conspicuousness was unparalleled in American literature; even Mark Twain, whose leonine features made him instantly recognizable, had not been so much in the public eye as Hemingway, whose rise to fame coincided with the heyday of "photojournalism." He was gorgeously photogenic, and his activities were suited for pictorial capture. Whether crouched over a greater kudu,[32] or posed beside a giant marlin hung up for weighing, or standing at the rail of an ocean liner, or focusing his binoculars on enemy fortifications at the front lines, Hemingway in his photographs displayed meaningful expectancy and fulfillment, and by extrapolation a life of extraordinary adventure. Although the public might occasionally see a photograph of him typing or writing at his stand-up desk, most often they saw him in nonliterary activity, frequently dangerous and nearly always glamorous. As Phillip Young has remarked, "far from presenting the literal record of a life which might counteract the legend, until the last years the photogenic Hemingway vastly confused the record by glamorizing it further."[33]

But many disapproved of the photogenic Hemingway. When some literary critics in the 1930s began to question his public personality, which they thought signified a defection from serious work and an unhealthy craving for celebrity, they frequently singled out the photographic record. Novelists, unlike movie stars, were supposed to be invisible to the public; their glory was in what they wrote, not in their faces. In 1936 John Peale Bishop, lamenting the deterioration of Hemingway's talent, felt that he had "turned into a composite" of his photographs of the previous half-dozen years, pictures of him "sun-burned from snows, on skis; in fishing get-up, burned dark from the hot Caribbean; the handsome, stalwart hunter crouched smiling over the carcass of some dead beast." This public man was not the Hemingway who had written *In Our Time* and *The Sun Also Rises*.[34] Edmund Wilson was equally censorious. The transformation of Hemingway from private writer to celebrity was obvious, Wilson said, in "the Hemingway of the handsome photographs with the sportsman's tan and the outdoor grin, with the ominous resemblance to Clark Gable, who poses with giant marlin which he has just hauled in off Key West."[35] Newspaper columnist Marshall Maslin's comparison was less flattering: he thought the photographic Hemingway looked like a combination of Wallace Beery and Pancho Villa. Referring to the photo in *Esquire* of Hemingway with his trophy lion, Maslin wondered "why a distinguished American author should take the trouble to go all the way to Africa to make an unprovoked attack on a lion—or even to pat one on the back."[36] Maslin's assumption, that distinguished American authors do not fritter away their energies and remain distinguished, was one that many detractors would later echo. These criticisms had no effect on Hemingway, who continued to pose for photographers; and they certainly had none on the newspapers and popular magazines, which printed his pictures in ever-increasing numbers.

No photographs accompanied the third and final African letter, "Notes on Dangerous Game," but it was even more self-congratulatory than the first two. Although he assumed a modest air—once referring to himself as a "greenhorn"—it is clear that this is only a matter of form rather than a reflection upon his skill. The standard by which the client should judge his effectiveness on safari, he said, was the number of times the white hunter had to fire his gun; with inexperienced or cowardly people, the white hunter fires as often as or more than the client. In an aside he rated himself:

> *You shot twice, Mr. P.* [Phillip Percival, the white hunter]. *Correct me if I'm wrong. Once at that leopard's mate when she broke back and you spun her over like a rabbit, and the other time when we caught the bull in the open and*

had two down and the third bull with four solids in him going at that same
gallop. . . . You figured he would make the bush so you shot and the gallop
changed into a long slide forward on his nose.[37]

As the aside also makes clear, Mr. P.'s shots came on multiple kills,
when it was less shameful to the client for the white hunter to fire.

Hemingway's admiration for Phillip Percival pervades the letter;
among other accomplishments, Percival was one of two white hunters in Africa who had never had a client mauled. (The other was
Baron von Blixen, another of Hemingway's pals, whom he called
"Blix.") Phillip Percival is "Mr. P." or "Pop," evidence of intimacy.
Hemingway advertised the warmth of the relationship in two more
asides. In one he mentions that he and Mr. P. went deep-sea fishing
after the safari; in the other he said he was going to write Mr. P.
because he "got to missing him." His intimacy with the white
hunter certified Hemingway as an insider whose observations on
big-game hunting could be trusted, professions of modesty notwithstanding. If his white hunter thought him a superb hunter,
who were his readers to doubt it?

Phillip Percival was of a type Hemingway characteristically admired: the professional with profound knowledge and competence
in his trade, especially if it was a dangerous one, like bullfighting,
war, or big-game hunting. Hemingway liked to think of himself as
a member of this fraternity of professionals, and twice in "Notes on
Dangerous Game" he implied that he was. During an account of
how Percival enjoyed going into the brush after injured game, he
interrupted: *"Excuse me, Mr. P. You see I do this for a living. We all*
have to do a lot of things for a living. But we're still drinking their whiskey,
aren't we?"[38] The phrase "still drinking their whiskey" recurs in
"The Short Happy Life of Francis Macomber," when Wilson, the
white hunter (based in part on Percival), defines it as an expression
used by a white hunter when a safari has gone to pot because of an
unworthy client. At first glance it might appear that Hemingway,
by using the phrase in the letter, might be voicing regret at using
his talents to write *Esquire* letters "for a living." It is, however, not
that simple. While he was implying contempt for his *Esquire* readers
(an attitude apparent only to insiders who would know the phrase),
he was not suggesting that writing for the magazine prostituted his
talents. Rather, he was asserting his claim to the same professional

pride in competence at his journalism as a white hunter could claim in serving a bad client.

"The main point about professionals that amateurs never seem to appreciate," Hemingway wrote, was that the professional "would rather take chances any day with his life than his livelihood."[39] While his reference was to white hunters, even a casual reader could see that the standard applied equally to Hemingway. The professional realizes that competence is everything; without it, and the reputation for it, he is without honor and proper pride. For the white hunter, taking chances with his life is necessary to maintain his professional standing; the same willingness to risk obliges the novelist who has taken the representation of grace under pressure as his literary domain.

None of the remaining *Esquire* letters equalled the African sequence in dramatizing Hemingway's masculinity, but several showed he was a pretty rugged fellow. In one he told how on a trip to Bimini he accidentally shot himself in both legs with a .22 Colt automatic pistol while trying to gaff a shark from the deck of the *Pilar*. He took the wounds stoically, and his fishing expedition was delayed only six days. "On Being Shot Again," the title of the letter, reminded his audience that he had been shot during the Great War.[40] Another letter was a ringside report on the Joe Louis–Max Baer fight. Because of Baer's incapacitating fear Hemingway called the fight the "most disgusting spectacle" he had ever witnessed. He confessed that he had felt fear on a mountain ledge, before bombardments, and after he was wounded in battle and saw a flash of eternity. Baer had been overcome by fear, making him a public disgrace; Hemingway had "been frightened many times"[41] but, as the *Esquire* letters amply documented, met his dangers with courage.

Occasionally Hemingway's manliness became pugnacious. In one letter he upbraided William Saroyan, who had claimed in *The Daring Young Man on the Flying Trapeze* that he could write as well as or better than Hemingway, Dos Passos, Faulkner, and Joyce. After noting Saroyan's literary weaknesses Hemingway asked: "Do I make myself clear? Or would you like me to push your puss in? (I'm drunk again now you see. It's a wonderful advantage when you're arguing.)"[42] In another letter he recalled his rage at a drunk in a boat who had taunted him while he was hauling in a marlin. "I would prefer to work on him drunk so it would be messier and less competitive," he added, "but I would be very happy to work on him sober so that he would remember it more clearly."[43]

Such pugnacity was backed up, according to press reports, by Hemingway's facility with his fists. A newspaper account in 1934 related what happened when he ran into Robert McAlmon, his first publisher, in a Paris bar. Hemingway asked McAlmon to step outside, where he proceeded to beat him up so badly that McAlmon had to be hospitalized. The reason for Hemingway's ire was that "McAlmon was at work on a book wherein he gave the 'lowdown' on Hemingway, and Hemingway, getting word of something he did not like, thought the two-fisted method the best answer."[44] *Commonweal* reported that Hemingway was a frequent target for people wanting to fight; among them were "three assorted members of the literati" who picked fights with him, much to their regret: "the last of the trio, a bad poet but a big man physically, fought Hemingway . . . and afterward was confined to his room for five days with a day and night nurse."[45] (The poet, not a bad one at all, was Wallace Stevens and, although he fought Hemingway, his injuries were mainly to his pride.)[46] Several periodicals reported a fracas when Hemingway refereed a fight in Key West. He was counting out a boxer, said *Time*, when his second threw in the towel. "Referee Hemingway threw it out. The second jumped into the ring, swung at the referee. Mr. Hemingway gave him a left jab to the chin, twisted his ear. Said Referee Hemingway, 'He must have lost his head.'"[47] Not all fights were reported publicly, at least not until years later. Leicester Hemingway tells of an occasion in Bimini when his brother, ridiculed about his fishing by a man he did not know, worked over his taunter so thoroughly that he needed medical attention. The victim turned out to be Joseph Knapp, publisher of *Collier's*, *Woman's Home Companion*, and other magazines. After this encounter Hemingway was called in whenever anyone started to throw his weight around on the island, and, according to his brother, he scored four knockouts in three weeks. A native band celebrated his prowess in a calypso song inspired by the Knapp fight.[48] These scraps reached a symbolic apogee in a New York nightclub. *Time* reported the event: "As hefty, two-fisted Author Ernest Hemingway sat in a swank

Manhattan nightspot, one Eddie Chapman, broker, sneered: 'So you're Hemingway? . . . Tough guy, huh?' and pushed him in the face. Said a friend at Hemingway's table: 'Swat him, but don't draw blood.' Hemingway swatted."[49] His swat must have been powerful: the New York *Sunday Mirror* headlined its account, "Hemingway by K.O. in Big Night Club Card."[50] The "big night club card" illustrated how his tough-guy reputation fed upon itself, each fracas inviting yet another one, to the delight of newspaper and magazine editors who knew a good story when they saw one.

During the mid-1930s several magazines published caricatures of the virile Hemingway. A "paper doll" satire in *Vanity Fair* offered costumes representing aspects of his public personality which the reader could cut out and paste on a body figure. "Ernie, the Neanderthal Man" wore a loincloth and held a club in one hand and a rabbit in the other; "Ernie as the Lost Generation" sat at a bottle-strewn cafe table; "Ernie as Isaac [*sic*] Walton" stood in a boat brimming with fish; "Ernie as Don Jose, the Toreador" took his bows over the carcass of a bull; "Ernie the Unknown Soldier" limped away on crutches from a bloody war scene.[51] Another caricature depicted him in a safari helmet with his shirt open to reveal his chest hair, holding a rod with a large fish on the hook, and sitting astride a dead bull surrounded by whiskey bottles.[52] Yet another portrayed him as a small boy in short pants, seated on the floor and putting a finger of his hairy hand into a candle flame. On the wall behind were scribbled, in a childish hand, "damn" and "hell."[53] More complimentary was a cartoon in *Vanity Fair* supposed to represent his essential qualities. It illustrated a hairy, tattooed fist grasping a rose, the two encased in a heart. Hemingway's status among the celebrated could be assessed from similar cartoons in *Vanity Fair;* three other personalities getting such treatment were Greta Garbo, Babe Ruth, and Mae West, whose visual recognition at that time was universal.[54]

III

Virginia Woolf's comment in 1927 that Hemingway was perhaps too "self-consciously virile" referred only to his fiction; in the 1930s the same charge was made, but it was not always clear whether critics were referring to his writing or to his public personality. If they were confused about the relationship of his personality to his literary achievement, they can hardly be faulted because so much of what he wrote then was exploitation of his personality. Responding to it so frequently, critics were enlarging his reputation even while they disparaged it.

The attacks on his virility began shortly after publication of *Death in the Afternoon*. Several reviewers were offended, in the words of Seward Collins, by Hemingway's "truculent he-mannishness."[55] One who took this line was Max Eastman, a some-time friend, in an article entitled "Bull in the Afternoon." Eastman felt that Hemingway, in his fiction a hard-boiled realist, overly romanticized bullfighting. Part of the explanation, thought Eastman, lay in the Great War, with its emphasis on "courageous killing." But of equal importance was a psychological compulsion:

> It is of course a commonplace that Hemingway lacks the serene confidence that he *is* a full-sized man. . . . Some circumstance seems to have laid upon Hemingway a continual sense of the obligation to put forth evidences of red-blooded masculinity. It must be made obvious not only in the swing of the big shoulders and the clothes he puts on, but in the stride of his prose style and the emotions he permits to come to the surface there.[56]

His "wearing false hair on the chest" in both art and life was designed to hide his sensitivity and feelings of inadequacy in the face of modern brutalities.

According to Eastman's memoirs, Archibald MacLeish interpreted the article as implying that Hemingway was sexually impotent and told Hemingway so. Eastman immediately wrote MacLeish to deny this reading, but Hemingway was already into the act with an ironic letter to the *New Republic*, in which he implied that his sex life was quite satisfactory.[57] He wrote Maxwell Perkins that Eastman was jealous of his manliness and literary skill, and, anyway, he could "beat shit out of any of them," meaning Eastman and his friends.[58] Eastman tried to clear the air in the *New Republic* three weeks after his article had appeared there. He denied that "Bull in the Afternoon" reflected on Hemingway's "manhood, courage, or what-not," and went on to say that he admired Hemingway's courage. When he had first met him early in the

1920s, he recalled, Hemingway had just been blown out of a bathroom and half-way down the hall by a gas heater explosion, yet he came out of it "with a smile on his face like a man on a toboggan." Eastman still felt, however, that the attitudes of *Death in the Afternoon* were poses, that basically Hemingway was "gentle and sensitive," and that "his roaring about whorehouses and bull's blood" was just so much "unreal interior bluster."[59] This did not please Hemingway either. Four years later the two men would bring their quarrel to its climax with a celebrated brawl in Perkins's New York office.

Unlike Eastman, Gertrude Stein had no illusions that she was writing only about Hemingway's work. Her comments, first published in the *Atlantic* in 1933, then in the best-selling *The Autobiography of Alice B. Toklas*, were personal and strongly uncomplimentary. She claimed that his literary success was due to her early tutelage but that he aped her techniques without really understanding them. Her stance in discussing these years was of the wise mentor amused by a naive protégé and tolerant of his immaturity. She has Alice express contempt for him, which allows her to condescend toward the younger writer, saying that while she recognizes his limitations she has "a weakness for Hemingway."[60] She tells how he often injured himself in sports, how he learned about boxing from Sherwood Anderson and bullfighting from Alice, and how he possessed little stamina. Why, she says, he "used to get quite worn out walking from his house to ours." He was even knocked out by a boy he was teaching to box.[61] These derogations of his sporting prowess impugned a reputation very dear to him. *The Autobiography of Alice B. Toklas* appeared just as he was beginning the *Esquire* letters, and his frequent boasting there about his sporting achievements may be reasonably seen as his attempt to neutralize the effect of Gertrude Stein's vituperations.

After savaging Hemingway the sportsman, she questioned his courage, precisely what Dorothy Parker five years earlier had said he possessed more of than any man she knew. Hemingway, said Stein, was "yellow." According to her, Hemingway once wrote a letter to Sherwood Anderson repudiating the older writer's work. When Anderson came to Paris, Hemingway was "afraid":

> As I say he [Anderson] and Gertrude Stein were endlessly amusing on the subject. They admitted that Hemingway was yellow, he is, Ger-

trude Stein insisted, just like the flat-boat men on the Mississippi river
as described by Mark Twain. But what a book, they both agreed,
would be the real story of Hemingway, not those he writes but the
confessions of the real Ernest Hemingway. . . . What a story that of the
real Hem, and one he should tell himself but alas he never will. After
all, as he himself once murmured, there is the career, the career.[62]

This portrait of Hemingway as callow, opportunistic, cowardly,
and boastful like the "pet Child of Calamity" in Mark Twain's *Life
on the Mississippi*, subverted every trait that counted most to him in
his private as well as his public character.

Hemingway reacted furiously, over and over, as though he could
not get enough of expressing his hatred. He took his first pot-shot
in a 1934 *Esquire* letter while discussing his symptoms of amoebic
dysentery. He had first misdiagnosed the disease; he thought the
ruckus in his bowels meant he had been chosen as the bearer of
Buddha about to be reborn. "While flattered at this, and wondering
how much Buddha at that age would resemble Gertrude Stein, I
found the imminence of the event made it difficult to take high
incoming birds and finally compromised by reclining against the
tree and only accepting crossing shots."[63] In other words, Gertrude
Stein looked like a 2,400-year-old Buddha, and the transition from
bowel pain to thoughts of her was associatively natural. Hemingway attacked her sexuality in the same year. For *Cahiers d'Art* he
wrote an appreciation of Joan Miro, whose painting "The Farm" he
had purchased years before in Paris. Miro, he wrote, took nine
months to finish the painting, "as long to make as it takes a woman
to make a child"—and "a woman who isn't a woman can usually
write her autobiography in a third of that time."[64] The allusion to
Stein's lesbianism stemmed from his conviction that she had attacked him because he was not "queer"; she was persuaded, he
thought, that anyone "who was any good was also queer."[65] He
attacked her as self-serving in his introduction to Jimmie Charters's
memoir of Montparnasse, *This Must Be the Place*, also in 1934. There
were three reasons, he said there, why a woman mentions in her
memoirs a former habitué of her salon: she is capitalizing on his
fame; she once liked him and has gotten over it; or she is rewarding
"loyalty to the establishment." The most likely reason was the first,
he thought: his name gave her memoirs cash value. This "self-made
legendary woman" needed him to "help the sale of [her] book" to

those strange people, "banded into clubs or guilds," who bought literary reminiscences.[66] (*The Autobiography of Alice B. Toklas* was published by the Literary Guild.) Although he did not mention her by name, the reference was clear to any knowledgeable contemporary. The reactions continued for years: in *Green Hills of Africa* (1935); five years later in *For Whom the Bell Tolls* ("'An onion is an onion is an onion,' Robert Jordan said cheerily and, he thought, a stone is a stein is a rock is a boulder is a pebble")[67]; finally and most extensively in *A Moveable Feast* (1964). Hemingway's keeping the feud alive made it, as *Time* said in 1937, "one of the most persistent literary squabbles of the generation."[68] It was also one of the most publicized, and it became part of the legend.

Eastman and Stein found fault not so much with Hemingway's fiction as with how he comported himself in life and in his nonfiction. But rather than persuade him to moderate his public personality, their criticisms led him to more strenuous assertions. If Eastman and Stein were convinced that he was less than "a full-sized man" and "yellow," he would prove them wrong by giving his audience further examples of his courage and stalwart behavior. His readers could decide who was telling the truth; they would draw the same conclusions about his "prowess in action" as *Time* did when, reporting his catch of a record marlin, it hailed his feat as a "convincing . . . rebuttal to the Eastman attack."[69]

IV

Near the end of *Death in the Afternoon* Hemingway wrote, "Let those who want to save the world if you can get to see it clear and as a whole."[70] This sentence was elliptical and oddly constructed, but its meaning was clear enough, defining what kind of man and artist he thought himself. He would not try to "save the world" in the currently fashionable way, through left-wing politics and socially conscious fiction; an honest writer should follow his own lights, avoiding reformist and revolutionary schemes, and if he did his proper work it would have greater practical consequences than any sociopolitical tract. Such opinions did not endear Hemingway to critics who turned to the left in the early years of the Depression. Between 1932 and 1936, when the Spanish civil war prompted his

"conversion" to the Popular Front, he and they would carry on a
running feud about the social responsibility of the artist. While this
issue might appear to be literary, it had more to do with Hemingway's public personality. Both he and his critics indulged in name-
calling, and because Hemingway was writing so much nonfiction at
that time with himself as hero, his personality naturally became an
important counter in the arguments.

Like Max Eastman, these critics characterized Hemingway's
stylized masculinity as an adolescent pose, and like Gertrude Stein,
they ridiculed his efforts to build a legend. They added a third
derogation: he was a "dumb ox" (the phrase is Wyndham Lewis's),
incapable of sustained reflection about ideas and woefully ignorant
of political questions. They began to compare Hemingway with
Byron, not as artists but as culture heroes. Clifton Fadiman was the
first of many: "Why is Hemingway news?" he asked. "It is because
this young Lochinvar out of the Middle West is a hero," who, like
Byron, had become a "model of behavior" for his culture. Both
writers had become famous as young men, expatriated themselves
and celebrated Mediterranean cultures, were attracted to and then
repelled by the military, emphasized their masculinity and ath-
leticism, achieved a "matinee-idol popularity," and were drawn to
"wild and romantic places." They both exalted "passion, action,
and violence" and idolized "a highly specialized, arrogant caste."
Fadiman felt that Goethe's remark about Byron—"Lord Byron is
only great as a poet; as soon as he reflects, he is a child"—applied
equally to Hemingway. He conceded Hemingway's importance "as
a purely literary figure," but argued that his standing as a culture
hero was a symptom of cultural malaise and social decay.[71]

Frequently Hemingway's detractors lectured him to change his
ways, to open his eyes to political realities, to think about the
present and the future, and, in Malcolm Cowley's words, to strike
"other chords."[72] A review of *Death in the Afternoon* by Granville
Hicks, a staunch leftist critic, was typical. Hicks said he had no
scruples about discussing Hemingway personally because Hemingway, knowing the drift of public interest, had made "a vigorous
effort to put as much of himself as possible into the book." Hemingway, said Hicks, was ignorant of the larger world; and his boastful
and oppressive masculinity—his celebrations of violence, drink,
sex, and sports—was hardly a way to "get to see [the world] clear

and whole." Only when he discarded his adolescent posing and contemplated more serious matters would he mature as man and artist.[73]

A few months after his essay comparing Byron and Hemingway Fadiman reviewed *Winner Take Nothing* with an appeal that Hemingway abandon his fixation on sports and sudden death and move to larger themes. But in a response, after bragging about his sex life, his wounds, and his military decorations, Hemingway toted up his seven books in nine years, hardly evidence of flagging talent. He would outlast his critics, and by writing skillfully and regularly would make them look foolish. He threatened to break one "lousy critic's jaw" every two years; Eastman would be his first victim and the rest would be drawn by lot.[74]

This he said privately. Publicly he used his *Esquire* letters as his forum for counterattack, much like a president carrying his campaign to the people. In his letter for September 1934, "Defense of Dirty Words," he argued that writers should use "true words," even though they risked having Heywood Broun "write something devastating about small boys, back fences, and the walls of privies" in his newspaper column.[75] Hemingway probably remembered Broun's calling *Death in the Afternoon* "adolescent" two years earlier, and Broun now had more to say. *A Farewell to Arms*, he replied in his column, might be the greatest American novel ever, but *Death in the Afternoon* was dreadful and marked Hemingway as a "complete snob and poseur." He was a dumb ox as well: "I do not like the man, and yet I must admit that I know no other phony in the whole course of English letters who could write so well about things of which he had not the slightest comprehension." Hemingway's "pose and pretense of being the professional tough guy" were irrelevant and obscene in Depression America, Broun felt, and he was finished as a writer of any consequence because the future belonged to the political and social novel.[76] Broun's response was a compendium of the criticisms after 1932 and pushed Hemingway to show his political sophistication.

In his letter for December 1934, "Old Newsman Writes," he took the role of a hard-bitten, shrewd journalist whose political analyses were trustworthy because he had seen revolution firsthand and knew what it was all about. Hemingway identified Broun as "the good grey baggy-pants of the columns" (you don't dignify your opponent by mentioning his name). He was a "jackal" because he scavenged the "meat" (news) others had killed, and the same went for most columnists. But the "old newsman" lately turned columnist could speak authoritatively because he had observed political violence in Germany, Italy, and Cuba, and in political judgments "you can depend on just as much as you have actually seen and followed." The "literary revolution boys," Broun and everyone else who called him ignorant, were amateurs and incompetents because their political knowledge was derivative; they had not "been there." Hemingway then went on to explain why revolutions failed to start or were aborted in France, Spain, Germany, Austria, Hungary, and Italy. Any communist revolution, he pontificated, must be preceded by a military debacle or it is doomed; "you have to see what happens in a military debacle to understand this." In case a reader missed the point, he ended, "Make a note of this, Baggy-pants."

An implication of "Old Newsman Writes" was that Hemingway could be a political novelist if he chose. But the writer's job was not to serve as an agent of political change; he should write as honestly as he could about the kind of people he knew. The vogue of socially conscious writing was the fault of "recently politically enlightened critics":

> All the critics who could not make their reputations by discovering you are hoping to make them by predicting hopefully your approaching impotence, failure and general drying up of natural juices. Not a one will wish you luck or hope that you will keep on writing unless you have political affiliations in which case these will rally round and speak of you and Homer, Balzac, Zola and Link Steffens. You are just as well off without these reviews.[77]

Heywood Broun was unimpressed by Hemingway's show of political savvy; he replied that the *Esquire* letter was only "bitter grapes [which] grow along the walls of the mansions of the isolated."[78] Taking Broun's side, Robert Forsythe attacked Hemingway for his truculence toward the columnist, his general inability to take criticism, and his lack of social consciousness. His title, "In This Corner, Mr. Hemingway," was a sarcastic reference to the novelist's reputation for pugnacity. (As it happened, a year later Hemingway told Maxwell Perkins that he was going to break Forsythe's jaw the next time they met.)[79] According to Forsythe,

Hemingway's reading was only in what people wrote about him, and any hint that he "may have slipped slightly south of genius is calculated to throw the great man into furious exercises on the punching bag." As a novelist, Forsythe thought, Hemingway had begun in a vacuum and was "ending in a vacuum" because he had no sense of political realities or social necessities.[80]

After "Old Newsman Writes" Hemingway's *Esquire* letters were increasingly concerned with politics, and reflected his addition of the role of political sophisticate to his repertoire. In his May 1935 letter he turned again to his experience as a political journalist, recalling his prediction of inflation in postwar Austria and Germany and his prophetic analyses of Clemenceau and Mussolini. These prognostications, accurate as they turned out, had been either censored or buried in the back pages of his newspaper, teaching him this lesson: "when, through following something closely, you were positive something was going to happen, the thing to do was to discover some way of betting that it would happen and keep your mouth shut about it."[81] The Cassandra posture, however, was too appealing to resist. His letters for September and November 1935 predicted a general European war in 1937 or 1938, and argued that the United States ought to stay clear. Much of the September letter, "Notes on the Next War," was a Machiavellian analysis of the Ethiopian crisis, which at the time was moving toward a military solution. Each of the major European powers, notwithstanding their denunciations of possible Italian aggression, would be pleased to see Italy fight in Ethiopia. France had apparently made a deal sanctioning an invasion of the African country in return for the cessation of Italian claims in North Africa; England would profit because Italy would have to use the British-controlled Suez supply route; both France and England would be glad to see Italy fight because she might lose, and even if she won, she would spend so much in men and materiel as to make her less troublesome in Europe; Germany would be delighted by a war in Ethiopia because it would support her own territorial demands; and Italy by waging war would divert the attention of her citizens from domestic problems.[82] After Italy invaded Ethiopia, Hemingway outlined for *Esquire* readers the strategies of each side, foreshadowing the role of military expert he would assume with the Spanish civil war.[83] Both this letter, "Wings Always over Africa," and "Notes on the Next

War" were condensed for the *Reader's Digest*, giving him a magazine readership larger than any he had ever reached.

V

That Hemingway was a serious artist more than a sportsman, world traveler, *bon vivant*, and political sage was obscured by the *Esquire* letters: in only five of the twenty-five did he discuss writing at any length, and even in these his literary observations were often subordinate. When he did address literary matters, his remarks were anti-literary by conventional judgment. In "Defense of Dirty Words," for example, the essay which first provoked Heywood Broun, he had defended "true words" in fiction after Westbrook Pegler condemned them. Pegler had praised Ring Lardner as an artist who could successfully anatomize the seamy side of life and yet refrain from indecorous language. Pegler was all wrong, said Hemingway; Lardner's refusal to "write dirty" was precisely what prevented him from becoming a great writer. He did not use "true words" because he felt superior to the people he wrote about, prizefighters and other professional athletes. Pegler was guilty of the same snobbery, and for the same reason: "they are intellectuals" who "feel superior to other pros because they make their money with their hands." The intellectual writer, a snob, cannot write well about professional athletes or soldiers because those subjects demand an empathy the highbrow lacks.[84]

Hemingway as "anti-'literary' writer" who "would rather fish than drink tea," in *Time's* admiring characterization,[85] struck Gilbert Seldes as ridiculous. Hemingway missed what was great in Lardner, Seldes wrote in *Esquire*, and his advocacy of "hairy he-words" was absurd. In any case, Hemingway was not competent to discuss literary questions: "Hemingway keeps away from literary cocktail parties and goes to a lot of prize fights, so that his opinions on the second subject ought to be more significant than on the first."[86] Seldes's rejoinder predictably got a rejoinder from Hemingway. Reading Seldes, Hemingway wrote in "Notes on Life and Letters," did not bring on *"blindness, insanity and death"* as it was alleged to do, but produced only a feeling *"no worse than a bad cold and if you get it at the start you can knock it with this stuff I'm going to give you. . . . There's no danger, men, as long as old Doc Hemingstein is in the magazine.*[87] "Old Doc Hemingstein"—the two-fisted, bluff, unpretentious sage who exposed incompetence wherever he found it.

The longest of his literary pieces for *Esquire* was "Monologue to the Maestro" in October 1935. The "maestro" was a young aspiring writer he had hired as night watchman on the *Pilar*. At sea he asked Hemingway about writing, and their conversation constitutes the letter. Hemingway lectured him on the value of experience for a writer, on seriousness and conscientiousness, and on the difference between reportage and invention. Use a pencil rather than a typewriter; stop writing while you know what is coming next; do not think about your work until you start writing the next day; if possible, reread everything each day before you begin. (These formulas would be repeated in the press over and over in later years.) He claimed that he "dislikes talking about it [writing] with almost anyone alive."[88] This was not true, to judge by his numerous literary discussions in print. No other novelist of his generation, in fact, made so many public pronouncements about literature as he did. But he had worked hard to establish his reputation as an "anti-'literary' writer" who despised salons, literary cocktail parties, and any place where aesthetic questions dominated. He tried to dissociate himself publicly from other writers, seeming to regard them as devitalized and too precious about "Art." Public discussion of literature on his part was therefore a potential embarrassment to the image he had cultivated with the public. By feigning reticence in this *Esquire* letter—and nearly every other time he spoke publicly of literature—he was able to discuss writing and avoid being taken for an aesthete.

VI

The *Esquire* letters tapered off early in 1936—he skipped February and March—with the final one appearing in May. His connection with *Esquire* had been useful for the magazine and himself: *Esquire* had displayed the name of America's most distinguished writer on its cover, giving it a special cachet; Hemingway reached a larger audience for his public personality than he could in nonfiction like *Death in the Afternoon*. These letters established him as the public writer of his time—by 1936 it was clear that he had beaten all challengers. In doing so, however, he had alienated critics representing the intellectual elite, and it was precisely his *Esquire* letters they found most distasteful.

The response of Edmund Wilson, in the 1920s one of his earliest admirers, was particularly scornful. Beginning with *Death in the Afternoon* and continuing throughout the 1930s, Wilson wrote, Hemingway lost control of his artistic faculties in aggrandizing his public reputation and personality. The "arrogant, belligerent, and boastful" Hemingway of the *Esquire* letters was "certainly the worst-invented character to be found in the author's work," and Wilson feared that this "obnoxious" character was the only one Hemingway had left.[89] John V. A. Weaver, a minor poet and *Esquire*'s drama critic, similarly disparaged Hemingway in *Ringmaster*, an expensive magazine that resembled *Esquire*. Weaver had met Hemingway in Paris in 1922, and the young novelist had become a symbol of artistic integrity for him because of his principle of being true to his artistic objectives, whatever the monetary temptations. Weaver's admiration had continued until the *Esquire* letters. "Just what, please, is the idea of all those smooth-paper articles which seem to be your only present output? Featured in a four-star position month after month they bring you, I understand, so much money that you bask around sapphire seas in a constant state of flagrant unworry." Weaver asked Hemingway for assurance he had not sold out, and for answers to accusations: "Everybody says you've gone soft; you're accused of being coin-conscious, lazy, cynical; of cashing in on your reputation, of racketeering your signature."[90] John Peale Bishop in the *New Republic* also felt that Hemingway had changed since 1922, when he too first met him in Paris. From those days until 1930, when he stopped seeing him regularly, Bishop was sure that Hemingway had "the most complete literary integrity." He recalled a time in Paris when the novelist, living in poverty, turned down an offer from the Hearst syndicate which would have made him financially independent for years; Bishop was certain Hemingway "could not be bought." But if money could not seduce him, fame had. The change for the worse into the "legendary Hemingway" reminded Bishop of the familiar Byronic parallel, and the deterioration of Hemingway's talent in the 1930s was due to his projecting his public personality and boosting his fame.[91]

These assessments by Wilson, Weaver, and Bishop were typical among literary critics in the mid-1930s. Hemingway's literary reputation had dropped after its high point following the publication of *A Farewell to Arms*. It reached bottom in 1936, then climbed to a peak again in 1940 after *For Whom the Bell Tolls*. Meanwhile he remained consistently in good standing with newspapers and magazines such as *Vanity Fair*, *Time*, and *Vogue*, which sustained his public reputation with favorable reports and anecdotes.

He was still a favorite of *Esquire*, too, even after his letters stopped. Arnold Gingrich, its editor, in a valedictory salute in 1937 handled the common charges of Hemingway's critics by responding in much the same terms as Hemingway favored in his letters. Hemingway had not sold out, but had forsaken "not one but many fortunes" in being "true to his long-since self-charted course." His interest in hunting and fishing was not adolescent but the expression of a devotion to the timeless and eternal. Responding to Gertrude Stein's "yellow" stigma, Gingrich said that Hemingway had the highest form of courage, "cold reasoning pituitary bravery." The incompatible charges that he was a roughneck and physically fragile, a snob and a hail-fellow-well-met, were fatuous. "Called a snob, . . . he is actually a Whitman democrat, who will turn his back on a duke to continue a conversation with a barkeep, and will spend hours by choice among dock characters of a type past whom the average intellectual would not care or dare to walk without a bodyguard. Called 'fragile,' his scarred and battered bulk has survived enough punishment . . . to have killed off a full grown ape." Gingrich concluded that "Papa" Hemingway, "a cross between D'Artagnan and Don Juan," was "the St. Anthony of modern letters" who had "turned his back on the tea-drinking, back-scratching, log-rolling literary world. . . ."[92]

Hemingway's twenty-five letters for *Esquire* confirmed what he suggested in *Death in the Afternoon*, that he was not going to accept the social role conventionally prescribed for serious novelists. This role demanded that the writer, in Dwight Macdonald's words, "work for a small audience that sympathized with [his] experiments because it was sophisticated enough to understand them."[93] The writer's influence would thus be great with the intellectual elite (if his work was good), but not beyond it. And as Norman Podhoretz has pointed out the success motive in American culture has generated an anti-success motive among literary intellectuals. The reasons for this, he argues, are both psychological and sociological. The study of literature "encourages great respect for activity which is its own reward"; "good" and "successful" are not necessarily synonymous, and this perception often leads to the belief that goodness and success can never go together. Professional students of literature imagine "they are entering an existence rich in spiritual satisfaction and turning their backs on one that has nothing to offer but empty material comforts."[94] But in *Esquire* Hemingway drama- tized himself as a man over long stretches enjoying travel, leisure, and other rewards of a considerable success. Anyone who could read, could read him, and without thinking himself an intruder among highbrows.

In one of his letters Hemingway told why he liked deep-sea fishing: "The Gulf Stream and the other great ocean currents are the last wild country there is left. Once you are out of sight of land and the other boats you are more alone than you can ever be hunt- ing and the sea is the same as it has been since before men ever went on it in boats."[95] In another he said, "When you like to shoot and fish you have to move often and always further out and it doesn't make any difference what they do when you are gone."[96] His search for "wild country" pervades the *Esquire* letters, putting him in a long American tradition—literary, historical, and mythic—of rugged individualists who tested their mettle in the fastnesses of nature. During the Depression, when there were added reasons to escape realities, Americans bought pulp magazines in record num- bers, with Western adventure stories about two-fisted natural men the most popular genre. Hemingway's *Esquire* letters offered the same kind of appeal; they represented a hard-living, hard-drinking, hard-fighting adventurer always in the end the master of his fate. And if "the strenuous life" is one of the strongest American ideals, as Edwin H. Cady has argued,[97] Hemingway's popularity in any period as a man of action is easy to understand. *Esquire* gave him the forum and the audience he needed to become a celebrity, and what- ever he did or said would now become capital for the mass media.

6

"All Angleworms in a Bottle"

GREEN HILLS OF AFRICA

Green Hills of Africa, Hemingway's second nonfiction book and the third installment, along with *Death in the Afternoon* and the *Esquire* letters, of what might be called his public personality trilogy, appeared in October 1935, after serialization in *Scribner's Magazine*. His purpose, he said in the foreword, was to discover whether literal truth could rival fiction in imaginative power, whether a scrupulous portrayal of his own safari could match in artistic intensity his own novels.[1] In his own mind, at least during the writing, *Green Hills of Africa* was superior to his fiction.[2] Few readers agreed, and fewer reviewers, nor did the book sell as well as Hemingway hoped. But *Green Hills of Africa* was a key document for his public reputation in the 1930s: it confirmed his fame as an African hunter, it was another showcase for his public personality, and, most of all, it reemphasized the significance of the heroic artist.

The principal character was Hemingway himself; supporting figures were P.O.M. (Poor Old Mama), his second wife, Pauline; Pop (here called Jackson Phillips), the white hunter; Karl, a resident of Key West; Kandisky, an Austrian living in Africa; and assorted natives. The book covers a portion of Hemingway's safari during the winter of 1933–34. He wanted to avoid the infelicities of earlier safari books, which Pop says have "all this damned Nairobi fast life or else bloody rot about shooting beasts with horns half an inch longer than someone else shot. Or muck about danger" (*GHOA*, 194). Hemingway did not entirely avoid these pitfalls:

there is nothing about Nairobi, but much attention to the size of beasts, and some to danger, too. He pursues and kills several kinds of game—lion, buffalo, oryx, sable, rhinoceros—but the central pursuit is his attempt to bag the elusive greater kudu.

Hemingway is always center stage. Edmund Wilson justly remarked that for a book about big-game hunting *Green Hills of Africa* provided little information about the animals other than that Hemingway wanted to kill them. "Nor do we learn very much about the natives," he added; "the principal impression we carry away is that the Africans were simple people who enormously admired Hemingway. Nor do we learn much more about his hunting companions. . . ; nor much more about Mrs. Hemingway except that she is fond of Hemingway."[3] Wilson noted the most obvious feature, that Hemingway was writing more about himself than about Africa. *Green Hills of Africa* is a book about Hemingway set in Africa, rather than a book about Africa with him in it.

Once more he exhibits the virility, self-confidence, and bumptiousness which had become typical of his public personality. In *Death in the Afternoon* there had been parity between his nominal subject and himself as subject, but *Green Hills of Africa* followed out the assumption of the *Esquire* essays that his most interesting subject was himself. By 1935, when he was reading proof on the book, he was convinced that it would succeed because it was "absolutely true autobiography."[4]

When Hemingway discusses hunting, he is in his familiar role of champion sportsman. He passes on practical tips for prospective safarigoers, informing hunters who wear glasses, for example, that they should carry several handkerchiefs for defogging, switching them from left pocket to right pocket as they become wet (*GHOA*, 56). He discusses the proper code for hunters, stressing the importance of killing cleanly (*GHOA*, 16, 148, 272). The accounts of stalkings and trackings serve as texts on the proper ways to stalk and track. He is proficient with weapons. Of the eleven animals he kills, he kills seven with his first shot (*GHOA*, 40–41, 76–78, 80–81, 118–119, 156, 230–232). Two misses were excusable: once he missed a buffalo because he was using an unfamiliar gun that was too heavy; another time, his native tracker frightened a sable and he had to take an inferior shot (*GHOA*, 100–101, 257). The loss of the sable made him assess his marksmanship. He was not, he says, so good with a shotgun as he often thought, but he was convinced that he shot with a rifle as well as anyone who had ever hunted. On the basis of *Green Hills of Africa*, no reader could disagree.

His boasting makes Pop and P.O.M. rib him about having the "braggies," ribbing he takes in comradely spirit. In the same motivational range, he is often in jealous funks over Karl's larger trophies, a jealousy exacerbated by his conviction that he is the superior hunter. Karl's shots had been consistently execrable, while only two of Hemingway's shots had been bad, yet Karl's trophies "made mine dwarfs in comparison" (*GHOA*, 86). He also shows himself to be unreasonably irritable, self-righteous, and not above white lies to inflate accomplishments.

This self-deprecation is part of the "true autobiography," but though he leaves his warts on, they are very small warts. Hemingway turns out immensely liked by everyone, and for good reason. In spite of his sulks he is a boon companion and an ideal safarist. He emphasizes the warmth of his relationship with Pop, his white hunter, a relationship more an abiding friendship than a business arrangement. Every time they gather round the campfire after a day's hunting they engage in the playful banter that Hemingway usually represents as conviviality among male equals who respect one another. Only intimates such as Pop and Hemingway could so mock each other's conceits and satirize each other's foibles without giving or taking offense. The two friends never use proper names. The white hunter is usually "Pop," sometimes "Mr. P.," to Hemingway, and Pop calls him "Colonel," "Old Timer," and "you damned bullfighter." (P.O.M. calls him "Papa." Karl, relegated to being another of Hemingway's outsiders, always calls Pop "Mr. Phillips.") Pop's esteem for Hemingway is not based on his stature as a writer. Pop is not literary at all—he has never heard of Joyce and thinks Homer wrote *Ulysses*. He admires Hemingway because he is an engaging companion and a good hunter, a man's man that a white hunter would take to, similar to himself. The native trackers, guides, and porters regard Hemingway as a white brother. After he has finally killed the greater kudu, they cluster around to shake his hand and pull his thumb. He wonders what the thumb-pulling means, and Pop tells him "it's on the order of blood brotherhood but a little less formal" (*GHOA*, 293). One native guide is so attracted to Hemingway that he has to be dragged out of the Land Rover at his village after the hunt. As the car pulls away, he cries "B'wana! I want to go with B'wana!" (*GHOA*, 289).

Hemingway's acceptability among nonintellectual folk like Pop and the natives makes him an insider once again. His welcome with Pop distinguishes him, moreover, from ordinary writers, whom he calls "writers in New York." These New York writers—his critics and uncertain others—are, he says, "all angleworms in a bottle, trying to derive knowledge and nourishment from their own contact and from the bottle. Sometimes the bottle is shaped art, sometimes economics, sometimes economic-religion. But once they are in the bottle they stay there. They are lonesome outside of the bottle" (*GHOA*, 21–22). The New York writers have limited experience and avoid challenges, and unlike Hemingway, they do not venture beyond their narrow literary milieu. Their only "nourishment," each other, is thin and enfeebling; his, coming from bullfighters, fishermen, white hunters, and the like, is hearty and enriching. These "angleworms," moreover, are unattractive to women and can never establish a satisfying relationship with one because their enclosure in the bottle prevents it. In *Green Hills of Africa* Hemingway has a fine relationship with P.O.M.

One of Pop's admirable qualities is that he drinks "a little too much as a good man should" (*GHOA*, 64), like Hemingway here and elsewhere. Campfire conversations with Pop are usually with a beer or whiskey in hand; and after killing the kudu he shares his beer with his African guide because "I knew he was another of the same" (*GHOA*, 241). Imbibing with the informal society of good fellows confirms acceptance. The drinking predictably offends Kandisky, the garrulous Austrian aesthete who serves as audience for Hemingway's pronouncements on life and literature. Clearly not in the fellowship, Kandisky says he abhors alcohol; it is "unnecessary" and "not good for the mind" (*GHOA*, 19).

Kandisky differs from Hemingway in more than drinking habits. He is a comic figure whose literary values caricature Hemingway's detractors in the intellectual elite, and his insistent questioning gives Hemingway the opportunity to work in his rejoinders to them. And here again, as in the *Esquire* letters, Hemingway is the unliterary, square-shouldered writer who dislikes talking about his craft and especially loathes aesthetic fripperies.

Writing, he tells Kandisky, is central to him because the rest of his life is meaningless unless he does a certain amount of it, but other activities—like hunting—are also important to his well-being.

In fact, he lectures, he enjoys hunting kudu as much as looking at paintings in the Prado, and by doing just what he wants he has created a life for himself which is consummately satisfactory. Unlike his critics, who call his activities adolescent or unbecoming or silly, he is a whole man whose life has its own art and symmetry, and he will not take on the conventional artist's role.

Hemingway frequently interrupts his narrative to comment on writers, his theory of art, his Paris years, and other matters relating to his professional life. In nearly all these interpolations he responds to his critics. His antipathy toward them becomes part of his public personality, and that rugged personality validates his charge that they are snobs and phonies. He makes himself out one of the last American writers with any integrity; the others "now wish to cease their work because it is too lonely, too hard to do, and it is not fashionable." Demands for social relevance have sapped the artist: "A thousand years makes economics silly and a work of art endures forever, but it is very difficult to do and now it is not fashionable. People do not want to do it any more because they will be out of fashion and the lice who crawl on literature will not praise them" (GHOA, 109). "The lice who crawl on literature" will have no effect on him. Those who have called him adolescent and denounced his fondness for violent sports are fashionmongers who would destroy him. He knows the worthiness of his way of life; he will resist the blandishments of the critical establishment that have seduced so many other writers.

The swing to the political left in the 1930s among intellectuals was in one way fortunate for Hemingway because it gave him a quasi-ideological basis for independence of their judgments. He could dramatize himself as the champion of the eternal and his critics as advocates of the ephemeral; while they dithered he tended the sacred flame of art. His roles as physical hero and art hero in *Green Hills of Africa* were congenial with one another because his life and art were unitary, not dialectical: he could preserve the integrity of art *because* he led his own life as he had before critics began to demand social relevance; he persevered in examining the value of life and the meaning of death. "To work was the only thing," he wrote, "it was the one thing that always made you feel good, and in the meantime it was my own damned life and I would lead it where and how I pleased. And where I had led it now pleased me very

much" (*GHOA*, 72). His life, he says again and again—nine times in
the first seventy-two pages—is absolutely satisfactory because he is
doing what he wants, and he will be the greater artist for it.

In his talk with Kandisky he tries to explain why American
writers become "something very strange":

> We destroy them in many ways. First, economically. They make
> money. It is only by hazard that a writer makes money although good
> books always make money eventually. Then our writers when they
> have made some money increase their standard of living and they are
> caught. They have to write to keep up their establishments, their
> wives, and so on, and they write slop. It is slop not on purpose but
> because it is hurried. Because they write when there is nothing to say or
> no water in the well. Because they are ambitious. Then, once they have
> betrayed themselves, they justify it and you get more slop. Or else they
> read the critics. If they believe the critics when they say they are great
> then they must believe them when they say they are rotten and they
> lose confidence. (*GHOA*, 23)

Hemingway attempts a sort of public exorcism-through-awareness
in this passage. The shabby little history was what critics had
attributed to him, but how could it apply if he himself understood a
writer's dangers so well? His self-confident enumeration of these
dangers conferred a kind of public immunity from accusations that
he had succumbed to them. His final point, about writers who are
made impotent by reading their critics, should have led to the
advice not to read them. But that was not possible, at least not for
Hemingway. His chosen means of practical resistance was to maintain a public reputation of sufficient size to be a buffer against his
critics, and to employ his public personality as a resource for counterattack.

It is in this connection that one may explain his curious reversion
to his Paris years in *Green Hills of Africa*. He gives himself in the
recollection a heroic bohemianism, public belief and sympathy
guaranteed. He had not been one of those boys whom doting parents had sent to Paris to try to become artists, and who, if they
failed, went home to America to join the family business. His
apprentice years were unsubsidized and discouraging:

> . . . We had taken the upstairs of the pavilion in Notre Dame des
> Champs in the courtyard with the sawmill *(and the sudden whine of the
> saw, the smell of sawdust and the chestnut tree over the roof with a mad woman*

> *downstairs)* and the year worrying about money *(all of the stories back in the mail that came through a slit in the saw-mill door, with notes of rejection that would never call them stories, but always anecdotes, sketches, contes, etc. They did not want them and we lived on poireaux and drank cahors and water). . . . (GHOA,* 70–71)

These recollections invested the Paris years with legend and glamour. O. O. McIntyre was not the last journalist who surrendered to this account. Not long after *Green Hills of Africa* appeared, he wrote in his newspaper column that Hemingway's life "shows what so often happens when a writer, indeed a worker in any line, blazes a trail with Something New. And it must not be forgotten that it was a long trek with lean, starving days—days in shabby Paris pensions and days without hope."[5] His situation was never so desperate as McIntyre (and Hemingway) suggested; he was not flush in those years, but the first Mrs. Hemingway got a steady income from a small trust fund. This was not common knowledge, but even if it had been, every sympathetic reader would have believed he had actually eked out his time as a young artist in a Parisian garret.

Green Hills of Africa, then, concluded the cycle Hemingway began with *Death in the Afternoon* and continued in *Esquire*. Although he published a few letters in *Esquire* after *Green Hills of Africa*, he did not add in them new features to his public personality. Just ahead was the Spanish civil war, nearly a decade of war, which led him to develop his public personality along different lines. *Green Hills of Africa*, for all that it was a book about hunting, was Hemingway's reassertion of the importance of his role as heroic artist after so much attention to nonliterary matters in the *Esquire* letters. The book in a sense brought his reputation full circle, back to where it was in 1929 when Dorothy Parker, among others, celebrated him as an incorruptible artist. With this difference: in 1935 it was he who was declaring his artistic incorruptibility, while his critics were saying the opposite. In 1929 he was the darling of the intellectual elite because critics exalted him as the great hope of modern American fiction; by the mid-1930s support from these quarters had fallen away, but through skillful exploitation of his public personality he had cultivated a larger and more heterogeneous audience he hoped would lastingly honor him.

7

"Fresh Air
on an Inside Story"

1936–1939

I

In the early morning of Labor Day, 1935, a hurricane battered the Florida Keys, leaving over five hundred dead, most of the victims impoverished Army veterans working for $45 a month at a U.S. government relief camp. *New Masses* wired Hemingway in Key West for a report on the disaster, and he responded with an impassioned article, "Who Murdered the Vets?" Why were the veterans sent to the Keys in the hurricane season to work for pauper's wages, and why were there no precautions to protect them? He confessed he did not know the answers, but he knew what political attitudes led the government to be so cavalier about the veterans' lives. "Wealthy people, yachtsmen, fishermen such as President Hoover and President Roosevelt" avoid the Florida Keys during the hurricane season because of the danger to their property, "but veterans, especially the bonus-marching variety of veterans, are not property. They are only human beings; unsuccessful human beings, and all they have to lose is their lives." The government that sent the veterans to the Keys respected property more than human life, and was thus guilty of manslaughter.[1]

His rancor toward the leisure class and the government (he implied they were interchangeable) and his implicit indictment of the system which had sent the veterans to the Keys in the first place marked a new departure for Hemingway. He had analyzed political questions in his *Esquire* letters, but always from a pundit's dispassionate point of view; in "Who Murdered the Vets?" he was more in the spirit of the 1930s, disenchanted and angry. His article for *New Masses* began a half-decade of activism: political and military reporting, speechmaking and fundraising, even writing and narrating a propaganda film.

His new political commitment in some ways made his public personality more salient than before. He did not become an ideologue; he rather made contempt for ideology a part of his public personality, as befitted the well-known exposer of sham. In this nonideological way he was antifascist and concerned for the oppressed, attitudes congenial with the Popular Front mentality of the late 1930s. Readers with various specific allegiances could support him. His expressions of political commitment were also consistent with his established personality. He accentuated his stoical heroism and his willingness to court danger, now at the front lines in Spain rather than on the savannas of Africa; his expertise at distinguishing the bogus from the authentic functioned now in politics rather than in fine wines and gourmet foods. The doings of the public personality became more dramatic, more serious, more heroic, and altogether more newsworthy.

II

The political consciousness of "Who Murdered the Vets?" did not prevent reviewers of *Green Hills of Africa*, published a few weeks after the *New Masses* article, from excoriating Hemingway for his resistance to ideas, his Byronic posturing, and his indifference to social problems, although Granville Hicks confessed that the article had put him "in a frame of mind to forgive everything, even *Death in the Afternoon*," and had predisposed him to find something good in *Green Hills of Africa*. He could not, however, and he advised Hemingway to forget about sports and to write a novel about a strike, because if he did he "would be bound to grow."[2] John Chamberlain in the New York *Times*, Edmund Wilson and T. S. Matthews in the *New Republic*, Bernard DeVoto in the *Saturday Review of Literature*, and Clifton Fadiman in the *New Yorker* all expressed similar distaste for the exhibitionism of *Green Hills of Africa* and urged Hemingway to write about something other than himself.[3]

Most reviews were unfavorable, particularly those written for the "serious" magazines, a symptom of the intellectual elite's distaste for Hemingway's public personality.

One of the most enthusiastic notices appeared in *Time*, which complemented its review with a large photograph of Hemingway and his wife, the caption informing *Time* readers that the Hemingways "prefer[red] African game to literary lice." *Time*'s reviewer was especially pleased that *Green Hills of Africa* threw "more direct light on [Hemingway's] personality than any book he has yet published," exactly the quality that highbrow reviewers disdained.[4] This difference of opinion was symptomatic. Beginning in the 1930s and for the rest of his career Hemingway had a special relationship with middlebrow periodicals, of which *Time* and its sister publication *Life* were the most influential. These periodicals never tired of Hemingway's public personality. Outside of Hemingway himself, they were its greatest propagandists, and not only in their book review sections. Their stock in trade was human interest, which meant that they were interested at least as much in the personalities of newsmakers as in their accomplishments, although achievement of some sort was a prerequisite to initial notice. As Andrew Kopkind points out, this way of seeing persons and events is typified in an apocryphal caption to a *Life* photograph of Hitler eating breakfast: "ADOLPH HITLER EATS cornflakes for breakfast, wants to conquer world."[5] With Hemingway the middlebrow periodicals found their ideal subject: his achievements were substantial and his personality colorful, and they were attractive to ordinary readers. And he was congenial because he encouraged these media in the exploitation of his personality.

The critical reception of *Green Hills of Africa* marked the low point of Hemingway's literary reputation in the 1930s. Edmund Wilson's judgment of it as his weakest book was shared by many other reviewers, particularly by those who viewed his work and personality from political and social perspectives.[6] In several reviews the conclusion was implicit that Hemingway was finished as a major writer. During the next five years, however, his reputation rose. His critics first gave a qualified approval to his new social consciousness and were less inclined to fault him for his public personality, and then, when *For Whom the Bells Tolls* appeared in 1940, they joined in almost unanimous praise. This reversal owed much to the excellence of *For Whom the Bell Tolls*, but it did not wholly stem from it, as may be seen from the revival of his literary reputation before 1940. Perhaps as important was his participation in the Spanish civil war, wherein his public personality took on a coloration more acceptable to the intellectual elite.

When the war broke out in July 1936 Hemingway was writing *To Have and Have Not*, and he chose to finish it rather than go at once to Spain. Walter Winchell reported in the late fall of 1936 that the novelist would soon leave for the front, and, prompted by Winchell's report, John Wheeler of the North American Newspaper Alliance contacted Hemingway to ask him to become the NANA correspondent.[7] NANA serviced over sixty major newspapers, including the New York *Times*, San Francisco *Chronicle*, Kansas City *Star*, Chicago *Daily News*, and Los Angeles *Times*, and Wheeler's offer, which Hemingway accepted, gave him a wide audience, by far the largest he had ever reached. He was to receive one dollar per word, a maximum of $1000 weekly, for his dispatches, according to *Newsweek* the highest fee any newspaper war correspondent had ever commanded.[8] Wheeler gave him *carte blanche* to write about whatever interested him, and in his own manner rather than that of the conventional news story.

Before he left for Spain Hemingway made clear where his political sympathies lay. Newspapers announced early in 1937 that he was serving as chairman of the ambulance committee for the Medical Bureau of the American Friends of Spanish Democracy, a group providing aid to the Loyalist side.[9] *Newsweek* reported accurately that he had contributed $3000 to purchase ambulances and inaccurately that he and a friend were personally going to deliver the vehicles in Madrid.[10] As so frequently happened with news of Hemingway's activities, this story got inflated. Martha Foley informed readers of *Story* (and *Time* later repeated her exaggeration) that the amount Hemingway contributed was $40,000, and that he had taken the NANA job to repay notes he had signed to make his contribution.[11]

He left in late February 1937 on the first of four trips he was to make to Spain during the war. With him was Sidney Franklin, the Brooklyn-born bullfighter whom Hemingway had praised in *Death in the Afternoon;* according to Hemingway, Franklin was going to "tag along and help Ernie get into trouble and out of it and fight

bulls in whatever arena we happen to pass."[12] His own purpose in
going, he announced at dockside, was "to make money the hard
way, as a working newspaperman."[13] As a reporter with an established reputation for hard drinking and hard living, he fitted an
image much beloved by Americans at least since the days of
Stephen Crane—perhaps one of the few original heroic images developed in postindustrial America—that of the dauntless, virile,
cynical newsman who beneath his bluff and tough exterior had
compassion for the oppressed. Such figures appeared in many mo-
tion pictures in the 1930s, notably in *The Front Page, Platinum
Blonde, It Happened One Night,* and *Nothing Sacred.*

One of the sources of Hemingway's public fame was his ability
to step outside his artist role and assume other guises. His world
appeared boundless, his aptitude for confronting experience unlimited. His mastery in so many arenas of activity suggested that he
was a modern Renaissance man, superior in whatever he turned his
hand to. He was, he often implied, more capable than most men,
even those who called themselves experts. As Robert F. Lucid has
pointed out, one of the fundamental characteristics of the public
writer is that he "asserts through a public representation of his own
life that he and the individual in the culture have common cause
against that institutional sphere which had, in an earlier time, given
such promise of respect and reward to them both."[14] Because
Hemingway was so many kinds of man, he was a model of resistance to institutional specialization, and he seemed to be cut from
the same cloth as the heroes of the preindustrial American past,
men who were at home everywhere and who had the force to
master any new situation. Orrin E. Klapp, in an analysis of social
types which predominate as models of character formation in
American culture, divides modern American heroes into five categories, each of which usually corresponds to a different *Wel-
tanschauung:* winners, splendid performers, heroes of social
acceptability, independent spirits, and group servants.[15] By 1936
Hemingway had amply documented his heroic stature in the first
four of Klapp's categories, and with the advent of the Spanish civil
war he added the fifth as well. His public personality was so protean that he managed to be many kinds of hero and yet not project
an image which was confused or inconsistent.

III

As NANA correspondent Hemingway filed twenty-eight dispatches from Spain, ten on his first trip in spring 1937, seven from his second in the fall of that year, and eleven during his third in spring 1938. (He was no longer reporting for NANA during his final trip in fall 1938.) The most striking characteristic of his dispatches was his advertisement of his own courage. Again and again he described how he narrowly escaped death from enemy aircraft, artillery, and rifle fire. His self-dramatization prompted Edmund Wilson to dismiss his dispatches as "inept,"[16] which they were not, but whatever their value as journalism, they contributed to his fame as a man who never lost his nerve. War offered special opportunities for displaying courage, and Hemingway's was all the more noteworthy because his danger was self-imposed: he was in Spain by choice, and as a noncombatant no one would have faulted him had he avoided danger.

Instead, he courted it. His headquarters in Madrid, the Hotel Florida, was less than two miles from the front lines in University City and was vulnerable to artillery shelling by Rebel forces, shelling he described as effective and lethal. Large rooms at the front of the hotel cost a dollar per day, he explained, while smaller and less comfortable rooms at the back were more expensive, the front rooms being more dangerous from their exposure. In an early dispatch he boasted about occupying a front room; after a shell exploded on the sidewalk he got another room twice the size, "a beautiful double corner room on that side" for less than a dollar.[17] In a dispatch on his second trip, he told how his room had come under artillery fire:

> They say you never hear the one that hits you. That's true of bullets because, if you hear them, they are already past. But your correspondent heard the last shell that hit this hotel. He heard it start from the battery, then come with a whistling incoming roar like a subway train to crash against the cornice and shower the room with broken glass and plaster. And while the glass still tinkled down and you listened for the next one to start, you realized that now finally you were back in Madrid.[18]

His frequent brushes with danger proved that he risked his neck to

get accurate information; he was not one of those correspondents
who relied on official handouts. His descriptions of whizzing bul-
lets, shells bursting only a few yards away, and Junker and Fiat
airplanes threatening overhead showed that he knew what he was
talking about because he had a combatant's perspective. Reporting
on the defense of Lerida he was jauntily ironic about how "easy" it
was to enter the town: "All you have to do is keep your legs moving
steadily and control a slight tickling sensation between your shoul-
derblades and the base of your neck as you cross the railway yard
and come under machine-gun fire from a tower 500 yards away."[19]
Discussing the Loyalist retreat in Catalonia, he reported that he
had "been doing the most dangerous thing you can do in this war.
That is, keep close behind an unstabilized line where the enemy is
attacking with mechanized forces."[20] An account of a Loyalist attempt to dislodge an enemy salient near University City outside
Madrid was largely about his difficulties in finding an unexposed
spot for observation. This attack, he said, was the second he had
witnessed "at the closest range" in four days. He and his party, two
filmmakers and another correspondent, first positioned themselves
at Loyalist headquarters, but were driven out by a volley of three-
inch shells. Still under fire they moved to the nearby woods only a
few hundred yards from the front lines, but trees hindered their
vision. Having scouted the terrain some days before, Hemingway
then led them to an elevated point where they could see the battle
clearly:

> Just as we were congratulating ourselves on having such a splendid
> observation post out of the reach of danger, a bullet smacked against a
> corner of brick wall beside Ivens' head. Thinking it was a stray, we
> moved over a little, and, as I watched the action with glasses, shading
> them carefully, another came by my head. We changed our position to
> a spot where the observing was not so good and were shot at twice
> more. Joris thought Ferno had left his camera at our first post, and, as I
> went back for it, a bullet whacked into the wall above. I crawled back
> on my hands and knees, and another bullet came by as I crossed the
> exposed corner.

Finally, one of the filmmakers found a less exposed post in a ruined
house from which they could observe more safely.[21]

Because of the admiration he roused in people who saw him in
action, Hemingway's NANA dispatches cannot be dismissed as

hyperbole. Many who observed him in Spain have testified to his coolness under fire. Claude Bowers, a historian and the American ambassador to Spain during the civil war, was impressed at the way he lived "dangerously but joyously" at the Hotel Florida.[22] To New York *Times* correspondent Herbert Matthews, Hemingway represented "much that is brave and good and fine in a somewhat murky world"; Matthews recounted how he and the novelist came under fire frequently during the battle of Teruel, and how they were among the first to enter the town.[23] Another correspondent, Vincent Sheean, praised Hemingway's self-possession, recalling a time when they were crossing the Ebro River in a boat in peril of being dashed against a bombed-out bridge. Sheean was not alarmed because "Hemingway was pulling us out of it. I had the kind of confidence in Hemingway that a Southern negro has in the plantation owner."[24] Yet another, Joseph North of the *Daily Worker*, who had little use for Hemingway's politics, praised his courage under fire.[25]

Hemingway reported after the battle of Brihuega, where the Loyalists routed the Italian "volunteers," that he had spent four days "going over the ground with the commanders who directed it and the officers who fought in it, checking the positions and following the tank trails," and he was prepared to argue that Brihuega would "take its place in military history with the other decisive battles of the world."[26] His assessment of the battle and what it portended was given extensive coverage by the press—for example, in both *Time* and *Newsweek*.[27] In other dispatches he summarized strategies and predicted military developments. All war correspondents do this, but Hemingway hinted that because he habituated the front lines and because he was a comrade of officers formulating strategy and executing tactics, he was a more reliable correspondent than most of his colleagues, who got their information second hand. His pride in his reputation as a soldierly correspondent showed in his angry reaction to what he thought was *Time*'s implication that Herbert Matthews had been the only journalist present at the taking of Teruel. He had not only been there, he informed his first wife, but he had in the first place arranged for Matthews and one other newsman to be present, and then had persuaded the censor to pass the other correspondents' stories.[28]

There was little political commentary in his NANA dispatches;

they were mostly given over to military reports and discussions of how the war affected soldiers and civilians. Although there was no doubt where he stood—he obviously favored the Loyalist side, and even at the time of his third trip in spring 1938, when Rebel forces isolated Madrid from Catalonia, he expressed optimism about the Loyalist cause, citing the sectional loyalties he thought would be aroused by the partition[29]—day-to-day journalism as such forbade the close examination of political questions to be found in his *Esquire* letters. He was a newsman, not the politically sophisticated "old newsman" of *Esquire*.

But an opportunity to be the "old newsman" again came early in 1938 with the launching of *Ken* magazine, and Hemingway took it. *Ken* was an avowedly political journal begun by the *Esquire* publishers to explain the *real* news; its editor, Arnold Gingrich, called it an "insider's magazine."[30] Hemingway was initially announced as one of the editors, but in a box next to his contribution in the first issue there was a retraction. According to Gingrich, Hemingway first asked to be an editor and then asked to be relieved when he learned that the magazine would take an anticommunist position.[31] He contributed thirteen articles (and one story, "The Old Man at the Bridge") in less than a year, all but one political. He was never happy with *Ken*'s anticommunism, and said so. Two anticommunist cartoons in the first issue had left a bad taste in his mouth; he argued that there could be "no anti-fascist magazine which does not maintain a popular front against fascism," and if *Ken* had been Red-baiting (as it certainly had), then whoever was responsible was "either a fool or a knave."[32]

In nearly all his articles for *Ken* he sounded a consistent refrain: the democratic nations must support the Spanish Republic if another world war is to be delayed or prevented; defeating the Fascists in Spain was the only way to give Hitler and Mussolini pause in their plans for conquest. Nearly equal to the Fascists among Hemingway's villains were the politicians in the English Foreign Office and their toadies in the American State Department. Out of expediency and a cynical desire to hang onto their jobs they were urging their governments to maintain a neutral position in the civil war. Hemingway singled out Neville Chamberlain, then British Prime Minister, as a particularly nefarious influence. He would have no honored place in history, and his role in international politics was shameful. "He acts as though what they [the Fascists] proposed were really what they intended to do, although every agreement they have ever made they have violated."[33] This evaluation of Chamberlain was astute and timely, coming as it did just three months before the Prime Minister negotiated with Hitler the Munich pact partitioning Czechoslovakia.

In his *Ken* articles Hemingway portrayed himself as an insider with information unavailable to others. This was a favorite Hemingway role in his nonfiction, especially in his political writing. In an article on treachery in war he lectured an unnamed writer friend (John Dos Passos) on his "good hearted naivete," which he condescendingly called "a typical American liberal attitude." Dos Passos had been disturbed that his Spanish translator was arrested for treason, and he could not believe the charges were true. Hemingway discovered that the charges had been proven at trial and the man rightfully executed. He doubted that Dos Passos would admit the justice of the sentence because, he implied, Dos Passos was not a political realist and not so informed as he about the mechanisms of war and politics. "But we who have seen this war for a long time have learned that there are all sorts of treachery just as there are all sorts of heroism in war. And very shortly the true story of the role played by treachery in the Aragon breakthrough will be able to be written."[34] He tantalized readers with the hint of inside information once again when he suggested that treachery had prevented an air-raid on Pamplona during the state funeral of Fascist General Emilio Mola, when the Loyalists could have wiped out most of the enemy leaders at one time. The reason this raid was not carried out "is another of the stories of the Spanish war which must wait a little longer to be written fully."[35]

Similarly, a late *Ken* article, "Fresh Air on an Inside Story," represented Hemingway as an insider outwitting another correspondent. The correspondent was a novice on a major newspaper who tried to circumvent censorship by smuggling out a dispatch claiming a state of revolutionary terror existed in Madrid. There was no terror in Madrid, Hemingway insisted, as he knew from personal observation and because "I had friends in Seguridad [Security] that I had known in the old days and could trust." The other correspondent, wanting to build a reputation as a "fearless exposer," had written his dispatch in his hotel room the day of his

arrival in Madrid and had asked a female correspondent leaving
Spain to post a sealed envelope out of the country. The envelope
contained his report, but he told her it contained a dispatch from
Teruel already cleared by the censor. Getting wind of the correspondent's request Hemingway insisted the woman have the censor
open the envelope because, he told her, "Never trust a man who
slicks hair over a bald head." The ruse exposed, Hemingway and
the other "hard-working, non-political, straight shooting correspondents who risked their lives daily" were infuriated by "this
outsider" who was trying to make them seem liars.[36] The point of
this story, besides the assertion that there was no terror in Madrid,
was evidently to publicize Hemingway's inside knowledge about
what was happening as well as to advertise his shrewdness and his
ability to detect sham.

In all his *Ken* articles he emphasized his opposition to fascist
tyranny. Those fighting for the Loyalists were dying for human
justice, he said, and the members of the International Brigades
were not soldiers of fortune, as they had been characterized, but
clear thinkers who recognized political realities and understood the
inhuman nature of fascism.[37] He gave a vaguely liberal interpretation of the war, stressing the unexceptionable goals of freedom
from want, the right of self-determination, and the pragmatic ad-
vantages to Western democracies of engaging fascism in Spain. His
political attitudes appeared succinctly in his preface to a collection
of drawings by his friend Luis Quintanilla, written about the same
time as the *Ken* articles. He wrote three prefaces to the volume: the
first the publisher rejected as too brief; the second was a pettish
rebuke to the publisher; and the third was at once a justification and
amplification of and an apology for the second. (All three appeared
with the drawings.) In the second he said he hated war, although he
confessed to having "a small talent for it"; what he wanted was to
have the war won so he could head straight for the Stork Club. In
the third preface he explained why his allusion to the Stork Club
was serious and not a joke, for he had learned that levity was to
some persons "unpardonable in a serious writer":

> When you have sat at a table and been served a plate of water soup, a
> single fried egg and one orange after you have been working fourteen
> hours, you have no desire to be anywhere but where you were, nor to

be doing anything but your work, but you would think "Boy, I'll bet
you could get quite a meal at the Stork tonight."

After going on for a couple of paragraphs about the food at the
Stork Club, he came to his point: the war in Spain was being fought
"so that everyone can eat as well as the best."[38] He had been drawn
to the Loyalist cause not to defend an ideology, but simply out of
compassion.

The *Ken* articles complemented Hemingway's NANA dispatches, which were confined to day-to-day military activities.
These forty-one journalistic pieces, appearing during a period of
less than two years, put forward a composite portrait of a man
fearless in battle, sophisticated and knowledgeable in war and politics, and committed to a humane endeavor. Although not a member
of the International Brigades, he dramatized his peril to be as great
as theirs, and his contributions to the Republic as important.

IV

When he returned in mid-May 1937 from his first trip to Spain, he
was greeted at dockside by reporters and by a *Life* photographer.
While the cameraman snapped, Hemingway briefed the reporters.
Contrary to his expectations, he said, he had found nearly all his
old friends in Madrid alive and in good health; he predicted that
Franco's troops would never take the city and that the Loyalists
would win the war.[39] His own plans were to give a speech to the
Second Writers' Congress and to continue working on his film, *The
Spanish Earth*, before returning to Spain in the fall.

His speech to the Writers' Congress at Carnegie Hall on June 4,
1937, exhorted writers to help resist fascism. Arriving late at the
meeting, according to *Time*, he kept muttering, "Why the hell am I
making a speech?" as he paced in the wings before going on stage.
Once he began, however, he "warmed up eloquently," and *Time*
reprinted a portion of his speech.[40] Writers had a particular stake in
the fight against fascism, he said, because it was the only form of
government which would not allow them to tell the truth. Telling
the truth in war is a dangerous business for a writer, "and the truth

is very dangerous to come by" because a writer may find death instead.

> Whether the truth is worth some risk to come by, the writers must decide themselves. Certainly it is more comfortable to spend their time disputing learnedly on points of doctrine. And there will always be new schisms and new fallings-off and marvelous exotic doctrines and romantic lost leaders, for those who do not want to work at what they profess to believe in, but only to discuss and maintain positions— skillfully chosen positions to be held by the typewriter and con- solidated with the fountain pen. But there is now, and there will be from now on for a long time, war for any writer to go to who wants to study it.[41]

Many writers and intellectuals supporting the Loyalist cause were serving either themselves or an ideology, and at no risk, while he exposed himself to the ultimate danger from his concern for justice and his need to discover truth.

Making himself a moral exception was typical in Hemingway's pronouncements on the relationship between literature and poli- tics. For example, in "Who Murdered the Vets?" he fancied how he might speak to a writer staying at a Miami hotel in the hope of witnessing a hurricane he could use in his next novel: "I would like to lead you by your well-worn-by-writing-to-the-literary-columns pants" to inspect the mangled and bloated bodies left by the hur- ricane. Perhaps the writer would learn more than he would sitting in his room reading the newspapers, "and you could make a note of it for your next novel and how is your next novel coming, brother writer, comrade s--t?"[42] This truculent digression had nothing to do with the effects of the hurricane or the government's negligence, but a great deal to do with how Hemingway conceived himself. It implied that he, rare if not unique among writers, had the integrity to enter threatening situations and to report them accurately, with- out the clichés of an imagination made decadent from self-seeking or straightjacketed by an ideological bias.

But the audience in Carnegie Hall that June evening evidently did not notice or did not mind Hemingway's self-flattery. They were simply delighted that he appeared and that he was antifascist. They enthusiastically applauded when he finished, and his pres- ence stirred at least one person there to believe that with Hemingway on the Loyalist side the victory over fascism was practically assured.[43]

Preceding Hemingway on the program, Joris Ivens had shown *The Spanish Earth*, the still unedited and unfinished film he was making at the front with Hemingway's cooperation. Produced under the auspices of an organization called "Contemporary Historians," which included John Dos Passos, Lillian Hellman, and Archibald MacLeish as well as Hemingway, the film was designed to propagandize the cause of the Spanish Republic and to raise funds for ambulances. As Hemingway had indicated in his NANA dispatches, he was with Ivens during much of the filming, and once that was done he agreed to write and narrate the commentary. In late June 1937 he and Ivens received a dinner invitation to the White House, where President and Mrs. Roosevelt were eager to see a preview of the film. A Broadway columnist reported the day after that the President had been so interested in his conversation with the novelist that he cancelled several appointments to prolong it.[44] Hemingway then flew off to Los Angeles where, under the sponsorship of Frederic March and his wife, he showed the film and raised about $20,000 for the Loyalist cause. *Life* magazine shortly thereafter published a four-page spread of stills from *The Spanish Earth* with captions taken from Hemingway's script.[45]

The film was strikingly photographed and well-edited. Hemingway's narration reduced the complex issues behind the civil war to the simple ones of peasants taking back land rightfully theirs and of uniting against a foreign invasion. When the script was published in 1938, its editor, Jasper Wood, asserted that much of the vitality of the film came "from the Hemingway personality which was injected into it."[46] Wood's introduction tended toward hyperbole, but it reliably indicated the direction of Hemingway's public reputation in the late 1930s. The film was Hemingway's "greatest contribution to society" because he and his collaborators had assisted more than anyone else in preserving world democracy. Hemingway was devoting his "entire self" to the cause in Spain, even giving "all the money he had" and borrowing more to aid the Loyalists. His dispatches were among the few truthful reports of what was happening in Spain because he risked his life "to give us something worthwhile and to tell the truth." The reason *The Spanish*

Earth was "so alive" was that "it was written in bomb-ridden hotels and in the seclusion of continually shelled trenches."[47] Hemingway publicly disavowed Wood's introduction because he felt it gave him too much credit for the film at the expense of Ivens and his camera-man, but it foisted the same heroic view of him he had conveyed more subtly in his NANA dispatches and *Ken* articles.

V

There was nothing heroic but much comic about Hemingway's scrap with Max Eastman on August 11, 1937, in Maxwell Perkins's office. Eastman had infuriated Hemingway years earlier with "Bull in the Afternoon" (see chapter 5), and when the two writers met by accident in Perkins's office, Hemingway, remembering Eastman's comment about "wearing false hair on the chest," bared his chest to reveal the luxuriance and authenticity of his hair, then unbuttoned Eastman's shirt for comparison. Eastman's chest was hairless. As Hemingway later told a newspaper reporter, this started playfully, but when he saw on Perkins's desk *Art and the Life of Action*, where "Bull in the Afternoon" was collected, he "got sore." What hap-pened next is uncertain, but Perkins, the only disinterested party present, reported to Scott Fitzgerald that Hemingway hit Eastman in the face with the book, whereupon Eastman charged and whether by design or accident fell to the floor on top of Heming-way. And that, said Perkins, was where the fight ended. Heming-way smiled, Eastman let him up, and it was all over.[48]

The versions given out by Hemingway and Eastman a few days later diverged from Perkins's account and from each other. Each antagonist agreed after the scuffle to keep the story quiet, but it leaked anyway. Once the newspapers had it they contacted East-man, and while he did not exactly claim to have thrashed Heming-way, he did tell reporters that after the novelist had thrown the book in his face, he wrestled with him and threw him across Per-kins's desk, pinning him and letting him up only when Perkins begged him to stop and Hemingway smiled and patted him on the shoulder.[49]

If Perkins's account can be believed, and he was known for his probity, Eastman somewhat exaggerated. He had not really manhandled Hemingway. But the evening papers using his version reported that he had soundly thrashed his opponent: one published a photo from the dust jacket of his book, *Enjoyment of Laughter*, which portrayed a laughing Eastman, and put it next to a cut of a sullen Hemingway; another paper announced that Eastman was planning to write an essay entitled "Enjoyment of Thrashing Ernest."[50]

Hemingway countered with his version. He had not thrown the book at Eastman but slapped him in the face with it, knocking him back onto a window seat. (The New York *Times* inaccurately reported that the comment in "Bull in the Afternoon" that offended Hemingway was, "Come out from behind that false hair on your chest, Ernest. We all know you.") He had merely slapped Eastman, because if he had hit him hard he might have knocked him through the window and out onto Fifth Avenue.[51] Eastman, in this version, shook with rage and called Hemingway "a big bully." "I was laughing at him all the time," Hemingway told reporters, "and I said, 'Max, if you were ten years younger I'd knock hell out of you.' He came for me then and I backed up against the desk, still laughing. I said: 'Make this guy stop being silly. He's too old.' I just held him off. I was trying to keep from hurting him."[52] He concluded by challenging Eastman to settle the dispute in a closed room; he would put up a purse of $1,000, to be contributed either to Eastman's favorite charity or to defray his medical expenses.[53]

Hemingway departed for Spain the day his version appeared in the newspapers, but before he left he gathered reporters on board ship and displayed Eastman's book of essays, smudged by "Eastman's noseprint where I slapped him in the face."[54] The reporter from the Associated Press, characterizing Hemingway as an "advocate of lean prose and fat muscles, who used to fight men in sideshows just for the fun of it," described Hemingway's feisty antics: "Two hundred pounds of good nature, lusty humor and red-blooded conceit was Ernest as he threw imaginary punches all over the cabin salon at Max Eastman. . . . And even though someone here and there looked skeptical, Ernest was not to be discouraged. 'Find out,' he growled, 'what I did to Philadelphia Jack O'Brien.'" What he ever did to Philadelphia Jack remains a mystery. When he returned from Spain, he threatened, he was going to take down Eastman's pants and spank him.[55]

The press had a field day with all this. An account of the fight was the lead item in Walter Winchell's column, and Hemingway's old antagonist Heywood Broun used it to start a discussion of the literary heavyweight championship. O. O. McIntyre reported the fight and recounted other famous literary brawls. Damon Runyon wrote that he knew of six engagements in Westchester County alone recently broken by girls appalled to learn that their fiancés' chests were hairless. The New York *Times* editorialized on the fight between "Slogger [sic] Hemingway" and "Kid Eastman," refusing to take sides. *Newsweek* and *Time* featured accounts, noting that Eastman claimed he had stood Hemingway on his head. *Time*'s account alluded to Hemingway's many scars and reported his denial that Eastman had given them to him.[56] John O'Hara, Hemingway's novelist friend, thought the magazine had not made clear that these scars preceded the Eastman fight. He had noticed scars on Hemingway's forehead two years earlier when he witnessed a friendly bout between Hemingway and former heavyweight champion Gene Tunney. For O'Hara, Hemingway's sparring match with Tunney was proof that he was a better man than Eastman: "I certainly would like to see Mr. Eastman after a friendly bout with Mr. Tunney. I certainly would."[57] The *New Yorker* took a more magisterial view. Writers think they lead dramatic lives, the magazine editorialized in its "Talk of the Town" column, and they want the public to know it, so they often tell things to the newspapers that are better left unsaid. Such was the case with the Hemingway-Eastman fracas—it was a childish affair which would amuse only lesser people who were "strongly moved by the embarrassments of the wise and great."[58] The *New Yorker* printed a cartoon showing a shirtless and hairy-chested young man being examined by a physician, who asks, "Writer?"[59]

Both Eastman and Hemingway exaggerated, but Hemingway exaggerated more. By luck or design Eastman had ended up on top of Hemingway, not cowering on a window seat. Hemingway's boisterousness at his press conference, his challenge to Eastman to meet in a closed room, and his vow to spank him revealed how deeply Eastman's version bothered him. It questioned a cherished reputation he had worked hard to establish, that of the rough customer who could handle himself in the clinches. All of his boasts and threats were calculated to reassert his public reputation as the toughest man of letters around. Had Hemingway been less concerned with his public reputation he might not have cut quite such a comic figure. But comic figure or not, his behavior confused the issue beyond hope of clarification. He succeeded in discrediting Eastman's account, without being able to impose his own. If nothing else, though, the hubbub kept Hemingway's name (and face) before the nation's newspaper and magazine readers for several weeks, and that alone was a decent enough accomplishment for a celebrity.

VI

The scrap with Eastman gave several reviewers of *To Have and Have Not*, which appeared two months later, a pretext for lecturing Hemingway on "his well known admiration for the hairy-chested man." Art demanded psychic not physical virility, one reviewer pontificated, and the new novel only confirmed Hemingway's failure to develop any but the latter. Another, conceding that Hemingway was so hairy and virile that "the hairs stick right through the pages of his book," urged him to write about men who had other interests than "boozing and womanizing." Yet another, loath to advance an opinion because he did not "want to get socked in the jaw," suggested that a wisp of Hemingway's chest hair should have been included with each review copy.[60]

Those who defended the novel were no less able than its detractors to resist the powerful pull of his personality. One of these, Elliott Paul, said *To Have and Have Not* was Hemingway's best novel, and claimed that reviewers who disliked it did so only because they were hostile to Hemingway himself. The "real" Ernest Hemingway, Paul's friend, was in any case unlike the larger-than-life figure prominently featured in the Eastman affair. He was shy, gentle, a good friend and companion, never belligerent or ostentatious, not hostile to constructive criticism, and "not at all sure of himself." He despised personal publicity, but newsmen whom he tried to accommodate frequently took advantage of him.[61] Perhaps the "real" Hemingway was diffident and modest, as Paul said—there are similar portraits by other friends—but he was not this person in his public personality, which was self-congratulatory,

oracular, often belligerent, always self-confident. The shy and un-
assuming man Paul described had little in common with the public
Hemingway, and for good reason. If he had come on publicly as
Paul claimed he did privately, he would never have become a celebrity at all.

To Have and Have Not brought one of the highest honors celebrities hoped for, a cover story in *Time* magazine. (Hemingway was
to appear once more on *Time*'s cover, and three times on *Life*'s.)
Time enthused over the new novel but, true to form, showed more
interest in the author than in his work. A thumbnail biography
sketched his childhood, his war experiences, his years in Paris, and
his activities during the 1930s, perpetuating many myths—that he
ran away from home at fifteen, enlisted in the Italian infantry, had
an aluminum kneecap as a result of his war wound, and so forth.
There were gossipy bits about his marriages, his Key West home,
and his distaste for "tea-fighting literary circles." *Time* gave more
space to a visual biography—sixteen photographs—than it gave to
text. The sequence included a baby picture; a family grouping from
childhood; pictures of the young sportsman fishing and hunting;
the injured war veteran convalescing in a wheelchair; the veteran
home from the front in Oak Park. There was the mature Hemingway: clowning with a bull in Spain; admiring a fish on board the
Pilar; and posing with the horns of a kudu in Africa. And there was
a recent photograph of him "watching through a window of Madrid's University City the effect of point-blank shell fire."[62] The
pictures amounted to a visual reprise of the well-known personality.

Hemingway's personality also figured in reviews of *To Have and
Have Not* by Alfred Kazin and Malcolm Cowley, whose leftist per-
suasions had formerly made them suspicious and hostile to it. Both
particularly praised the ending, where Harry Morgan's dying
words seemed to be a rejection of individualism and a summons to
some kind of group solidarity, and both were pleased that Hemingway had changed from sportsman and playboy to an activist out-
spoken against fascism. In both his books and his life, said Kazin,
he had "worked his way out of a cult of tiresome defeatism."[63] The
story behind the novel, Cowley thought, the story of the change in
Hemingway himself, might prove more interesting than the novel.
Of one thing Cowley was certain: Hemingway's espousal of the

Loyalist cause had transformed him.[64] For Kazin and Cowley, Hemingway's public personality no longer seemed a dangerous, irresponsible force. Enlisted in the battle for human justice, the public Hemingway was a valuable asset precisely because he commanded a large following. The reception of *To Have and Have Not* by critics like Kazin and Cowley prompted Edmund Wilson a few years later to state, perhaps to overstate, that "the Left . . . received his least credible piece of fiction as the delivery of a new revelation."[65]

Much the same spirit of accommodation prevailed in the reception of *The Fifth Column and the First Forty-Nine Stories*, published in 1938. Reviews were enthusiastic about the stories and silent about the public personality. This was especially true among leftist reviewers, whose rapprochement with Hemingway was evident in Edwin Berry Burgum's review in *New Masses*. The collected stories, said Burgum, were "the record of the road Hemingway has travelled through the confusions of modern life to a clearer insight into the relation between democracy and art."[66] No jibes at his personal behavior, no lamentations about the deterioration and waste of his talent.

Most reviewers who liked the stories were less enthusiastic about *The Fifth Column*, Hemingway's play about wartime Spain; it seemed to them a diversion, although harmless, not an important work. The story of the play's composition, however, came in for much attention, and it was a capital demonstration of Hemingway's penchant for self-advertisement. Late in 1937 newspapers reported that he had just finished the play at the Hotel Florida, "the famous hotel which has been so severely punished by Rebel shells"; he had written it at least partly because his fellow correspondents urged him to.[67] When the play was published in the short story omnibus, Hemingway emphasized in an introduction that he had written it under perilous conditions. If the play was not good, he said, maybe the thirty shells that struck the hotel while he was writing were at fault; hedging, he added that if it was good perhaps the bombardment had made it so.[68] It was not a good play, but his story of writing it under fascist guns was good copy, and newspapers and magazines used it many times. *Life*'s retelling, a few years later when the play was being mounted for a Broadway production, was typical. Preparing *The Fifth Column* for the stage was easy for

Hemingway in comparison with his difficulties in writing it: "Daily he expected a bomb to land in his typewriter. The room next door was wrecked by a shell." Characteristically, *Life* accompanied the story with a photograph that had nothing to do with the play. It showed Hemingway guzzling from a fifth of White Horse scotch, with the caption: "Ernest Hemingway takes a warming swallow of scotch before breakfast in his Madrid hotel. In Spain's sub-zero weather, he sometimes had to wash his face with whiskey."[69]

By 1939 critical enthusiasm for Hemingway and his work almost reached the zenith of a decade earlier. There was a minority report, however, and it came from two of the nation's most distinguished critics, Lionel Trilling and Edmund Wilson. Both saw a separation in Hemingway between the "artist" and the "man": when the "artist" was in control, as in the early stories and novels, his work was honest and had admirable clarity; when the "man" dominated, as in most of his writing in the 1930s, he became shrill, belligerent, and dishonest. Trilling ascribed the ascendancy of the "man" over the "artist" in the 1930s to pressure from the left, pressure which moved him to vindicate himself by exhibiting the proper social consciousness, thus bringing the "man" with all his contradictions into his writing.[70] Wilson was more acute in one respect than Trilling, who failed to acknowledge Hemingway's emphasis on his public personality in the half decade before his antifascism. With a few exceptions among the short stories, it was no longer possible, thought Wilson, to distinguish between Hemingway's latest fictional heroes and the "false or publicity Hemingway" which had grown out of his self-advertisements. His antifascism was simpleminded and derived from his compulsion to aggrandize his public reputation, now as a dedicated warrior against fascism rather than as a fearless hunter stalking lions. Both warrior and hunter, as Hemingway dramatized them, were "in the nature of a small boy's fantasy, and would probably be considered extravagant by most writers of books for boys."[71]

Hemingway again took umbrage, and he tried to keep Wilson from collecting the article in a book. According to Wilson, the book was to be published by Scribners, but the firm broke the contract for fear of offending its prize author. Hemingway then delayed another publisher with the demand that his lawyer get an injunction on the grounds that every other sentence in the piece was libelous. These allegations, which Wilson said made him think Hemingway was not quite sane, were finally trimmed to two or three minor errors of fact, which Wilson corrected, and the article finally appeared in book form.[72] Wilson's article was sympathetic to Hemingway save on one count—it made fun of his public personality—and it was of course this one count that most upset Hemingway.

In truth, however, nothing Wilson said could have damaged Hemingway's public reputation. Wilson's essay, in the *Atlantic*, and Trilling's, in *Partisan Review*, were aimed at an audience of intellectuals; Hemingway's public reputation depended on a different audience, the readers of magazines like *Esquire*, *Time*, *Life*, and *Newsweek*, periodicals with a far larger readership than the *Atlantic* or *Partisan Review*. As long as these popular magazines were lionizing him, Hemingway's public reputation was secure.

By the end of the 1930s Hemingway's public personality was so well established, and his reputation so large, that he could bully his way through critical controversies, often assisted by the mass media, especially *Time* and *Life*. A case in point was his squabble with Archibald MacLeish. Early in 1940 MacLeish gave a speech to the American Association for Adult Education, which the *New Republic* published, arguing that novelists who had written about the World War, specifically Hemingway and Dos Passos, sincere and skillful though they were, had educated a generation to refrain from making moral judgments in the false belief that moral issues were fraudulent. Their novels, MacLeish argued, had caused the undergraduates of America to become cynical pacifists.[73] *Life*, sensing a good story, asked Hemingway to respond. With his penchant for taking criticism personally, he accused MacLeish of a bad conscience and of insufficient antifascist militancy. "Having fought fascism in every way that I know how in the places where you could really fight it, I have no remorse neither literary nor political. Suggest that MacLeish read my play *The Fifth Column* and see again the film *The Spanish Earth*. If MacLeish had been at Guadalajara, Jarama, Madrid, Teruel, first and second battles of the Ebro, he might feel better." Writers who had written about the Great War, he added, while they believed all wars were vile, had been outraged at the stupid way that one was fought, and if the Germans in the meantime had learned to mount a successful campaign and the

Allies had not, no writer could be blamed.[74] MacLeish's remarks
were not directed at Hemingway personally but spoke only to the
effect of his fiction, and so Hemingway's bluster was irrelevant.
But *Life* gave Hemingway the edge in its representation of the
argument. MacLeish's remarks in the *New Republic* ran to several
thousand words; *Life* condensed them to a few sentences, without
their full contextual sense. Predictably, *Time* did the same, and
both magazines turned the occasion into another Hemingway celebration.

As the 1930s came to a close, Hemingway could look back on a
decade in which, largely by his own efforts, he had become a full-
fledged celebrity. His literary reputation nearly reached bottom in
the middle of the decade, then rose toward a peak it would reach in
1940 with *For Whom the Bell Tolls*. His public reputation suffered no
such vagary. It ascended throughout the decade with no sign of
faltering. The large, heterogeneous audience he had so assiduously
cultivated, the substantiality he had given to his public personality,
and the heroic framework he had provided in his self-
advertisements, all had made him the most famous and most charis-
matic of living writers, and guaranteed that as he moved into
middle age, he could feel confident of his stature as America's
public writer.

8

"Task Force Hemingway"

1940–1945

I

Hemingway had no need to belabor his critics after publication of *For Whom the Bell Tolls* (1940); it was virtually an unqualified success, the most favorably received of his books to date. Clifton Fadiman, John Chamberlain, and J. Donald Adams, who had criticized his "immaturity" during the 1930s, hailed the book as his finest novel, a literary landmark of the twentieth century, and a sure sign that he had sloughed off the tiresome poses of the previous decade. Edmund Wilson's enthusiastic response was typical: "The big game hunter, the waterside superman, the Hotel Florida Stalinist, with their constrained and fevered attitudes, have evaporated like the fantasies of alcohol. Hemingway the artist is with us again; and it is like having an old friend back."[1] Less than six months after publication the novel had sold nearly a half-million copies, and it became the best-selling novel in years, outdone in the recent past only by *Gone with the Wind*. With *For Whom the Bell Tolls* Hemingway won a competition in the one arena where a writer's success may be accurately measured, and he strengthened his claim to the title of champion writer of his time.

Even before the novel was published, there was public speculation about which movie studio would get the rights to it and how much it would have to pay. A week before publication Louella Parsons reported that Hemingway was asking $150,000, and that he was conferring with Gary Cooper in Sun Valley about playing the role of Robert Jordan.[2] When a few days after publication Paramount bought the rights for $100,000 plus ten cents per copy for the first 500,000 sold, newspapers and magazines reported that he had received the largest sum paid by the film industry for any book.[3] This put him in the class of the top performers in entertainment—the highest paid baseball player, the actor whose income from a picture broke records, the singer whose songs were consistently number one on the Hit Parade. These were the celebrities with whom he was competing for public attention by 1940.

Publicity about the film version did not end with the settlement of rights; the casting had to be done, and, again according to Louella Parsons, Hemingway was active in the decisions. She reported in November 1940 that he wanted Gary Cooper to play the leading role, and that Cooper was "dying" for the part; late in the month she wrote that Hemingway suggested his friend Robert Capa for the gypsy, Raphael; and early in 1941 she told her readers that Hemingway was a house guest of Gary Cooper in Hollywood while he conferred with "Paramount biggies" about the film. He would make all final decisions about casting, she announced.[4] A few months later *Time* said that Paramount was urging Hemingway himself to take a screen test for a part in the film,[5] but nothing ever came of it. It was *Life*, however, with its insatiable curiosity about celebrities, which gave him his most flattering publicity in connection with the film when it featured a "photo-essay" on his meeting with Ingrid Bergman in San Francisco, one of three such human interest pieces on Hemingway *Life* was to publish in the year following the appearance of *For Whom the Bell Tolls*.

According to *Life*, Bergman was on a skiing holiday at June Lake in the Sierras when she learned that Hemingway was in San Francisco and anxious to meet her; he had seen her performance in *Intermezzo* while writing the novel and decided that she was the actress to play Maria. She also was eager to meet him, and drove nearly all night to Reno to catch a morning plane to San Francisco. Hemingway was "obviously pleased" with her, and *Life* published several photographs of the novelist and the movie star cozily drinking and chatting at Jack's Restaurant.[6] The millions of *Life* readers got a glimpse of the private lives of two famous persons, and they witnessed the mingling of two worlds ordinarily discrete. An encounter between two celebrities increases the fame of each—largely because it is a useful relationship for the mass media—and an individual may be identified as a celebrity when he mixes easily with other celebrities. At that time, to judge from *Life*'s slanting of the occasion, Bergman had more prestige to gain than Hemingway; she had come to see him, driving most of the night to do so; and he got top billing in the headline, "Ernest Hemingway Meets Ingrid Bergman."

Later in 1941 *Life* published a four-page spread on Hemingway and Gary Cooper hunting in Sun Valley. Cooper was taking a vacation after completing two films, said *Life*, and relaxing with him were his family, the director Howard Hawks and his fiancée, the producer Leland Hayward and his actress wife Margaret Sullavan, "and, notably, Author and Hunter Ernest Hemingway, 'the tough guy' of American letters." The text reported that Cooper and Hemingway were "expert hunters, crack shots and good friends," and they spent their days hunting and fishing and in the evenings celebrated with friends at the Lodge. As with most *Life* features there was more space given to photographs than to text, and over a dozen shots portrayed novelist and movie star engaged in the typical activities of Sun Valley.[7] Though taken by Robert Capa, the photographs were not remarkable, the text less so; the interest of the feature lay solely in the fame of its subjects.

Shortly after *For Whom the Bell Tolls* came out Hemingway married Martha Gellhorn, a staff writer for *Collier's* and a former correspondent in Spain. *Life* dispatched a photographer to the newlyweds' honeymoon spot in Sun Valley to take a series of "intimate pictures of a great American at work and play." As usual, the magazine gave short shrift to work—there is a single photograph of Hemingway writing—and emphasized play. The feature included a photograph of the happy couple after the wedding, others of them dining with friends, dancing, relaxing on the terrace of their room at the Sun Valley Lodge, hunting, and posing with downed quarry. In the text Hemingway the celebrity was valued as highly as Hemingway the artist: "Today, in prime physical vigor, 210 pounds in weight, a good boxer, a crack wing shot and an excellent soldier, he is the acknowledged master of his art."[8] In a companion feature *Life* paid some attention to his artistic achievement in *For Whom the Bell Tolls* with a spread of photographs, chosen by Hemingway, designed to serve Paramount as a graphic scenario.

But even here the proof of the novel was the author not the book. Hemingway was the ideal writer to capture the essence of the Spanish war, *Life* opined, because in his many sojourns there he "had been imbued with the Spanish people and their country"; because he was intimately acquainted with their political life, having "sat with Republican leaders . . . in Madrid when, for the first time, a constitution for the Spanish Republic was penned (1931)"; and because, when the war broke out, he "threw his heart into the defense of Spain's humble people" and shared their danger and suffered their agonies. His "astonishing knowledge of warfare and maneuvers" gave the novel an authority it would not have had in less capable hands.[9]

Look, whose editorial policies were similar to *Life*'s, made its first contribution to his public reputation in the spring of 1941, when it printed a synoptic biography accompanied by photographs of him in hunting getup and at the front lines in Spain. *Look* praised him as the greatest living American novelist, but predictably gave most attention to his personality. The anecdotes were the tired ones—he ran away from home at fifteen, in the war transferred to the Italian infantry after a stint in the ambulance corps, was seriously wounded, lived in Paris as an impoverished young writer, wrote *The Fifth Column* under enemy bombardment, and so on. There was a correlation between Hemingway's fame and the frequency with which such anecdotes were repeated in magazines like *Look*. The familiar anecdote is for the celebrity like the slogan for the consumer product in that it encodes a message about his personality and authenticates impressions through corroborative repeating. The celebrity is a celebrity in part because he is familiar, because his admirers think they know him. Such anecdotes lead to legendary conclusions, as in *Look:* "It's certain that Hemingway has not given much thought to the risk involved [in his dangerous adventures]. He has never worried about personal danger. He is probably as tough as any of the tough specimens who people his books."[10] That many of the "specimens" in his books were not really very tough at all was irrelevant; *Look* was not interested in literature but in a personality, and since Hemingway had so frequently portrayed himself as a rugged character, that and not his fiction was the touchstone for his fame.

Life's photographs and *Look*'s anecdotes confirmed the heroic roles of *Death in the Afternoon* and Hemingway's other nonfiction of the thirties. The world traveler had an intimate knowledge of Spain; the arbiter of taste and *bon vivant* enjoyed the pleasures of Sun Valley; the sportsman hunted and fished with skill; the manly man was a "tough specimen"; the insider was privy to the formation of the Spanish Republic; and the warrior against fascism, the military expert, and the stoic and battle-scarred veteran combined to produce the heroic artist who had written *For Whom the Bell Tolls*. *Life*'s attention to Hemingway as the familiar of other celebrities was a new emphasis. He courted flattering invasions of his privacy by *Life* and other popular vehicles, and the media were delighted to feature a respected writer together with entertainment stars and sports heroes; they could extoll Hemingway as the greatest novelist of his time and not risk going over the heads of their audience.

The record of marriages and divorces among movie stars has been a staple of American journalism since about 1920, and the press attention given Hemingway's divorce from Pauline, his second wife, and his marriage to Martha Gellhorn shows how successful he had been in making himself the public equal of the more conventional popular celebrities. Besides the *Life* coverage of his honeymoon, newspapers and magazines published stories about the divorce and remarriage,[11] syndicated columnist Walter Winchell reported the details of the alimony settlement,[12] *Harper's Bazaar* ran a full-page photograph of the "co-adventurers" taken after their wedding,[13] and the tabloid New York *Mirror* featured a human interest story on Hemingway's love life. The feature began by saying that although writers' lives are not usually very interesting and "don't make good subjects for stories or plays," the axiom was not true for Hemingway, whose "life and romances—particularly this last one—are something for the movies." The rest of the lengthy feature was a "scenario" for a movie of his life, employing the standard biographical information and misinformation, but presented in a manner suggestive of popular romance. Readers of the *Mirror* learned, for example, that when it appeared Hemingway's marriage with Hadley, his first wife, was beginning to founder because of his fascination with Pauline Pfeiffer, "Hadley was ready to fight to keep Ernest for their son, John, and herself." Each of his three wives was described in detail, and their photographs appeared with the article so that readers could make their own comparisons.[14]

If the print media knew their business, readers of *Life*, *Look*, and the New York *Mirror* were more interested in the kind of woman Hemingway was attracted to, what he liked to drink, what he did for relaxation, and why he allowed his younger sons to drink beer and wine with their meals—according to *Life*, he encouraged it on the theory that they would learn moderation[15]—than they were in learning why he was a great and respected novelist. During the 1930s Hemingway had been able largely to control the sort of information made public about him, because he was doing much of the publicizing, but after 1940, when the mass media adopted him in force, he had less control. The media never violated his public personality and always paid their respects to his artistic genius, but they tended to ignore even more than he had the centrality of his literary vocation. He became under their patronage a caricature of himself, a composite of the roles he had developed earlier without even the secondary focus on his creative life that he had always maintained, albeit tenuously, in his self-advertisements. Ironically, because of the success of his efforts, because he had been able to compel a nearly universal acceptance as the champion writer of his time, he encouraged the natural tendency of the media to regard him merely as a colorful character and man of action.

II

When asked by an interviewer from the *New Yorker* about the sales of *For Whom the Bell Tolls*, Hemingway announced that he and his new wife were going to the Orient early in 1941 to "put some of that dough back on the line."[16] *Look* interpreted this comment to mean "that the money had come out of the fight for democracy, and it was going back into the fight. And its owner with it."[17] This was exaggerated; the Hemingways were indeed going to the Far East as correspondents, he for *PM*, she for *Collier's*, but with no apparent intention of joining the fight against the Japanese. His commission with *PM* was to report on the Sino-Japanese conflict and to assess future developments in the Far East. Ralph Ingersoll, *PM*'s editor, claimed that Hemingway, as always the insider, was the first American correspondent ever allowed to visit the front lines of the Kuomintang, and that his great fame as novelist, war correspondent, and military expert gave him a "unique basis" for discussing the war with political and military leaders.[18] His seven dispatches in *PM* show him at his best as a military expert and a political pundit—his analyses were crisp and shrewd, and his forecasts accurate. This reportage was unique in his nonfiction, moreover, in that his public personality was only vestigially present, subordinate to discussions of the political and military situation. Why this should have been so is not clear, but perhaps it had something to do with his unfamiliarity with the Orient, his position as observer rather than participant, and especially his perception of his audience—*PM* was a liberal and serious newspaper whose readership could be expected to be more issue-oriented than that of a standard metropolitan daily. But his self-effacement was temporary; when he became a correspondent for *Collier's* three years later, he advertised himself as vigorously as he ever had in his *Esquire* letters or NANA dispatches.

Time reported several months after Pearl Harbor that Hemingway had told a journalist in Cuba that he was going to get into the war but that he had refused to elaborate on how, when, or where. "I am and always have been a soldier," he said. "For that reason I prefer action to talking about the war. . . . I'll talk about that when I get back from it, if I come out alive from this struggle for the liberty and dignity of man."[19] The cadences of this comment were the familiar ones of the celebrity with the well-established public reputation for courting danger and opposing fascism, but the surprising thing was that in the first two years after American entry into the war Hemingway did not seem to be taking part at all. By the middle of 1943 the absence of news about him was so noticeable that in her syndicated newspaper column Elsa Maxwell wondered why this "two-fisted romantic" had been so little heard from.[20] The answer would not become public knowledge until after the war. Shortly after Pearl Harbor he had outfitted his fishing boat, the *Pilar*, with radio equipment, a machine gun, a bazooka, and a load of high explosives, manned it with a crew of nine, and cruised the Caribbean in search of German U-Boats. His plan was to be ordered alongside a surfaced enemy submarine, in the habit of marauding for supplies among defenseless fishing boats, and then blow it up, perhaps by dropping explosives down the conning tower. Fortunately for the life expectancy of Hemingway and his crew, as Malcolm Cowley later remarked, no enemy submarine ever came close enough to hail the *Pilar*.[21] Secrecy about this mission was imperative; hence it was the only time during Hemingway's career when his more adventurous activities went unreported, at least for a while. This neglect was compensated for later, when the story was made public; because it was a good story and seemed to typify his swashbuckling character, it was later told over and over in journalistic rehashes of his life and ultimately became a familiar part of his legend.

Early in 1944 *Collier's* announced that he would soon go to Europe as its war correspondent, ending the two-year drought in news about him. While in New York waiting to embark for London, he was interviewed by Earl Wilson, whose column of gossip about show business appeared in newspapers across the nation. Wilson, a self-proclaimed "worshipper of Hemingway," thought his idol was "America's greatest writer," but in his column he showed no interest in him as an artist, never so much as mentioning a single title of his books. Instead, he passed along to his readers observations related to one another only in that they were somehow about Hemingway. They learned that while in New York he boxed in Brown's Gymnasium, that his stomach was "like stone," that at home in Havana he liked to box barefoot on cinders, that he had a "tin leg" from his wound in the First World War, that he had plenty of hair on his chest and was wearing a beard, and so on.[22] Wilson's column, like most of its kind, was purely anecdotal; one item followed another at random, leading to no conclusion or insight. Such columns do not report news so much as they exploit personality. Names and not achievements are the province of the gossip columnist, and his importance is measured by his ability to sport the biggest names. Just because the columnist presents anecdotes haphazardly, however, does not mean that the celebrity emerges as indistinct; he is recognizable precisely because he is so superficially drawn. The portrait may have little to do with what the celebrity is *really* like, but a great deal to do with how he is publicly perceived. And typically, Wilson's gossip column reinforced conceptions of Hemingway that had circulated for years.

The only real news about him was that the rugged veteran of two past wars was on his way to a third.

From the 1920s through the 1950s gossip columns were important vehicles for creating celebrities and keeping them in the public eye. They were so influential that press agents were employed by celebrities at handsome retainers because they had connections with the columnists and could insinuate items now and then. Hemingway had no press agent, and did not need one: hardly a year went by after 1944 until his death when such journalists, usually Earl Wilson or Leonard Lyons, did not write columns about him. They always followed the same form—the series of anecdotes emphasizing the dramatic and exciting quality of his life and the vigor of his personality. The anecdotes changed from time to time but the source of their meaning did not; they all recapitulated the roles he had established during the 1930s. This attention was not uninvited: Hemingway freely granted interviews to columnists when he was in New York, and on occasion their columns carried a Havana dateline, signifying that they had been his guests at the Finca Vigia, his Cuban home.

Each syndicated column was read by millions, but its influence was not limited to its own readership. There was an osmotic effect whereby an item in one column might be taken up by another, producing a total saturation. Wilson's column—or it may have been Lyons's, since his column on the same day as Wilson's reported the same information about Hemingway sparring at Brown's Gymnasium and wearing a beard[23]—was the source of at least three more reports in the mass media about the hirsute, pugilistic novelist-correspondent. All three rehashes seemed to be occasions more for publishing photographs of Hemingway than for anything else: *Time*, in its "People" department, a glossy version of a gossip column, announced that he was "sporting a lush bush," and to let readers see for themselves, ran a picture of him sitting at a night-club table;[24] *PM*, below a photograph of him standing in a ring bare-chested and wearing boxing gloves, declared that "our invasion fleet will have some hair on it, with Ernest Hemingway in there punching as correspondent for *Collier's*. . . . He's been boxing barefoot for months, and his trainer says he's practically all muscle";[25] *Newsweek* used the same photograph as *PM* and the same observations about beard and boxing which had appeared in Wilson and Lyons.[26]

By calling attention to Hemingway's imminent departure as *Collier's* correspondent in Europe, the columnists gave him an advance publicity bound to increase the audience for his dispatches; and they implied that because his boxing put him in shape for his assignment, because he was so tough and eager for action, readers could expect him to be in the thick of the fight, discovering things less rugged correspondents would miss. His beard—unconventional at that time—was a symbol of his reputation for individualistic behavior, but as Orrin Klapp has pointed out, a little eccentricity is a valuable asset to a celebrity because it helps distinguish him from others competing for public attention.[27] The logic of all this publicity in 1944 was that since columnists took interest in Hemingway, he had to be important; a corollary was that since they did not take such interest in other writers, he had to be the champion.

III

Hemingway reached London about three weeks before the invasion of Normandy, but he almost missed D-Day because of injuries a week after he arrived. The automobile in which he was riding collided with a water tank during a blackout, pitching him into the windshield and giving him head wounds that required minor surgery and fifty-two stitches. Faithful as always despite his commission as a correspondent for a rival magazine, *Life* featured a photograph of him recuperating in a hospital, his head turbaned by bandages but his spirits undimmed. The accompanying article gave the details of the accident and an accurate inventory of his injuries; but then the magazine embroidered the story so as to confirm his fame as a man of almost superhuman capacities. According to *Life*, five days after the accident he "was out of his hospital bed and, over the protests of his doctors, in an attack transport headed for the invasion beachhead. Doctors had removed some of the stitches in his head, but he had pulled the rest out himself, leaving big, raw wounds."[28] This account was consistent with past anecdotes, but it was not true. The accident occurred nearly two weeks before D-Day—not five days as *Life* stated—and he had no need, temporal or medical, to pull out his stitches. The film director John Ford once said that in a Western when truth and legend conflict, the director

should print the legend, because it was more interesting and because people believed it. Like the West in its heyday, Hemingway
was developing his legend with almost every public move, and with
the help of many eager imaginations.

He recovered sufficiently from his injuries to make the Normandy invasion, and his first *Collier's* dispatch was an account of the
landing on Fox Green Beach of the eighth wave of the invasion
force. Since D-Day occurred more than a month before his dispatch appeared on the newsstands, he was not reporting fresh
news; but as in Spain, his assignment was to write about what
interested him without any necessary attention to day-to-day oper-
ations. His comportment under fire and his military expertise were
the subjects he felt his readers would be most interested in, and
these he emphasized. His dispatches most frequently took the form
of a short story: they focused on the microcosm, they were laced
with dialogue, and they had a heroic protagonist, namely Hemingway. In this first dispatch, "Voyage to Victory," he liberally employed the pronoun "we" rather than "the soldiers," "the Allies," or
"they," giving the impression that he was a member of the attacking
force. While this technique made for immediacy, it suggested er-
roneously that he waded ashore with the troops, as when he wrote
"This is simply the account of how it was in a LCV(P) on the day
we stormed Fox Green Beach."[29] He even implied that he was the
unofficial leader of the party. The officers nominally in charge were
confused by the circling boats and unsure of the location of their
assigned beach; and then their only map blew away in the wind.
Fortunately, Hemingway had memorized most of the map and was
able to find the landmarks. To complicate matters more, the infantry officer in charge, against Hemingway's advice, ordered a landing at a spot enfiladed by machine-gun fire, and the transport had to
turn back when it became obvious that they might be killed. The
officer refused to make another try at a different location, ostensi-
bly because he had been given orders to wait, even though
Hemingway in the meantime had found a place where they could
land safely:

> "Let's cruise along it to the right and see how it is up at that end," I
> said. "I'm pretty sure we can get in there when he wants to get in.
> You're sure they told him he shouldn't go in?"
> "That's what he says."
> "Talk to him and get it straight."[30]

The other party in this exchange was the Navy lieutenant in command of the boat, and throughout the dispatch he deferred to Hemingway's military knowhow. Finally, after a daring rescue of men in a foundering transport, the troops were landed at "a good spot we had picked on the beach."[31] "Voyage to Victory" was competent journalism in its portrayal of the confusion during a sea invasion, but it was also a superb self-dramatization wherein Hemingway's personality competed for attention with D-Day itself. It confirmed him in the thick of the fight, with both grace and control under pressure. His willingness to assume command was a preview of other legendary things to come.

Some years later, *True*, "the Man's Magazine," featured an article entitled "Hemingway's Longest Day," a narrative of his Normandy adventures. *True* quoted an unidentified member of a D-Day combat team: "that wild man who dumped us on the beach" had taken command of the team when it came under murderous enemy mortar fire and had led it to a safe location under the lee of a hill, supervised the securing of the position, and then started to crawl back to the beach in order to pass on his assessment of the situation to the command headquarters. At that moment the enemy started firing again and the combat team lost sight of him, and they assumed that "this Hemingway guy" had been killed.[32] This was fiction presented as fact; he did not land with the troops but went back to England after the party left the LCV(P). Hemingway himself was probably the source behind the story. Its author was William Van Dusen, an acquaintance who saw him in Paris a few months after the invasion; Hemingway evidently told him this fable at that time, for he had told almost the same story to his brother Leicester shortly after D-Day.[33]

If his adventures on the Normandy beachhead were fictitious, his capture of six German panzer soldiers in August 1944 probably was not. Newspapers announced that he and an aide flushed the six soldiers out of a basement in the battle area by lobbing grenades into the house;[34] a few days later they reported that he narrowly missed death when he was blown into a ditch by an antitank shell.[35] Shortly thereafter he advised readers about his activities with the French *maquis* as they pushed toward Paris alongside and often in front of regular Army units. Although he did not state that he was

leading the irregulars (that would have been against the Geneva
Convention), he left the impression that commanding them was
exactly what he was doing. They usually addressed him as "Cap-
tain," but as "Colonel" when strangers were present; by either title
he was clearly running the show. After joining the guerrillas, he
explained, he led them into Rambouillet, still in unsecured territory, and from there sent out reconnaissance patrols to gather intelligence which could be sent back to the infantry regiment command
post. After regular army units moved into the town they were
almost immediately withdrawn, leaving it unprotected except for
Hemingway's irregulars:

> I do not know if you understand what it means to have troops out ahead
> of you and then have them withdrawn and be left with a town, a large
> and beautiful town, completely undamaged and full of fine people, on
> your hands. There was nothing in the book issued to correspondents
> for their guidance through the intricacies of military affairs which dealt
> with this situation; so it was decided to screen the town as well as
> possible and, if the Germans, observing the withdrawal of the Ameri-
> can force, advanced to make contact, to provide them with the neces-
> sary contact. This was done.[36]

It is unclear from the dispatch how long he and his troops held the
town, but it was certainly several days, long enough for casualties.
When an Army unit finally arrived to occupy Rambouillet and
relieve its defenders, the irregulars, still under Hemingway's leadership, joined patrols into German territory. He was deliberately
vague about the details of these missions because, he said, they "are
not publishable at this time. Sometime I would like to be able to
write an account of the actions of the colonel both by day and by
night. But you cannot write it yet."[37] He could not write it because
it would be self-incrimination, a confession of his violation of the
prohibition against correspondents engaging in combat and leading
troops. What he did not mention was that Colonel David Bruce of
the OSS was in Rambouillet all the time he was; one could never
have known from him that any ranking officer was there. This
omission may have been a matter of security and censorship, and
his cryptic reference to his balked wish to write of "the actions of
the colonel" may have referred to Bruce, but if it did no reader
could have guessed. Hemingway seemed to be talking about him-

self when he spoke of the colonel, since that was one of his honorific titles with the irregulars. And he habitually left associates' names out of dispatches.

When General Leclerc's armored column finally arrived in Rambouillet on its way to Paris, Hemingway by his account went to transmit the intelligence he and his troops had gathered. Instead of being gratefully received he was rudely dismissed by the general and forbidden to move toward Paris until the entire French column had passed. Undaunted, he led his troops in an "evasive action," first to a local bar and then by back roads until they rendezvoused with the tanks at the head of the column; and in that leading position they moved toward Paris. His dispatch closed with him at the crest of a hill overlooking Paris, "gray and always beautiful" as it spread out below him.[38] It is impossible to view these two dispatches on his tour of duty with the *maquis* as much more than further self-advertisements. *Collier's* readers learned little about the European war, but they learned a great deal about Hemingway as soldier. He never mentioned certain important events occurring at the time—the FFI uprising in Paris, the Allied landing on the Mediterranean coast, or the attempt to encircle the German Seventh Army near Caen. His perspective might be explained by the fact that he did not witness these other events, and had only minimal contact with the American Army, but his choice of joining the *maquis* and defending Rambouillet was symptomatic of his tacit assumption that as *Collier's* correspondent he was reporting on himself as much as on the war.

Nor did he write about what he did after he saw Paris from the head of Leclerc's column. He did not have to; there were plenty of others willing to do so for him. The story of his liberation of Paris became one of the most familiar legends of his wartime service. Because it epitomized so well his freewheeling, picturesque behavior, it was recounted again and again in books, newspaper columns, and magazine articles. The most common version of the story was this (often told with slight variations): "Task Force Hemingway," increased to over two hundred guerrillas and a fleet of assorted vehicles, moved toward Paris until near Versailles Leclerc's column was slowed down by skirmishes with German troops, as Hemingway had anticipated. Having scouted the area beforehand, he knew which back roads were free of enemy resistance and led his troops away from the column and by these roads into Paris. While Leclerc was still tied down on the south bank of the Seine, Hemingway's men were already fighting German stragglers at the Arc de Triomphe, and when Leclerc finally entered Paris, according to one report, "he noticed a large sign hanging from the door of a cathedral: 'Property of Ernest Hemingway.' "[39] Hemingway headed straight for the Hotel Ritz to liberate it, and when Robert Capa arrived at the hotel that night after entering Paris with the first units of the Free French Army, he was greeted by Hemingway's driver, who said, "Papa took good hotel. Plenty stuff in cellar. You go up quick."[40] Like the earlier story of Hemingway on the beaches of Normandy, this of him being first into Paris and liberating the Ritz was dramatic and colorful, perfectly suited for journalists who wanted to convey the flavor of his personality, but like the earlier story it was just not true. He arrived in Paris with Leclerc's troops, and if Brigadier General S. L. A. Marshall is to be believed— Marshall was with him and was the official Army historian for the European theatre—he did not even liberate the Hotel Ritz.[41]

After the liberation of Paris, the war ground on as the Allied troops advanced toward Germany, and Hemingway, after a brief respite at the Ritz, attached himself to the Fourth Division of the American First Army and advanced with it. According to John Groth, an artist sketching scenes of battle at the front, Hemingway was still leading his irregulars, now from "Schloss Hemingway," an abandoned farmhouse with no Allied troops between it and the Germans and with six miles of open country on its flanks. On the divisional maps a symbol designated the part of the line being held by "Task Force Hemingway."[42] In a briefing speech that was to be quoted often in the future, General R. O. Barton, the Division Commander, said: "Old Ernie Hemingway is out there sixty miles ahead of everything in the First Army. . . . He's been sending back information. But now what do you think he says? He says that if he's going to hold where he is, he'll need tanks."[43] Groth reported that Hemingway always carried two canteens full of cognac when out "Kraut hunting," and when he arrived at a captured pillbox he would set up a bar, oblivious of the intermittent fire. (In other versions of this story, he carried one canteen of gin and another of vermouth for mixing martinis.) His courage under fire was best exemplified, Groth thought, by his imperturbability one evening when an officers' mess was shelled by German artillery. During the meal a shell landed directly outside the mess, breaking the windows and cutting off the lights. Everyone dived to the floor, everyone except Hemingway, who continued eating in the darkness as if nothing had happened. When a candle was finally lit, everyone except Hemingway put on his helmet and waited nervously for the next shell to land.[44] By now it was inevitable that this story would be added to the Hemingway legend, as of course it was.

His final two *Collier's* dispatches, datelined from the vicinity of the Siegfried Line, were not so self-dramatizing as those about his activities around Rambouillet, perhaps because he was already under Army investigation for violations of the Geneva Convention. (He was cleared of the charge of engaging in unlawful combat, and instead of being court-martialled, was awarded the Bronze Star.) Though he did not write about "Schloss Hemingway," he indicated that he was still in the vanguard of the troops advancing on Germany, and he gave the impression that he was the only correspondent so far forward. In the first of the two dispatches he quoted a conversation at the front with a GI who asked him what he was doing there when he could be enjoying himself behind the front lines:

> ". . . What are you doing here if you don't have to be here? Do you do it just for money?"
> "Sure," I said. "Big money, lots of money."
> "It don't make sense to me," he said seriously. "I understand anybody doing it that has to do it. But doing it for money don't make sense. There ain't the money in the world to pay me for doing it."[45]

At that moment a German shell exploded nearby, ending the conversation, and readers were left to draw their own conclusions about why he was there. Any Hemingway fan could see through the façade of cynicism and knew that he was there because of his interest in war, and because he had taken the study of courage, his own and others', as his province. To state this outright would have been bad form, as well as unnecessary.

An unnamed correspondent quoted in the New York *Times* later testified to Hemingway's extraordinary self-possession in war. "He is about as battle wise as a man can be," he said; "he knows about ten times as much of what is likely to happen [in battle] as even the most experienced of the other war correspondents."[46] He was "bat-

tle wise" because he so assiduously sought out action, and in his
Collier's dispatches he emphasized how perilous his tour of duty
with the Allied thrust had been. As his final dispatch indicated, he
was with the unit that first moved into Germany and breached the
Siegfried Line, and using his familiar "you," he offered to tell about
it: "If you want to know sometime, get someone who was there to
tell you. If you wish, and I can still remember, I will be glad to tell
you sometime what it was like in those woods for the next ten days;
about all the counterattacks and about the German artillery. It is a
very, very interesting story if you can remember it."[47] This was a
fitting close to his *Collier's* dispatches, and to all his adventures in
the European theatre. He had "been there," in the thick of battle,
and by his own and others' reports he had acquitted himself honor-
ably. By his well-publicized performance he had confirmed his
standing as the nation's foremost civilian expert on war and on the
behavior of men in battle. Most important, he had maintained his
standing as the public writer of his time by being equal to a prominent role, and so zestfully and so skillfully, in the major episode of
the world's greatest war.

9

"I Started Out Very Quiet and I Beat Mr. Turgenev"

1946–1952

I

In all of Hemingway's career as a public writer, the nearly eight years between his return from Europe early in 1945 and the publication of *The Old Man and the Sea* are the most difficult to characterize. He was more a celebrity than ever, but for the first time since 1932 he was not taking the lead in displaying his public personality. The sportsman and *bon vivant* of *Death in the Afternoon*, *Green Hills of Africa*, and *Esquire*, the fearless correspondent and antifascist who sent back reports from the front lines of the Spanish civil war to the readers of *Ken* and the nation's leading newspapers, and the soldierly leader whose *Collier's* dispatches charted his pursuit of the Germans across France, were not followed by a new Hemingway striking out in another direction. One explanation of his quiescence may be that others were ready to produce his publicity for him. He was featured, for example, nine times in the "People" section of *Time* between 1945 and 1948, and on four of those occasions the magazine included photographs of him. Only two of these notices contained real news; the rest were miscellaneous bits of information that *Time* felt would be interesting because he was such a celebrity. *Time*'s readers learned, for example, that a panel of magazine illustrators had chosen his as "one of the six 'most startling and exciting heads in the world'"; that he was "having the time of his life" shooting with his friend, "Poloist Winston Guest"; that he was traveling in Italy; and that one of his favorite drinks was a " 'Reviver' or 'Death in the Gulf Stream,' " a powerful concoction made with a few drops of bitters, the juice of one lime, and a tall glass of Holland gin.[1]

Time was not alone in gossiping about him. During this period he was also a favorite subject for Sunday supplements. A female reporter who interviewed him for the New York *Post Weekend Magazine* announced that he looked "virile enough to make bobby-soxers swoon by the droves," and that he was called "Papa" because he was "a little bigger, more alive and warmer" than other men. The *Post* was fascinated by his glamorous life in Cuba, his athletic prowess, and his personal courage. The biographical sketch—as usual, filled with fictitious anecdotes—was designed to show that he was "a man who has as much of what he calls guts as do any of his heroes."[2]

These Sunday magazines dwelt much on Hemingway's marital affairs. When his third wife, Martha, divorced him in 1945, the New York *Sunday Mirror Magazine* featured a piece on how the "bell tolls for three of Ernest's wives," complete with a description of them and a summary of dramatic moments in his life.[3] The Hearst supplement, the *American Weekly*, paid the most extensive (and fantastic) attention to his women. Hemingway had a "short hair" ideal of femininity, the magazine revealed, quoting a description of Maria in *For Whom the Bell Tolls*, and all of his wives had conformed, including his fourth, Mary Welsh. Each wife was discussed in the feature, with particular attention to Martha. She had met him in Key West in 1941, the magazine related (despite its acknowledgment that *For Whom the Bell Tolls*, published in 1940, was dedicated to her), after she went into a bar with her mother and saw a stool with his name on it and decided to wait for him. She "had had more than her share of disappointment in love" at the time, "and Hemingway loomed as a romantic figure entirely aside from his literary prowess," mainly because of his reputation as a "prizefighter par excellence." When he came into the bar, "Hemingway took one look at her and was head over heels in love" and they were married shortly thereafter. But after three years she tired of "trying to be 'Maria' Hemingway," and the marriage failed. Fortunately, concluded the magazine, his new wife looked more like Maria than the others had.[4] Most of this story in the *American Weekly* was inaccurate, as well as banal; it was also ignorant of even the most rudimentary things in Hemingway's fiction—for instance, short hair on women was to him always a sign of violation of femininity (example: Brett in *The Sun Also Rises*); long hair was his ideal. But the *American Weekly* was not interested in the real person, or even in producing figments consistent with that real person's bent. The Hemingway legend was becoming eclectic in the worst sense.

Another cause of Hemingway's relative retirement from publicizing himself may have been his writing problems. He had always had misgivings about becoming a "public character," and his anxiety was now growing. During the 1930s he had been able to write a good deal of fiction at the same time he was promoting himself in nonfiction. But between the appearance of *For Whom the Bell Tolls* in 1940 and *Across the River and into the Trees* in 1950, he published no new fiction, and he was having only indifferent success until early 1949 with his various literary projects. He also had a sense of impending doom that made him all the more anxious to get on with his creative work.[5] His letters in these years frequently complained that he was tired of all the personal publicity he had received, and he said more than once that he was afraid talking about himself could lead to the extinction of his creative energies.[6]

But again, his retirement from publicity was relative. He still granted interviews to Earl Wilson and Leonard Lyons, he still posed for photographers, and he actively assisted Malcolm Cowley and Lillian Ross in preparing magazine profiles about him. The nonfiction of this period—a pair of articles and a scattering of short magazine pieces on such topics as his friendship with Marlene Dietrich and his method of working—did not suggest that he wanted admirers to think of him in a new way. In both articles, "The Great Blue River" and "The Shot," he reappeared as champion sportsman.

"The Great Blue River," published in *Holiday* in 1949, discussed marlin fishing in the Gulf Stream off Cuba. Here once again the author's life was rich, full, and satisfying. He was close to "the finest fishing I have ever known"; he went at things casually; the Cuban climate was magnificent; the flora and fauna were lush and varied; he competed at the local shooting club with members of the Brooklyn Dodgers. And he was still the democratic free spirit who could hobnob with "lottery ticket sellers you have known for years, policemen you have given fish to and who have done favors in their turn, [and] bumboatmen who lose their earnings standing shoulder-to-shoulder with you in the betting pit at the jai-alai fronton. . . ."[7] Photographs published with "The Great Blue River" portrayed a tanned, bare-chested, and ruggedly handsome Hemingway piloting the *Pilar* and fishing for marlin off the stern.

If he was anxious for privacy, this *Holiday* item did not help. His account of the pleasures of Cuba invited journalists to give further details of how he lived, and they did so in quantity. *Harper's Bazaar*, *Vogue*, and *Flair* dispatched photographers to the Finca Vigia to take pictures of the famous novelist at home. The photo-essay in *Harper's Bazaar*, "The Hemingways in Cuba," included photographs of him and his wife, and others of the interior of their house so readers could see its gracious furnishings.[8] *Vogue*, which described him as "a famous presence in Cuba," pictured him clad in shorts with a tall drink in hand, sitting next to a leggy model on a couch at the Finca Vigia,[9] while *Flair* published its photograph of him under the headline, "Roaring Charm."[10] Earl Wilson wrote several columns about why his "great unshaven hero" resided in Cuba and about his splendid life there, citing the climate, the jai-alai games, and the excellent fishing and shooting.[11] Leonard Lyons also visited Cuba to get similar coverage.[12] Mrs. Hemingway wrote an article for *Flair* in which she made the usual day at the Finca Vigia sound like paradise. There was no routine, she said, and freedom and comfort were the only principles for selecting their activities.[13] This attention to Hemingway's life at the Finca Vigia made him into a Cuban landmark, a tourist attraction. General articles on Havana in *Holiday* and the *Saturday Evening Post* featured photographs of him as well as of traditional highlights like the Havana Cathedral and the Malecon.[14]

"The Shot," published in *True*, also opened with his life in Cuba, but in this instance his focus was dangers, not pleasures. Headlined as an account of antelope hunting, it began with a long anecdote about a pair of gunmen who came to the Finca Vigia to borrow $500 so that one of them could escape arrest for an assassination he claimed he did not commit. This man, whom Hemingway recognized, said he was a friend of one of the novelist's friends, an honest government official, and so Hemingway gave him $200. This anecdote was important as an illustration of Hemingway handling danger, thus it got serious treatment: "I didn't see these two Negroes until they were by the table . . . I had been watching the reflection of the bamboos and the Alamo trees in the pool and when I looked up and saw these two by the table I knew that I was slipping. They had come up a piece of dead ground but I should have seen them come around the corner of the shower house."[15] The violent milieu Hemingway had described so well in *To Have and Have Not* was one he demonstrated he could master. The anecdote was formally a short story with Hemingway as protagonist, and for readers who also read "The Great Blue River," the vicarious thrills at his peril must have combined well with the vicarious enjoyment of his sensuous life.

The remainder of "The Shot" suggested his early *Esquire* letter, "Shootism vs. Sport." As before he disdained hunters who used mechanized equipment and overwhelming firepower; the "dude" who got his game in this way was not a sportsman. The real sportsman hunted on horseback and on foot and relied on shooting skill, like Hemingway. After three days riding in the mountains he crept close enough to a herd of antelope and then dropped the largest buck with what he modestly called a "lucky" shot from 200 to 250 yards.[16] As usual, there were photographs of him in action.

Hemingway was once again addressing the kind of audience that supported his public reputation, an audience with a presumably limited interest in imaginative literature as such. *True*'s policy was to exclude fiction, but it was interested in "true adventure" and striking personalities, real things that happened to real people. "The Shot," headlined on the cover and the lead article, was followed by a profile of Detroit Tiger pitcher Hal Newhouser and an account of "them reckless Lees of Tucson," a family that included "the best professional mountain-lion hunters in the United States." Hemingway may have written "The Shot" primarily for the money—he got $3,500 for it—but he was putting out the old sort of publicity for the same sort of people. He was insensibly forced by the demands of his fame—he could not resist speaking in its terms any more than he could declare his private life off-limits.

II

The publication of *Across the River and into the Trees* in September 1950, and other events of that year, had special significance in the history of Hemingway as public writer. The buildup given the novel prior to publication was of a piece with the Hemingway legend. Scribners announced late in 1949 that he had written *Across the River and into the Trees* in the shadow of death. During a visit to Italy he had contracted a nearly fatal case of blood poisoning from a fragment of shotgun wadding which lodged in his eye, and the threat of death made him put aside the work of "large proportions" he had been writing and take up the new novel, which he completed after he recovered.[17] This story was more fancy than fact, but it seemed typical.

About 150 newspaper and magazine critics reviewed *Across the River and into the Trees;* most found it poor,[18] especially the magazine reviewers. Some, like Maxwell Geismar and Chandler Brossard, said Hemingway had irretrievably deteriorated as an artist and was finished as a writer of consequence.[19] John O'Hara, Evelyn Waugh, and William Faulkner came to his defense, and the critical issue became a spectacle played out in magazines like *Time* and *Collier's*. The publication of the novel produced a cultural event rather than a literary reception.

Across the River and into the Trees was not of the stature of *For Whom the Bell Tolls*, but it was not an unmitigated disaster, and so the critics' hostility was excessive. The violent reaction resulted from three factors: Hemingway's previous novel had been an overwhelming success, and it was ten years in the past; his public reputation attracted attention and caused strong antipathies as well as loyalties; Colonel Richard Cantwell, the hero, seemed to be only Hemingway under another name. The last two factors were particularly important, figuring in many of the unfavorable reviews.

The assumption that Colonel Cantwell was a mask for Hemingway allowed many reviewers to attack him and the work at the same time. There were indeed striking correspondences: both Cantwell and Hemingway served with the Italian Army as young men and were decorated for valor; both loved hunting; both addressed women they admired as "Daughter"; both had particular affection for Paris and Venice; both had been divorced from a war correspondent; and both were among the first to enter Paris in the 1944 liberation. Typical was Norman Cousins, who characterized *Across the River and into the Trees* as "a bleating boast for the sentimental brute," and concluded that it was "a disturbingly autobiographical summation."[20] Alfred Kazin called it "one of the most confused and vituperatively revealing self-portrayals" he had ever read. The Colonel's prating was nothing more than "the oracular and naive self-importance of an American big-shot who has been in all the countries and seen all the twentieth-century wars and has charmed a whole generation into believing that toughness is the same as valor."[21] Isaac Rosenfeld came up with the most ingenious criticism of all. It was not enough, he said, to call the novel a bad book and ascribe its failure to Hemingway's public role; to do this made for an artificial separation between the artist and the man that "succumb[ed] to the strategy" Hemingway had devised, namely, "at the expense of the man, to flatter the art." That strategy, so successful in the past, had miscarried with this novel. Hemingway had finally revealed too much about himself, "he let himself be lulled and dulled by the fable of himself," and he had exposed "the sickness and fear and sad wreck of life behind the myth."[22] If Hemingway had in the past created a public personality which suggested he shared his heroes' virtues, then these critics would in reverse infer from Colonel Cantwell that Hemingway was unbalanced, unbearable, and at the end of his tether.

Among the defenders, Ben Ray Redman in "The Champ and the Referees"—the title left no doubt where he stood—chastised the attackers, in an appropriate sporting metaphor, for "having failed to keep their eyes on the ball," for confusing literary criticism with a vendetta against Hemingway.[23] In the New York *Times Book Review* John O'Hara likewise drew upon the language of sports, assuring readers that Hemingway had "real class," and that "he may not be able to go the full distance, but he can still hurt you. Always dangerous. Always in there with that right cocked." O'Hara's review said little about the new novel and was mainly an excuse to rehearse events in Hemingway's career and to take swipes at literary critics and academics, but it opened with the remarkable assertion that Hemingway was "the most important, the outstanding author out of millions of writers who have lived since 1616 [the death of Shakespeare]."[24] Two weeks after that bombshell, the

Times published an entire page of letters about his review. Only one of the eighteen correspondents agreed with O'Hara; typical comments were: "real crass," "always in there with that right half-cocked," and "what makes Shakespeare better?"[25] *Commonweal* professed to be dumbfounded by O'Hara's statement and compared the feeling it produced to the speechless sensation induced by the pronouncements of the Russian ambassador to the United Nations [26]; *Time*, treating O'Hara's comments as juicy gossip, featured excerpts from his review not in its "Books" section but in "People"[27]; and *Collier's* editorialized on his hyperbole, adding its own negative opinion of the novel for good measure. *Collier's* printed a caricature of Hemingway, bare-chested, muscular, and bearded, standing like Popeye the Sailor with one foot on Shakespeare's chest in front of a heap of bodies, including Milton, Dostoevski, and Swift.[28]

According to Evelyn Waugh, the reviews of *Across the River and into the Trees* were "smug, condescending, derisive," and he wondered "why do they all [the critics] hate him so?" His "boisterous manners" had something to do with it, but even more, his critics detected in him a quality of "Decent Feeling" which was anathema because of the "high, supercilious caddishness" which was dominant in literary circles. "Behind all the bluster and cursing and fisticuffs," he added—and it was clear he was speaking of Hemingway as much as of Colonel Cantwell—"he has an elementary sense of chivalry—respect for women, pity for the weak, love of honor—which keeps breaking in," and these were qualities which offended his detractors.[29] Waugh's defense of Hemingway, like O'Hara's, was picked up by *Time* and partially reprinted in "People."[30] One of those who read the *Time* version was William Faulkner, who dispatched a letter supporting Waugh (and Hemingway).[31]

In its own review *Time* found little to like in the new novel, the only occasion on which the magazine criticized Hemingway since its disapproval (quickly reversed) of *The Sun Also Rises* almost twenty-five years earlier. But the extensive quotations from O'Hara and Waugh in the "People" section suggested that the magazine's editors were reconsidering their own judgment. Hemingway, after all, was still the writer they were most interested in, and they had the stake of long commitment in maintaining his public reputation now. There was no other literary figure, and few other persons in any line, who even approached him as good copy. In any case, in its review *Time* characteristically featured his personality, and Hemingway himself supplied the personal data. *Time* cabled questions to him in Cuba and published his answers in full, and this feature made up considerably more than half their review. He referred to himself in the third person, as Hemingway, H., Hem, or Hemingstein, treating himself not so much as an individual as an institution. After brief comments about his novel, he gave evaluations of various military commanders (duplicating Colonel Cantwell's) and summarized his experience in World War Two "on various projects" at sea, in the air with the RAF, and on land with the Fourth Infantry Division. "Hemingstein was only a guest of this division," he wrote, "but he tried to make himself useful." He said he would not be able to give the details of the actions he was in because *Time* had limited him to $25 cable tolls.[32]

His own efforts in *Time* to sustain his fame as military expert and heroic artist were complemented by *Newsweek*'s review. *Newsweek* praised the novel, and the book editor, coincidentally named Cantwell, informed readers that "an understanding of Hemingway's military career [was] necessary to evaluate [the hero] correctly."[33] *Newsweek* repeated the details of his conversion of the *Pilar* into a Q-Boat and of his leadership of the irregulars at Rambouillet,[34] which were common knowledge by 1950.

Hemingway was as testy as ever in his replies to his critics. He told Harvey Breit that the novel was "done with three-cushion shots," and that in his writing he had progressed through arithmetic, plane geometry, and algebra, and was now into calculus; if his critics did not understand what he was doing, then "to hell with them. I won't be sad and I will not read what they say. They say? What do they say? Let them say."[35] These comments were part of a long interview on the order of his *Time* communique, in which he talked about boxing, politics, poetry, and other random topics. In a more truculent mood, he told Earl Wilson he would like to take a poke at some of his critics: "I am not angry at nobody or his cockeyed, lousy, lying brother. . . . Sometimes I would like to throw at a character, from close and short. But what happens afterwards? The jaw is broke (you can hear it go like a bag of marbles), then the law suit." These comments, like those to Breit, were reprinted in *Time*, making its readers the best-informed per-

sons in the country about developments in the ongoing controversy.[36] Hemingway had regular access to channels of
communication closed to other writers, and to his critics, and he
could broadcast his rejoinders to a national audience.

The publicity given *Across the River and into the Trees* was far out
of proportion. Even best-selling novels—which this one was—
rarely receive so much public attention. But Hemingway the personality got even more attention than the novel, and made the
novel's reception more a cultural than a literary event. The reaction
in *Night and Day* is a case in point. *Night and Day*, billing itself as
"America's Picture Magazine of Entertainment," featured short articles about celebrities and photographs of Hollywood starlets. In
its March 1951 number, along with features on Errol Flynn, Shir-
ley Temple, and the inevitable starlet, the magazine published an
article entitled "Is Papa a Flopa?" *Night and Day* said the critics were
dead wrong when they claimed Hemingway was finished. "Papa,
as Hemingway has been better known to each of his four wives,
didn't much care about the critics," the magazine reported. "He
hunted and fished as usual, gave high-powered interviews to the
press with bits of advice like 'keep punching' and 'go in fighting,'
and lounged in the sun at his palatial home in Havana, Cuba. The
man who inspired a father complex certainly did well financially."[37]
This feature demonstrated the attraction of Hemingway's personality on even the most unlikely periodicals. The resort to his private
life, the implication that his financial success was a sufficient rejoinder to critics, and the layout of the feature with the text almost
hidden by photographs of him eating and drinking showed how his
public reputation had the effect of transforming literary questions
into personal ones.

III

Hemingway's career as public writer was a necessary prelude to the
controversy over *Across the River and into the Trees*, but a pair of
magazine pieces which appeared during the two previous years
were especially instrumental in the collision between his public and
literary reputations. One was Malcolm Cowley's "A Portrait of Mr.
Papa," published in *Life*, the other a *New Yorker* profile, "How Do

You Like It Now, Gentlemen?" by Lillian Ross. In 1949 *Life* was at
the peak of its influence and was probably the most important
single source of information for a popular audience. Its publication
of Cowley's long and admiring biographical article—which, unlike
earlier *Life* features on Hemingway, was not tied to a recent book or
film—certified his preeminent cultural position. The *New Yorker*
profile differed considerably in tone from the Cowley piece and
from almost every other past treatment of Hemingway's personality. Ross's attitude was difficult to identify; if it was admiring, as
she insisted, there were many who disagreed, and with reason. The
profile's effect was immediate and dramatic. Reviewers of *Across the
River and into the Trees* who viewed it as evidence of Hemingway's
disintegration as artist and as personality itself repeatedly used the
profile as evidence.

Cowley's "A Portrait of Mr. Papa" in *Life* ran to about 9,000
words and was the most comprehensive study of his life to that
point (January 1949).[38] Hemingway aided Cowley in preparing the
essay—he invited the critic to interview him during a two-week
visit to the Finca Vigia and suggested others whom Cowley might
contact for information—but he did not read the piece until it was
in print. When he did, he pronounced it "OK" although "not aw-
fully accurate,"[39] though it was more accurate than most previously
published biographical sketches. Some years later Cowley said that
the only inaccuracy Hemingway ever specified was the story of his
carrying canteens of gin and vermouth during the war; he scoffed at
the idea he would waste a canteen on vermouth.[40] There were
minor errors, mostly concerned with Hemingway's boyhood. He
did not, as Cowley claimed, take boxing lessons at age fourteen
from a professional named Young A'Hearn; Cowley undoubtedly
heard this story from Hemingway, as several others did around this
time. Nor did he talk himself into a job with the Kansas City *Star*
after his graduation from high school; his uncle Tyler arranged it
for him. But these were trifles compared with the apocrypha of his
running away from home to become a hobo, leading an Arditi
company, becoming a professional boxer and bullfighter, and so
on, that had circulated in the past.

After the feature appeared, Cowley complained to William
Faulkner that the *Life* editors, who chose the photographs and supplied their captions, had done him a disservice. The pictures and

captions were "pretty God-awful," he said, and "surrounded, sub-merged, and . . . changed in import" the text itself.[41] There were indeed many pictures, fifteen in all, and they portrayed Heming-way in characteristic activities: in boxing gear at ringside; in aviator costume, preparing to step into an RAF bomber for a mission over France; drinking from a bottle of White Horse scotch before de-parting for the Spanish front; and strolling toward a Cuban bar "to get a double Daiquiri and visit with some of his fishermen friends." There were portraits of him at various ages—in a wheelchair after being wounded in World War One, breakfasting at the Finca Vigia, and posing with each of his wives. Yet the pictures were not out of place, for the text of "A Portrait of Mr. Papa" also stressed Hemingway as colorful personality and vigorous man of action.

Cowley's profile, gracefully written and eminently readable, was a sophisticated version of the anecdotal form used by the gossip columnists; it was a series of stories unconnected by a controlling theme or insight. Readers heard about Hemingway's conversion of the *Pilar* into a submarine-hunting Q-Boat, his leadership of the French irregulars at Rambouillet, his leading the Allied troops into Paris, and his presence at the front lines throughout the eighteen-day engagement in the Huertgen Forest, but the only conclusion Cowley drew was that if Hemingway ever wrote a book about World War Two, it would be "certain to contain more first-hand accounts of combat than any of the war novels that have so far appeared."[42] Similarly, his extended treatment of Hemingway's life before World War Two made little effort to relate the man to his work, and at no point was there more than a sentence or two about his stories and novels. "A Portrait of Mr. Papa" differed from Earl Wilson's columns principally in being more accurate and more lit-erate. It appeared in a magazine that adored Hemingway and that would not have been interested in a formal article by even an established critic like Cowley. In the two decades between 1941 and Hemingway's death, *Life* published sixteen major features about or by Hemingway, more coverage than it gave any other literary figure. It twice published his fiction, but the great majority of these features focused on his personality. He was made to order for *Life:* a best-selling novelist generally accepted as a major writer who dealt with important contemporary themes and who was col-orful and photogenic.[43]

At about the time "A Portrait of Mr. Papa" appeared, Cowley was urging William Faulkner to approve a similar *Life* treatment. Faulkner's resistance showed the difference in attitudes toward publicity of private and public writers. Faulkner said he would cooperate with Cowley only if he was given the right "to blue pencil everything which even intimates that something breathing and moving sat behind the typewriter which produced the books." That, he was certain, would never be acceptable to *Life*. "I imagine the last thing on earth they will pay their good money for," he added, "is a piece about somebody's mere output even though art, since I imagine they dont care two whoops in the bad place about art but only about what they would call 'personalities.' "[44] On the other hand, when Hemingway asked Cowley to withhold certain material from "A Portrait of Mr. Papa," he merely wanted him to be consistent with the public personality he had developed. Cowley wanted to say that in Oak Park "he was a literary boy, not a sports boy," which was true, and Hemingway requested that he omit that observation, which Cowley did.[45] It was a small point, but it would have clashed with the man of action that he had been so careful to project and which, in other particulars, Cowley had corroborated.

"A Portrait of Mr. Papa" presented *Life*'s five million subscribers and perhaps twenty million readers the public personality they knew well. For Hemingway as a public writer at mid-century, *Life*'s tribute was the nearest thing to naming a popular laureate. A little more than a year later Lillian Ross's *New Yorker* profile, "How Do You Like It Now, Gentlemen?" offered a different portrayal. Some readers considered it a devastating critique of Hemingway's essential fatuousness and an exposure of the humbuggery of his public personality. Others, notably Ross herself, felt it was a sympathetic and even loving portrait of a fascinating man and great novelist. Although it is probably the best-remembered of all the personality analyses appearing in his lifetime, its importance to his public reputation at that time was less than its durability would suggest. The *New Yorker*'s circulation was nothing like that of *Life* or *Time*, and its readership was on the whole more "intellectual" than theirs. Public reputation, in any case, is created by repeated exposure, and no single magazine piece, even an unsympathetic one— and Ross's profile is certainly not *clearly* that—could much impair his standing as public writer. What the profile did affect, if only tangentially, was his literary reputation.

Unlike previous observers, Ross was not much interested in Hemingway's heroic exploits. She hoped to capture something more intimate, something more indicative of his essential nature. She wanted, she later said, "to give a picture of the man as he was, in his uniqueness and with his vitality and his enormous spirit of fun intact."[46] To achieve this she spent two days with him in New York late in 1949 before he sailed for Italy. He had just finished writing *Across the River and into the Trees*, and by his own admission was in a period of tired irresponsibility "after the terrible responsibility of writing."[47]

In spite of his weariness with writing, more of the serious artist came through in the Ross profile than in any journalistic piece since Dorothy Parker's profile twenty-one years earlier. The later one is studded with conversations on literary topics, and a lengthy portion is given over to his visit to the Metropolitan Museum of Art. At the museum he becomes "excited" and discourses on the capabilities of each painter and what could be learned from his work. This Hemingway was hardly the "dumb ox" of Wyndham Lewis, or the heroic adventurer of Malcolm Cowley. He was, instead, a man who took art very seriously and who gave much energy to creating it and understanding it.

This unusual emphasis on Hemingway as artist was somewhat obscured by his idiosyncratic behavior. He speaks occasionally in a kind of mock-indian language, leaving out articles and pronouns and sometimes verbs, for example: "Not trying for no-hit game in book." Several times he says, "How do you like it now, gentlemen?" a gratuitous remark that Ross was at a loss to explain, although she notes that the phrase seemed especially important to him. He stops in the middle of Fifth Avenue to take imaginary shots at a flock of real pigeons. When he goes to Abercrombie and Fitch to buy a new coat, he "menacingly" says to the clerk, "Want to see coat." He does not like the fit, and "tearing the coat off," says, "I'm tall on top. Got any other coat?" as if he expected the clerk to say no. Some of the singularities in his behavior were familiar. He laces his conversation with metaphors drawn from sports, so that even his pronouncements about literature and painting have something of the flavor of the gymnasium. He drinks prodigiously, including three double bourbons at the airport, several bottles of champagne (with caviar) at his hotel (some of it early in the morning), and at the Metropolitan Museum repeated bracers from a flask.

Lillian Ross was trying not to perpetuate the standard image of his personality but to demythologize him, to place his familiar traits in the context of the actual man. When she describes his reunion with Marlene Dietrich, for example, she does not stress the glamour of their meeting, as *Life* had done years earlier regarding his interludes with Gary Cooper and Ingrid Bergman. Their talk is about grandchildren and how Miss Dietrich cleans her daughter's apartment with towels from the Plaza Hotel. Hemingway's edgy reluctance to buy new clothes, the cushion of paper under the nosepiece of his glasses, the sophomoric way he behaves when he runs into his old friend Winston Guest—these details made him seem much more accessible than the gallant author-adventurer sketched with broad strokes in Malcolm Cowley's article.

His most striking characteristic in the Ross profile was vanity as to things great and small. He was proud of his trim waist and his taut stomach muscles; his son was a Harvard student; he himself was the champion writer of his time; his new novel was better than *A Farewell to Arms* and he was prepared to defend his title with it. The literary heavyweight championship was obviously on his mind because he returned to the subject three more times in the two days. He had won the crown in the 1920s, he said, defended it in the 1930s and 1940s, and was happy to defend it in the 1950s. He confided that he had "started out very quiet and beat Mr. Turgenev. Then I trained hard and I beat Mr. de Maupassant. I've fought two draws with Mr. Stendhal, and I think I had an edge in the last one." But he would not get into the ring with Mr. Tolstoy unless he went crazy or continued to get better.[48]

The most significant aspect of the Ross profile was that it minimized the mythic qualities of his public personality while laying bare and accentuating the grandeur of his literary ambition. He had rarely been modest about his achievements, but before 1950 he had allowed his fame as public writer merely to imply that he was the champion writer too. But now what was left, for *New Yorker* readers, was a Hemingway bereft of the protective legend, and insistently staking his reputation on *Across the River and into the Trees*.

There are basic ambivalences and ambiguities throughout the profile. Hemingway's eccentricity, for example, is a function of his vitality and his appetite for experience. His diction and syntax are strange but he explains that they are a variation on a joke language he uses at home among friends. He drinks a great deal but his consumption of champagne and caviar is more ritualistic than profligate. His attempt to buy a new coat is hilarious, but he charmingly finds the business of proper appearances a bore. His discussions of literature and art are dogmatic and curiously phrased, but he is serious and informed about them. Much of the profile confirms Ross's contention that she admired Hemingway because he "had the nerve to be like nobody else on earth."[49]

She includes three incidents, however, which convey less his eccentric charm than his egotistical boorishness. When she was arranging the interview, he had mentioned he hoped to see a boxing match when he came to New York. When he arrives she tells him that a friend of hers has tickets to a fight that evening and would like to take them. He asks who is fighting and when told launches into a diatribe against "bums"; "a bad fight is worse than no fight," he says. He ignores her kindness and her friend's generosity. At the beginning, when Ross goes to meet him at the airport, she finds him looking "bearish, cordial, and constricted," with one arm around a "wiry little man" named Myers. Myers was a businessman who had been Hemingway's seatmate on the flight from Havana, and the novelist had shown him the manuscript of *Across the River and into the Trees*. At the airport gate Hemingway, squeezing Myers and shaking him to punctuate a point, explained how much he liked the book. All the "wiry little man" could do was gasp "whew" and then walk away "unsteadily" when he was released. Ross's emphasis on Hemingway's bearishness and aggressive self-confidence made this other than engagingly eccentric. From the overbearing Hemingway of this episode readers assumed Ross was trying to ridicule him throughout.

Near the end of the profile she describes a luncheon Hemingway held in his hotel room for his publisher, Charles Scribner, "a dignified, solemn, slow-speaking gentleman with silvery hair." At one point Scribner asks Hemingway if he has some letters he had written to him; the novelist's reply—that he carried them everywhere he went, along with his copy of Browning's poems— seems in context more unkind than playful. A short while later Scribner attempts to tell a story about his inept hunting in England. Hemingway takes advantage of his pauses to talk about his desire to compete in the Monte Carlo and San Remo shooting championships.

> "I finally got one," Scribner said timidly.
> "Got what?" asked Hemingway.
> "A rabbit," Scribner said. "I shot this rabbit."
> "They haven't held the Monte Carlo shoot since 1939," Hemingway said. . . .[50]

Ross's use of "timidly" to describe Scribner's comment borrows from Hemingway's own literary technique. She rarely uses a modifier to describe how people speak, but when she does it has force. Here it emphasizes Hemingway's imperious manner and his compulsion to call attention to himself.

Years after the profile Ross called it "a sort of Rorschach test on Hemingway" in which readers found what they wanted.[51] But few people besides Ross found it sympathetic. According to her, Hemingway liked it and told her so; others—including A. E. Hotchner and Phillip Young—testified that he was upset, even horrified, by it.[52] Nearly coinciding with the publication of *Across the River and into the Trees*, the profile encouraged personal remarks in the unfavorable reviews that were to come.

Dwight Macdonald said the profile illustrated how much Hemingway "had accepted the public personality that had been built up by the press" in the past; worse, he apparently "gloried in the grotesque (but virile) Philistine" Ross made him.[53] On both counts Macdonald was wrong—Hemingway's usual public personality was hardly there, and he was not a philistine there, either. Macdonald was not alone in being confused about the relation of the profile to Hemingway's public personality. Morton Dauwen Zabel, in his review of *Across the River and into the Trees* for the *Nation*, pronounced his distaste for the "dismal exhibitionism" of the public personality, especially as Ross represented it. After reading the profile, he wrote, "one was left wondering what could survive for the serious business of art and writing," and the answer provided by the new novel was "very little."[54] This was hardly fair: Ross had written about only two days in Hemingway's life, two days when he was on vacation. Joseph Warren Beach shared Zabel's sentiments. "It is painful to find that a serious artist, in the fulness of maturity and fame, can be such a boyish—and bearish show-off, . . . that an experienced man of the world should be willing to expose to the world so many intimate personal secrets, or that a man who has seen so much and thought so much about life should be so shamelessly self-confident and self-absorbed."[55] These comments show why many intellectuals found Hemingway's public personality deplorable. Literature was "serious business," and Hemingway's comportment and personality were not compatible with serious business. Moreover, his eagerness to be a public man, his exposure of "so many intimate personal secrets," was a violation of the artist's proper social role. It was expected that movie stars would make public spectacles of themselves, but for a distinguished novelist to do so lowered him and by contagion his art to their vulgar level.

The simplification of the Ross profile by Macdonald, Zabel, Beach, and others expressed the disdain among literary intellectuals toward the public Hemingway. The profile had been published in what was at least marginally one of their own periodicals (Macdonald had worked for the *New Yorker*, and Edmund Wilson was its regular book reviewer); therefore, they believed it must be an exposé. These critics, prizing complexity and ambiguity in literature, consistently simplified Ross's profile, refusing to see that it, too, was a complex study—one of the few dealing with Hemingway's personality that was (or ever would be) worth rereading.

But the effect of the profile on Hemingway's public reputation was not great: celebrity thrives on simplicity, and "How Do You Like It Now, Gentlemen?" was complicated. He had never before been so open about his ambition as he was to Ross; he knew that he was speaking for publication, and he seemed to know that nothing Ross wrote could hurt him where it counted. He was right. His literary reputation in 1950 fell to its lowest point since 1935, but his standing as public writer was not weakened. He had created his public personality and built his public reputation in part to protect himself from the vicissitudes of critical opinion, and by the time of the Ross profile and *Across the River and into the Trees,* no critic and no single magazine piece could undermine his position.

In those days Hemingway was frequently solicited by business firms for endorsements of their products. Ross reported that he was offered $4,000 by an agency called Endorsements, Inc., to become a "man of distinction" in a whiskey advertisement. He turned it down only because he was a "champagne man" and did not like the brand of whiskey.[56] Yet he endorsed the Parker Pen in an advertisement on the inside front cover of *Life; Time*'s commenting on it in "People" shows that such a practice was not quite familiar among literary figures.[57] Sometimes his endorsements alluded to his adventures and avocations. In the official program of the Ringling Brothers and Barnum & Bailey Circus he called the 1953 circus the best he had ever seen. The elephants, he said, were well-trained and almost seemed happy. "They do not spread their ears and raise their trunks and come crashing through the brush."[58] In yet another advertisement appearing in *Life,* spread over two full pages, he suggested that readers should taste a Ballantine Ale "on a hot day when you have worked a big marlin fast because there were sharks after him." The Ballantine copy called him "internationally famous as a deep-sea fisherman" as well as the "greatest living American writer."[59] He was also a natural for travel advertisements because of his globetrotter reputation. For Pan American Airlines he encouraged his countrymen to spend their next vacations abroad to understand more clearly the destiny of their own country. He testified to Pan American's reliability, telling travelers that they could feel just as confident as he had when he flew the airline into the heart of China.[60]

A testimonial of a different sort was his "Tribute to Mamma from Papa Hemingway."[61] "Mamma" was his old friend Marlene Dietrich, and his tribute to their friendship was part of a long feature about her in *Life.* His remarks were generous, as the occasion demanded, but what was notable was not so much what he said as the fact that he could as it were validate Dietrich. He did not write the piece merely to publicize his own stature—his admiration for her was obviously genuine—but the *Life* editors, from a sense of his superior position in at least their hierarchy, published his comments as a boxed insert under a separate headline, indeed like an endorsement.

IV

The early history of Phillip Young's *Ernest Hemingway*, published in 1952, belongs with an account of Hemingway's public reputation because it indicates his wariness about being characterized in terms of anything other than his nonfiction. Young used the theories of Sigmund Freud and Otto Fenichel to explain the psychology of Hemingway's fictional heroes and, to an extent, the behavior of the novelist. Freud had discovered while treating victims of World War One that men severely wounded in battle had a compulsion to repeat their wounding experience in dreams, thereby contradicting the theory of the pleasure principle. He explained this "repetition compulsion" by a theory of the death instinct, which proposed that the goal of all life was to return to a state of non-life. Man's destructive urges, argued Freud, were an adaptation to this instinct: he destroyed other things in order not to destroy himself. Otto Fenichel, Freud's disciple, elaborated the theory. The victim of a "traumatic neurosis"—one triggered by a serious physical wound—suffered from insomnia and nightmares, felt a compulsion to relive in his mind the traumatic experience, and in order to adapt to it had to develop a "complicated system of bindings and primitive discharges." These theories seemed to Young to describe exactly the psychological profile of Hemingway's fictional heroes, and also to explain why he himself was so eager to study violent death and to confront it in the African bush and on the battlefields of Europe. He had suffered a traumatic neurosis after his wounding in 1918, and his work as well as his life were reflections of how radical that neurosis was.[62]

There was much more in Young's book than this, but it was his psychologizing which got him into difficulty with Hemingway, who wanted the book suppressed. In the foreword to the revised edition of his book, Young recounts the lengthy, tortuous, and sometimes hilarious negotiations between novelist and critic which preceded the first edition. Hemingway had discovered the forth-

coming book when Malcolm Cowley, who had served as a publisher's reader for it, commended it to him. His reaction was swift.
He did not want the book published and proposed to stop it by
refusing permission to quote from his works. His objections were
threefold: (1) no biography should be written during his lifetime;
(2) Young was invading his privacy; and (3) the whole thing was a
personal attack.[63] Young's book was not a biography, and although
it had a biographical dimension, he used only information which
had already appeared in print. Nor was it an attack; Young's admiration for his work was evident throughout.

   As to the invasion of privacy charge, a critic who writes about
the work of a living writer and refers at all to him beyond his work
is more or less guilty of such an invasion. But of all writers
Hemingway had the least grounds for invoking personal privilege:
he had often written intimately about himself, and he had abetted
others in writing so about him. Yet he told Young that it damaged a
serious writer to be told he had a neurosis, damaged him possibly to
the point where he would be unable to write. He added that such a
diagnosis could also "[damage] him with all his readers . . ." (Young
paraphrases Hemingway's correspondence).[64] This last assertion
may best explain his opposition to the book. Neither the right to
privacy nor the accuracy of Young's reading was really at issue.
What was being contested was the explanation for the way of
Hemingway's public life. In his nonfiction he had argued that he
gambled with his life because that was his duty as heroic artist.
Popular commentaries had almost always followed his lead.
Coronet, for example, concluded a feature in 1949 by asserting that
"his checkered experiences on five continents—dishwasher, sparring partner for a prizefighter, soldier, bullfighter"—had made his
fiction authentic.[65] But when Young argued that "in the light of a
Freudian explanation, . . . our understanding of him as human *or*
hero, man *or* legend, may be deepened and properly enriched"
(italics added),[66] he cast doubt on the validity of Hemingway's self-
portrait. If his swashbuckling exploits were an adjustment to a
neurosis, they could not easily be refracted through the lens of an
uncomplicated heroism as well.

   Hemingway overestimated Young's ability to "[damage] him
with all his readers," inasmuch as the audience for Young's book
was not going to be the one which gave Hemingway his public

reputation. Nevertheless, for over a year he insisted that he would do everything he could to prevent publication. When he relented, he did so out of necessity and reluctantly, although with typical generosity. Because of the suppression Young could not get a teaching job, and he finally threatened to publish the book with the quotations paraphrased. Hemingway yielded, gave his permission to quote, directed Scribners to credit Young for his share of permission costs, and even offered to lend him money. On that happy note the difficulty ended, and the book was published, without diminishing Hemingway's public reputation in any perceptible way.

His fears of its possible effect, however, again suggest why his public personality was so important to him. He had fashioned it partly to keep the private man unseen, to disguise who he really was. Young's explanation of it as a mask was more vexing than a simple debunking. Attacks on his public personality could be parried and even turned to advantage, but an interpretation of it as a psychological smokescreen was much more difficult to counter.

The strenuousness with which he opposed Young may have also been a carryover from his displeasure at the reception of *Across the River and into the Trees*. Some reviewers of the novel none too subtly implied that he had lost his bearings. Young's book, as Hemingway perceived it, made the same argument. In his "African Journal," written in the mid-1950s, he has his wife remark about how upset he had been "when that man wrote a book about how you were crazy"[67]—surely an allusion to Young's book.

V

Hemingway had no reason to complain about the reviewers' response to *The Old Man and the Sea*. By any standard the novel was a triumph. Nearly all reviewers praised it, and many called it a masterpiece, the crowning achievement of his career. After reaching a low point in 1950, his literary reputation turned so sharply upward two years later that at least one reviewer could again refer to him, without irony, as "the champ."[68]

The Old Man and the Sea was first published in a single issue of *Life*—September 1, 1952—and commonly sold out within eight hours after its appearance on newsstands.[69] In its editorial preface *Life* complained that Hemingway had been unfairly attacked in the past by "certain critics, members of the intelligentsia and lesser writers envious of his success." These "literary barflies" needed to swing at "the biggest man at the bar" to build their own egos. They had attempted to make Hemingway over in their own image, but without success: he was his own man, a supreme individualist impervious to the bleats of these "improvers." Looking for symbolism in his fiction was a "highbrow practice" that did no justice to the perfection of *The Old Man and the Sea.* But perhaps there was just a bit of symbolism: Hemingway as the Old Man, his story as the great marlin, and his critics as the sharks. The symbolism was not complete, for the sharks could do nothing to damage this marlin.[70]

Life's admiration for Hemingway was predictable, partly because of its past favor and now because of its payment for the novel (variously reported to be between $30,000 and $65,000). Its editorial, however, surpassed in assertiveness any of the magazine's prior homages. *Life* had little use for "highbrows" and "members of the intelligentsia"—terms it used with undisguised opprobrium— and its editorial assured readers that Hemingway shared this contempt. Why else would there be such antagonism between writer and critics? "Success" was a key concept in *Life*'s system of values— by which it meant conspicuous public acclaim—and Hemingway's success was the reason intellectuals defamed him. Moreover, because he was no highbrow, because he resisted conventional definitions of the writer's role, he had a rapport with the public which caused his enemies, in their envy, to gnash their teeth all the more. The most remarkable thing about this editorial was not its certainty that Hemingway belonged to *Life* and its audience more than to the "intelligentsia," although that proposition had never been so baldly put before; rather, it was *Life*'s willingness to employ its editorial space to carry on Hemingway's campaign against his critics, and to adopt his tactics in doing so. *Life*'s audience was not known for its interest in literary reputations, and while the magazine's evaluation was characteristically framed in personal terms, it was only being faithful to Hemingway's own example. His public personality gave him a forum to respond to criticism, and a way to create an audience independent of the standards of literary tastemakers; now he had the pleasure of seeing one of the nation's most powerful media take up these tasks for him.

The immediate audience for *The Old Man and the Sea* was certainly among the largest for any initial publication. *Life*'s circulation was nearly five and a half million copies, the Book-of-the-Month Club chose the novel for its September 1952 selection, and the trade edition remained on the best-seller list for twenty-six weeks. This popular reception, coupled with the critical acclaim, closed an uncertain phase in Hemingway's career as public writer. He had suffered no diminution of his public reputation during the previous eight years—he was in 1952 more famous than ever—but his public personality had lacked its previous dynamic quality. The dedicated young writer of the 1920s had given way to the sportsman and *bon vivant* of the early 1930s, who was in turn succeeded by the social activist of the Spanish civil war and the combat-wise veteran of World War Two, but no new Hemingway had emerged in the postwar years. He produced little nonfiction in this period, and none of it further developed his public personality. *The Old Man and the Sea* marked the beginning of a new public role, perhaps his most famous. The battered but undefeated figure of Santiago merged with the image of his creator, producing a sage who seemed to speak with the authority of all the ages.

10

"Papa"

1953–1960

I

Hemingway's face was a familiar sight on magazine covers in the years after *The Old Man and the Sea*. Although occasionally appearing on the covers of periodicals with a continuing interest in literature—the *Atlantic*, *Saturday Review*, *Wisdom*—he was more frequently featured by magazines with only a minimal interest in high culture. These included *True*, *Look*, the Luce magazines *Time* and *Life*, *Fisherman*, *Popular Boating*, the Sunday supplements *Parade* and *This Week*, and the gossip magazine *See*. What this signified, beyond the obvious fact that he was the best-known writer of his time, was that he had transcended his literary calling and become a figure of importance to his entire culture.

One of his cover appearances for *Look* came early in 1954, when the magazine announced, under a photograph of the novelist in safari garb, that inside the magazine "America's great author takes you on safari—in 16 pages of words and pictures."[1] The pictures nearly outnumbered the words. Hemingway wrote captions to the photographs and a single page of text describing the first few weeks of his safari; on the other hand, there were thirty-three pictures which had been selected from 3,000 taken by a *Look* photographer. The feature took up about one-third of the total editorial (non-advertising) space in the issue.

Look readers learned nothing about Hemingway as a writer of fiction; none of his works was mentioned. They learned only a little more about the experience of a safari. They learned a great deal about how he looked after killing a leopard or when he was relaxing in camp after a day's hunt. The emphasis on photographs in the *Look* feature was consonant with the public interest in him as man of action and as sportsman. Prose could not convey his courage so successfully as a photograph, spread over a page and a half, of a rhinoceros bearing down on him. And no paean to his hunting prowess could compete with another photograph of that same rhinoceros, now dead, being inspected by its hunter.[2]

Hemingway's return to Africa in 1953 was an event of public note, reported to curious readers by newspapers, gossip columnists, and *Time*.[3] Even though it had been twenty years since his only other trip, his fame as safarist had never dimmed. In part his own efforts in his *Esquire* letters and *Green Hills of Africa* and now in *Look* accounted for this, but of perhaps equal importance was the notion, firmly planted in America by Theodore Roosevelt's famous safari in 1909, that a hunting expedition in Africa epitomized the strenuous life. For Hemingway as for Roosevelt, an African safari was a demonstration of one's mettle as a robust man of action. Whatever their private motivations, the safaris signified publicly that each man could alternate with equal success between civilized and "natural" pursuits, and that each had a manly vigor denied to all but the most heroic figures in the society.

Hemingway's safari had a spectacular conclusion. As the *Look* feature was appearing on the newsstands, a private plane he and his wife had chartered went down in the bush near the Murchison Falls in Uganda. The whole party survived, and after an uneasy night avoiding curious elephants, they hailed a passing boat (the same one Humphrey Bogart piloted in *The African Queen*). At Butiaba they boarded another plane which was to fly them to Entebbe for medical treatment, but on takeoff it too crashed. The Hemingways once again escaped, though not without injuries.

The news of the first crash came over the Associated Press ticker in midafternoon on Sunday, January 24, 1954. The presumption was that he had perished, and newspapers across the country began to assemble obituaries. In New York, the *Herald Tribune* by early evening had its Early Bird edition on the stands with a full obituary. The *Mirror* gave its entire front page to the story and featured a long account of his marriages; it also promised a sequel the next day giving the lowdown on "Hemingway, a he-man who packed a punch—and proved he could take it." When the news came, first, that the aircraft was only slightly damaged, and then early the next morning, that he had escaped not only one crash but a subsequent one, all the New York newspapers changed their leads and tenses, still giving the story front-page coverage.[4] His presumed death seemed appropriately in character, a violent end in the land with which he was closely identified; but his miraculous escapes were even more fitting. The man who had tempted death in action so many times had once again cheated it. As an editorial in the New York *Times* commented, the fact that the story of his crashes made headlines around the world was "an extraordinary tribute to the popular stature of a literary figure,"[5] but it was equally a tribute to his prior success in impressing his personality upon people everywhere.

The newspaper accounts of the mishaps were only the beginning of the publicity. At Entebbe, where he held a press conference a day or two after the crashes, Hemingway arrived (so the newspapers said) clutching a bunch of bananas and a bottle of gin and breezily proclaiming, "I feel wonderful. . . . I think [my luck] she is running very good."[6] This statement inspired Ogden Nash to write "A Bunch of Bananas," subsequently set to music and recorded by Jose Ferrer and Rosemary Clooney. It began, "A bunch of bananas and a bottle of jeen, / Keeps the hunger out and the happiness een, / I got a bunch of bananas and a bottle of jeen— / My luck she is running very good," and continued for five more stanzas describing the crash and its aftermath.[7] "A Bunch of Bananas" had only a brief popular success, but even this depended upon easy public recognition of the person and event involved, especially since the words do not use Hemingway's name.

Journalistic accounts of the accidents said again and again that Hemingway was indestructible. *Newsweek* concluded that, although he had pursued death all his life, "you can't kill 'Papa.'"[8] In his newspaper column Robert Ruark made the same point: "The man is unkillable. He has been trying for years to polish himself off the hard way and never quite succeeds."[9] Earl Wilson hailed him as "invulnerable Papa,"[10] and Ed Sullivan quoted Toots Shor on Hemingway's toughness: "'He's one of our indestructibles,' marvelled Toots. 'When he's high, his favorite diversion is going around to waterfront saloons and challenging longshoremen. If it's in the daytime, he goes around to fight gyms and picks on the professionals.' "[11] Leonard Lyons assured his readers that "The Champ" was calm before the prospect of a violent end, having faced it so many times before. He always sought new and dangerous experiences, Lyons added, in order to achieve "the fuller life which helped enrich his talents."[12] Characteristically, these commentators were encouraging their readers to think of Hemingway in terms of traditional heroism. The hero miraculously turns defeat into victory; he emerges with his fame enhanced and with renewed vigor for confronting his next ordeal.

His indestructibility was affirmed by a subsequent *Newsweek* report that, disobeying his doctor's orders to take a complete rest following the accidents, he had undertaken an expedition up Mount Kilimanjaro.[13] This story was as false as the account in a German newspaper that his plane crashed into Mount Kilimanjaro while he was looking for the frozen carcass of a leopard, but both reports partook of the desire among journalists to heighten even the most dramatic moments of his life. The reason for this hyperbolic treatment of what was already arresting was implicit in the persona he had created. As one magazine columnist approvingly put it, "Hemingway is a more fabulous character than any he ever created."[14] He was himself hyperbolic, and if journalists took liberties with the truth, they did so to achieve the same effects that Hemingway sought. The journalists emphasized moments which simplified his personality, and the naive hero worship Hemingway inspired was usually characterized by reductions. He had to be made transparent and available for his admirers; and hyperbole insured that no realistic ambiguity survived.

After the initial publicity about the crashes Hemingway reawakened interest by publishing in two numbers of *Look* his own account. The transformation of his brushes with danger and violence into a narrative with himself as protagonist was not, as we have seen, unprecedented for him—he had done it successfully in *Green Hills of Africa* and in his war dispatches—but writing about the airplane crashes presented a new problem. In his nonfiction he had almost always taken care to advertise himself as omnicompetent, as one who because of his acumen and fortitude was capable of mastering dangerous circumstances. But as an airplane passenger he was necessarily more passive, his role in the drama less self-evidently heroic. To compensate, he adopted a tone of muscular jocularity. Explaining why the pilot did not land in the water at the time of the first crash, he said that because the plane had fixed wheels it might pitch over on contact, and, since he had ascertained that "the drink" was full of crocodiles, this kind of emergency landing was "considered by experienced defiers of the laws of gravity to be extremely inadvisable."[15] He was also droll in describing the second crash. The aircraft, bouncing down a deeply rutted runway, suddenly "became violently air-borne through no fault of its own. This condition existed only for a matter of seconds after which the aircraft became violently de-air-borne and there was the usual sound, with which we were all by now familiar, of rending metal."[16] His jauntiness could not help but give readers the impression that he was a man whose imperturbability was unshaken where most men would have quailed. If he was not in control of the aircraft he was certainly in control of himself.

The airplane crashes were the occasion for the *Look* articles, but less than half the 17,000 words had to do with them. Otherwise he gave his opinions about drinks, landscapes, African game, newspaper columnists, hotels, and assorted matters, including ramblings about his restaurateur friends Toots Shor and Sherman Billingsley. Readers who were also Hemingway admirers would have been disappointed had they gotten only an account of the crashes. This they could get from the newspapers; what they wanted was more of the Hemingway personality. Indeed the *Look* articles had no important content beyond the personality. This focus, noticeable in the first *Look* feature about his safari and nearly exclusive in his account of the crashes, was a distinguishing feature of his nonfiction thereafter. Even when he returned to reportage in 1960 with "The Dangerous Summer," his narrative of the *mano a mano* between Spain's two greatest matadors, the duel was subordinated to his intensive self-examination.

This self-absorption was encouraged by the magazines. He once made news because of what he did; now he made news because of who he was. And after 1952 curiosity about him had quickened because of the success of *The Old Man and the Sea*. Its publication in *Life*, the attendant publicity, and the hosannahs which greeted it combined to bring Hemingway more than ever to the center of the national stage. Most important, he became an elder statesman of literature, the best-known member of a brilliant literary generation which was already beginning to recede into history. If he had been French he would have been an *Immortel*. As a sage he had unlimited license to direct attention more or less exclusively to himself.

II

When Hemingway finally was awarded the Nobel Prize for Literature in 1954, the journalistic response confirmed what had been clear for years—that he was the most renowned and honored American writer of his time. He had been passed over in earlier years, so the story went, because his work was not sufficiently idealistic to conform to the provisions in Alfred Nobel's will. *The Old Man and the Sea* seemed to remove that obstacle. It was rumored that the 1953 prize had been awarded to Winston Churchill instead of Hemingway because of the Prime Minister's advanced age, but the next year the African crashes persuaded the Swedish Academy that it should not delay in making Hemingway a laureate.

He received the news with characteristic grace and spite. He told Harvey Breit, who interviewed him via international telephone, that the award should have gone to Isak Dinesen, Bernard Berenson, or Carl Sandburg; he would accept it, however, with the humility proper to the occasion. Privately he felt the award was long overdue and that the Swedish Academy had not been judicious in earlier selections. He was particularly piqued that William Faulkner had received the prize four years earlier, and did not hide his irritation from Breit. "I do not know what Man (with a capital M) means," he said. "I do know what a man (small m) is. I do know what man (with a small m) means and I hope I have learned something about men (small m) and something about women and something about animals."[17] This was an allusion to Faulkner's acceptance speech, which asserted that "Man"—in the abstract, capitalized form—would not only endure but prevail. In his own acceptance speech, Hemingway could not resist another allusion to Faulkner, who had been baroquely ornate. "Having no facility for speech-making and no command of oratory nor any domination of rhetoric," Hemingway began, "I wish to thank the administrators

of the generosity of Alfred Nobel for this prize." His resentment of
Faulkner came from his competitiveness, and it showed the importance of the literary heavyweight championship to him. Faulkner's
selection by the Swedish Academy in 1950 seemed to deny
Hemingway's claim to the title, an especially irksome affront at the
time when *Across the River and into the Trees* was getting its hostile
reception. The Academy's slight bothered him even after 1954.
Two years later he told an interviewer, "One shouldn't win the
Nobel Prize, then rewrite the Bible and become a bore—I accepted
the Bible in its original version," a dig at Faulkner, whose *A Fable*, a
novel with systematic biblical parallels, had appeared in 1954.[18]

The Nobel Prize honored Hemingway's stature as an artist in the
international arena, but in reporting the event the American press
predictably responded more to his cultural importance as a personality than to his literary accomplishment. The New York *Times'*
assessment—that the story of his life was an important part of the
public history and the legends of twentieth-century American
life—was typical of newspaper coverage, and this observation
served in the *Times* and elsewhere to introduce a reprise of its
notable moments.[19] *Newsweek* characterized him as "nothing less
than a monument,"[20] and *Time* ran its announcement of the award
under the headline, "Heroes: Life with Papa." He was a hero, a
legend in his own time, as the magazine explained: "As a globetrot-
ting expert on bullfights, booze, wars, women, big-game hunting,
deep-sea fishing and courage (which he once defined as 'grace under
stress' [sic]), his personality has made as deep an impression on the
public as his novels."[21] *Time*'s only attention to literature was its
calling him a "supercraftsman"; *Life* went a bit further and acknowledged that in pursuing his many interests he had never neglected
his writing, and it even named the titles of three novels, but this
homage was muffled by nearly two dozen photographs chronicling
his turbulent life.[22] Hemingway was now the supreme winner, the
champion of literature and of every other activity in which he
competed. As Robert Ruark put it, "He has lived the life he wanted
to live, the way he wanted it. And he has profited thereby, in fame
and money"[23]—a crude but accurate summation of the calculus of
Hemingway's appeal.

As an artist Hemingway occupied an honorific position in the
culture, but one with limited status outside the intellectual elite.

Because his work had been successful commercially, and particularly because he had made himself a celebrity, he had increased his own public status enormously. The Nobel Prize publicity confirmed this enlarged status, not, paradoxically, because it ratified what an important artist he was—although it did that too—but because it signified what an important *man* he was. By winning the Nobel Prize, he showed he could play for the largest stakes and win; as champion his domain included literature but was not limited to it, and to the public literature was still subordinate to "life." The institutional recognition afforded by the Nobel Prize was the final step in making him a full-fledged culture hero. Thus when *Life* headlined its report of the award, "The Old Man Lands Biggest Catch," it made coy reference to his fiction but also emphasized the cultural significance of the event. As a culture hero he embodied values cherished by the society, ones related to what were believed to be frontier virtues—a taste for adventure, intrepidity, and a hearty, vigorous masculinity—and which were generally assumed to be collateral to any great accomplishment.

III

After the plane crashes and the Nobel Prize, journalists rushed to capitalize on Hemingway. Sometimes the attention was grossly exploitative, as in *Focus*, another of those magazines given over to photographs of starlets and gossip about celebrities. *Focus* quoted Hemingway as saying he would not sue his critics because he could not spare time from his writing; the statement was dubious, but the main reason for printing it was to justify a photograph of his famous face, flanked by pictures of show business personalities Sophie Tucker and Carol Haney.[24]

Other magazine features were more substantial if not more accurate, although in these, too, text was ancillary to photographs. *See*, "The Exciting Picture Magazine," tried to explain what made him a unique and significant figure, and concluded he could be understood only in terms of his unquenchable appetite for new experiences and his readiness for danger. As evidence *See* adduced flyblown anecdotes from the Hemingway legend—for example, that he ran away from "the respectable woman's world of his mother to become a boy hobo," but it added remarkable variations to the familiar litany. Without indicating they were fiction, *See* presented plot summaries of "The Light of the World," "The Battler," and "The Killers" as accounts of his own experience; it also said he had suffered from gangrene on one of his African safaris.[25] *Picture Week*, another magazine like *Focus*, called Hemingway "the last one of his kind in a world that is rapidly making pure, rough-cut adventure a rare thing for a man to come by."[26] This helps one understand why *See* chose to treat his fiction as fact, disregarding the artist in favor of the man: the supposedly actual man was more compelling and reassuring than characters in his fiction. As a result the fiction literally became stuff for the personality.

The most ambitious magazine attempt to explain the public personality in the 1950s was "Who the Hell Is Hemingway?" *True*'s "bonus book-lengther," the cover story for its twentieth anniversary number. *True* advertised its profile as "an astonishing and intimate portrait of America's great soldier of fortune," although nothing in it was astonishing or intimate. It was a pastiche of well-known anecdotes by several hands (with a few samples of Hemingway's nonfiction), leading to the standard conclusion that he was a "swashbuckling" adventurer, "living it up and writing it down."[27] *True*'s false claim of intimacy at least showed that intimacy with the celebrity was a value the magazine believed its readers wanted. Intimacy to *True* meant the elaboration of the public man—the man Hemingway had claimed to be throughout his journalism and other nonfiction. He had convinced people because the public man represented to substantial segments of his culture things admirable and worthy of emulation. Doug Kennedy, the editor of *True*, introduced "Who the Hell Is Hemingway?" and explained why this literary man had been chosen for the cover of the anniversary issue. His world was inhabited by "beautiful dames" and "rugged guys," and he was without peer as a hunter, fisherman, drinker, and reporter of violence. He could "tell the next guy to go to hell—and make it stick." Therefore he was a "fitting symbol" for *True*'s twentieth anniversary issue because "of all men, living or dead, Ernest Hemingway stands for much of what we, at *True*, admire. Hemingway represents a hairy-chested maleness, an irreverence for the conventional, a dislike of the traditional. He is, truly, a rogue male."[28]

In the 1950s Hemingway the sportsman continued to appear in magazines celebrating his virility. In one of its early issues, *Sports Illustrated* featured a photo essay extolling his sporting accomplishments, which according to the magazine included working as a sparring mate for "itinerant fighters," killing a charging rhino at point blank range, entering the arena to fight a bull, and being a "two-fisted drinker."[29] *Sports Illustrated* later gave readers his recipe for "fillet of lion" in a feature describing favorite dishes of famous persons; and in a series on "celebrity foods" *This Week*, a national Sunday supplement, reported that he particularly enjoyed deerburgers and tenderloin of lion.[30] His unsuccessful efforts to catch a 1,500-pound marlin for the film production of *The Old Man and the Sea* attracted attention from newspapers and magazines, which ran photographs of him with 1,000-pound specimens he did catch.[31] Even *Wisdom*, an expensive clothbound magazine with relatively naive pretensions to high culture, featured an article about his sporting interests which concluded that he was "a man's man," and there was the familiar accompaniment of photographs showing the sportsman in action.[32] *Argosy*, by overt policy a man's magazine, called Hemingway "the world's greatest writer and authority on hunting, fishing, drinking and other manly occupations," with evidential tales of his sporting and drinking prowess.[33] The republication of Hemingway's prose in popular magazines also helped prove his identity as champion sportsman and masculine paragon. *Look* and *Argosy* reprinted portions of *Green Hills of Africa*, and *True* featured "The Great Blue River," his *Holiday* article on marlin fishing from a few years before. *Fisherman* supported an article about Hemingway as a champion angler with a reprint of an early Toronto *Star* dispatch on trout fishing; *Field and Stream* reprinted "Big Two-Hearted River."[34]

This Week put Hemingway together with leading ladies, as *Life* had done years before with him and Ingrid Bergman. It told how Hemingway while chatting with the film star Ava Gardner at a practice bullring in Spain saved her from injury by grabbing the horns of a charging bull and flinging it aside. The feature included a large photograph of the actress smiling worshipfully at him.[35] *This Week* also published Marlene Dietrich's appreciation of Hemingway, "The Most Fascinating Man I Know," wherein she said "He has found the time to do the things most men only dream about"—

and compared him with "a huge rock, off somewhere, a constant and steady thing, that certain someone whom everybody should have and nobody does."[36] Dietrich was right—one could "have" Hemingway only imaginatively—but she was also wrong in that everyone at least had him imaginatively as "a constant and steady thing."

The approbative consistency with which periodicals over a broad cultural range treated his personality was no less remarkable than the frequency. Always he was brought forward to show how splendid life could be if one only had imagination enough to make it so. As a *Cosmopolitan* writer put it, Hemingway was "aware of an important, but socially obscured psychological principle: Life can be indescribably rich when you do the things you really want to do, ignoring the always cogent arguments that insist it would be foolish or useless to do them."[37]

Cosmopolitan's encomium implied the cultural function Hemingway—and other celebrities—performed. The mass media, particularly movies and television, relentlessly emphasized life's potential glamor, luxury, and excitement—potentialities closed off to most persons by circumstances and their ordinariness. The celebrity provided an easy and uncomplicated access to surrogate experience, and being neither remote nor mysterious to the public because of the media's unstinting attention to his private life, he seemed almost an intimate to his admirers. This explains why Hemingway's doings were so frequently chronicled by journalists, but it does not account for their consistent adoration. The celebrity occupies a tenuous position: his fame may evaporate as the public wearies of him; or, because he has a dangerous relationship with social norms—he is a celebrity, after all, because he is different—he may overstep the boundary between what is acceptable and what is not and thus expose himself to public censure. The public could not easily tire of Hemingway because he was a model of protean change, and because he had personally fashioned the impressions the public had of him. For all his boisterousness and braggadocio, moreover, he did not violate important social norms. He had a record of substantial achievement, in literature and otherwise, which had been certified by the highest authorities. Unlike many celebrities, his triumphs were real and his accomplishments genuine: no press agent could have engineered the Nobel Prize for him.

The mass media treated him so respectfully, in short, because he was a hero as well as a celebrity in a time when, as pundits were fond of pointing out, heroes were becoming exceedingly uncommon. The commonplace of the 1950s that Americans had sacrificed their adventurous spirit and eagerness for challenge to become Organization Men made him stand out all the more as a supremely individualistic hero. Yet for all the emphasis on his uncompromising uniqueness, he was never portrayed as perversely eccentric or odd. The ubiquitous assertions that he was "a man's man" were a shorthand way for journalists to assure readers that his heroism was of a familiar kind. He was, without paradox, familiarly beyond classification—as the ideal American male in the movies has been described, "manly, good-looking, easy-mannered, equally at home in an alley brawl and a drawing room, daunted by nothing."[38] The admiration he inspired and the expression of it in the consistent legend signified the pull of a traditional pattern of unconvention.

IV

In much written about him during the 1950s Hemingway the hero merged imperceptibly with Hemingway the sage, thus restoring to him one of the artist's most venerable functions, one radically diminished for serious writers since at least the time of Flaubert. Modern writers might still aspire to transform the consciousness of their race, but because of their art's increasingly private and "difficult" nature, and especially because powerful competing modes of communication had usurped some of their functions and much of their audience, they no longer enjoyed the cultural preeminence they once did. As a novelist Hemingway subscribed to Flaubert's specification of a restrained, indirect, and subtle art, but this chafed that part of him which wanted more in the way of public influence. His solution—arrogating to himself the role of mentor in his public personality—used the competing media for his own purposes. Paradoxically, however, because he was an artist whose literary genius was universally recognized, his stature as a sage was considerably augmented. Performing one of the artist's traditional roles, but in the untraditional way of speaking outside his art, he prescribed modes of consciousness and implied by example how his admirers could live their lives as successfully as he had his. And his culture, granting the validity of his special insight because he was an artist, eagerly welcomed these prescriptions.

The guise of preceptor was already familiar for Hemingway, but it became more evident in these years. A month after featuring news of his Nobel Prize, *Time* honored him with a cover story, its supreme accolade. The piece contained the old anecdotes but it hinted at a new stress or aspect in the personality. For over a quarter-century he had been a swashbuckling man of action, the "lion-hunting, trophy-bagging, bullfight-loving Lord Byron of America." He was still "a character—not the sallow, writing type with an indoor soul, but a literary he-man"; yet now he was "battered and mellowing." He had read Darwin when he was ten years old—there were 4,859 volumes in his library at Finca Vigia— Marlene Dietrich called him there long-distance to discuss problems. He looked older than his fifty-five years, wearing "a patriarchal beard that gave him a bristled, Neptunian look."[39]

What *Time* was edging toward was a characterization of him in his last and most famous incarnation, "Papa," the grand old man of American life and letters. The nickname was familiar; P.O.M. had called him that in *Green Hills of Africa*, and journalists had occasionally used it since. But after 1954 it became virtually a trademark, as recognizable as "Bogey" or "Ike" from the same period. He had earned his paternal stature by triumphing in the rough and tumble, and now as a cultural sage he could dispense wisdom with an air of benevolence and with the unassailable authority of age and long experience.

One of a sage's traditional duties is to instruct the young in proper ways of thinking and feeling. In "Hemingway Talks to American Youth," *This Week* described him before a group of high school students in Ketchum, Idaho, where he outlined his ideas on "work, fear, failure and success." His responses to the young people's questions were suitably homiletic. Asked by a student whether young Americans were better suited to face the future than young people of other countries, he replied: "As far as facing the future as adults, if you follow something far enough your possibilities are unlimited. You settle for less, you get less. The big thing is not to settle too easily."⁴⁰ A drawing in the feature showed him leaning forward in his chair and gesturing with his hand, while the teenagers clustered devotedly at his feet.

Compilations of extracts from his nonfiction and from interviews also stressed his role as a public sage. *Wisdom* offered "From the Wisdom of Ernest Hemingway" as a companion piece to articles on various aspects of his life and work.⁴¹ *Playboy*, a widely successful magazine by the 1960s, published his philosophizing in three January issues (1961, 1963, 1964); *Playboy*'s January number was always its most ambitious, for which the editors saved their best features. In "Hemingway Speaks His Mind" (1961) the editors assured readers that "a philosophy of life as trenchant as his prose" was to be found in these observations by "America's foremost literary figure." Each extract was headed by its topic—for example, "On Honor," "On Cowardice," "On Bullfighting." These were all statements of the public man, derived exclusively from his nonfiction and published interviews. Kinds of experience that he had examined again and again in his fiction—love, for example— got gnomic treatment: "ON LOVE: 'It is an old word, and each man takes it new and wears it out himself.' "⁴² Writers render experience, sages utter aphorisms, and it was the latter whom *Playboy*'s readers met in the magazine.

If in his first *Playboy* appearance Hemingway was brought forward as Nestor, in the next two he sounded more like Kahlil Gibran. The two later features were not compilations of earlier pronouncements; according to *Playboy* they were unpublished material he gave to the Wisdom Foundation of California shortly before his death. They are inflated and banal aphorisms loosely related to one another by general headings, such as "On Love and Women," "On Living with Meaning," and other grand categories, the format of "Hemingway Speaks His Mind." In one a truism becomes a revelation: "People are always seeking shortcuts to happiness. There are no shortcuts"; another platitude becomes poetic: "In a calm sea every man is a pilot"; there is an empty gesture toward principle that is characteristic only in its aggressiveness: "I will wage warfare against any writer whose work appears to me careless." Hemingway had never made a show of patriotism, yet in *Playboy* he was fulsome: "There can be no great literature in

America until her writers have learned to trust her implicitly and love her devotedly." The author of "A Clean Well-Lighted Place" and "The Gambler, the Nun, and the Radio" hardly seemed one to extol faith, but this Hemingway did: "As a weak leg grows stronger by exercise, so will your faith be strengthened by the very effort you make in stretching it out toward things unseen."[43]

The later two *Playboy* features belong properly to the history of Hemingway's posthumous reputation, but they deserve mention here because they are related to the development of his public reputation as "Papa." The desire to be oracular and to enter fully into this role in these pieces resulted in what is unmistakably the most egregious writing of his career, but their place in his canon was not much to the point. More important was that *Playboy*—the success of which suggested its editors knew well the tastes of its readers—treated these collections as if they had just been handed down from Mount Sinai. *Playboy* gave them grand titles—"A Man's Credo" and "Advice to a Young Man"—implying that they were profound and essential reflections on life, printed them on heavy-stock colored paper, and decorated them with elaborate representations of Hemingway's likeness, all of which contributed to the impression of a momentous event. *Playboy* published excellent fiction and nonfiction in this period, and that it made so much of Hemingway's philosophic posturing is evidence not of its bad taste so much as of a common and unquestionable assumption that he was a sage.

The photographic Hemingway matched Hemingway the sage; his pictures, as always, managed to convey the new emphasis in his public personality. The beard he grew in Africa came out white, making him look patriarchal and wise, as did his prominent wrinkles. His appearance made him look old while he was in his fifties, still in what should have been the prime of life. *Pageant* said that its five pages of photographs of him at home in Cuba showed "the hero, and also the author, of a lifetime of violent living and violent novels in a somehow tragic new role: that of an aged, tired, white-haired but still redoubtable lion."[44] The famous photographer Yousuf Karsh, whose portrait of him first appeared in the *Atlantic* and later in other magazines, chose a more literary but equivalently heroic metaphor. He looked like "a giant cruelly battered by life but invincible," like Ulysses departing on his last voyage.[45]

V

Being a sage had its disadvantages. Hemingway complained in 1955 to Earl Wilson that since "the Swedish thing" it had become fashionable "to crash our gate."[46] Those who made the pilgrimage to the Finca Vigia included fledgling writers seeking advice, tourists hoping for a glimpse of the famous adventurer and writer, and, in one journalist's inventory, "wealthy sportsmen of the international set, movie stars such as Ava Gardner and Gary Cooper, baseball players, West Point generals, priests, prize fighters, jockeys, matadors, and Spanish exiles."[47] He might have added magazine writers and newspaper columnists bent on getting interviews.

One of those who made the trek was Earl Theisen, the photographer on the ill-fated African trip. During an eight-day stay in 1956 he took over twelve hundred photographs of the Hemingways for a forthcoming *Look* feature on "Papa" at home. He was followed in turn by a *Look* editor who persuaded Hemingway to write an article to accompany the pictures about " 'how things go now' down at the Finca."[48] The title Hemingway gave the piece, "A Situation Report," reflected the narrowed focus of his late nonfiction: his subject was unabashedly himself.

He began the article with a series of waspish complaints. Old friends were dying and "the jerks and twerps, the creeps and the squares and the drips" were prospering and multiplying, making it difficult to avoid their company. There were so many visitors to the Finca Vigia that he could not work and was being run out of his own home. But there were few places to go. Spain and Africa were being overrun, and it was more and more difficult to find places in them yet unruined. His old haunts in Wyoming, Idaho, and Montana were also spoiled, "and nobody who knew them in the old days could live in them now."[49] One of the perquisites of old age, particularly for a sage, is license to deplore the present, to bewail its inferiority to the past. Men were not what they used to be, and everything had changed for the worse since the old days. This is a standard, even expected, attitude for a patriarch. By lamenting the inferior present, Hemingway was not only exercising his rights as "Papa," but also proclaiming his own heroic stature as one of the most luminous figures of that golden age before decay set in.

He prefaced his article with a long quotation from Cyril Connolly's *The Unquiet Grave* that puts useful light on his complaints. Connolly argued that a writer's only task was to produce a masterpiece, and any excursion into such writing as journalism or movie scripts was folly. "Writers always hope that their next book is going to be their best," Connolly wrote, "for they will not acknowledge that it is their present way of life which prevents them ever creating anything different or better." Hemingway's use of this quotation amounted to a public self-indictment. Too much energy and time was going to peripheral concerns, namely to being a celebrity and maintaining his public reputation by indulging the visitors and solicitors like the *Look* editor. He vowed not to write any more journalism until his book was finished (he said he had completed 850 pages of it), yet the vow was being broken even as he wrote "A Situation Report." His complaints in the early 1950s about having too much publicity, expressed in letters to friends, surfaced again in the *Look* piece. During the 1930s he had been able to advertise his public personality and be a celebrity without those activities interfering too much with his creative work; in the 1940s and especially the 1950s he had less success in maintaining this balance. He was the acknowledged champion, but the price of his success was the distraction of celebrity.

A *Look* reader might have sensed in the opening comments of "A Situation Report" his determination to cease being a public figure, and if so, could only have been confused by the rest of the article, where Hemingway was as robustly public as ever. He spoke of the pleasures of fishing in Cuba and the difficulties of fishing in Peru (where he had gone to catch a giant marlin for the filming of *The Old Man and the Sea*), making casual references along the way to the *Pilar*, confident that his readers would know he meant his own boat. He praised "Miss Mary," Mrs. Hemingway, with a long list of her virtues and accomplishments, still making his private life public. And he recounted the events of an evening spent in the Floridita Bar with a group of Navy Chief Petty Officers, old friends of his, who had, to his relief, rescued him from some callow midshipmen wanting to talk about Ezra Pound. An amiable anecdote that strains for wit (at one point, one of the Navy men says that "Ernie" wrote *"The Mooney Sixpence"* under a "synonym"), its only real purpose seems to be to illustrate how much the Navy men admired him.[50] Earl Theisen's photographs of him on board the

Pilar and following the domestic routine of the Finca Vigia emphasized the public figure, too.

Forgetting his vow to suffer no more interruptions, he continued to grant audiences to journalists, including old friends Leonard Lyons and Earl Wilson as well as feature writers from such magazines as *Bachelor* and *Cosmopolitan*. Another who came to Cuba to interview him was George Plimpton, founder and editor of the *Paris Review*. Unlike most of his interviewers, Plimpton was interested more in Hemingway's ideas about literature than in his sundry opinions or in the routine at the Finca Vigia, and the interview he got had a markedly different tone from others Hemingway had given. Plimpton praised Hemingway's charm, but there was a consistent touchiness in his responses. Several times he chided Plimpton for the inferiority of his questions, and he assured his interviewer that he would be severely penalized for interrupting his work to give the interview. He dodged some questions by falling back on old formulas—the "iceberg theory" of prose, for instance—and avoided others with non-sequiturs. Nothing in the interview shed much light on his fiction or his literary attitudes. Behind his elusiveness and testiness was his conviction, expressed to Plimpton several times, that it was bad for a writer to talk about his craft.[51] Yet his nonfiction was often full of literary talk amidst reports of his current attitudes and activities, and when Leonard Lyons or Earl Wilson or a writer for a popular magazine came to interview him, he often rewarded them with quotable material about his writing.

Why was he disingenuous with Plimpton? Plimpton's questions had something to do with it, and so did Hemingway's estimate of the audience that would read his answers. Journalists who interviewed him were rarely interested in literature except in a general way, and they accepted uncritically whatever he said about it. His remarks in these situations were consistent. He frequently talked about his schedule for writing (from just past dawn until about noon), his methods (he wrote standing up, in longhand with a pencil except when he used the typewriter for dialogue), and the difficulty and loneliness of what he usually called his "trade." Nothing he said was very speculative, and his interviewers apparently did not press him, eager as they were to go on to nonliterary matters of more interest to their readers. He usually said just enough to convey the impression that he labored mightily, and that he was able to enjoy the rest of his time because he labored mightily. Thus he reminded journalists that his literary vocation was central to his well-being. He did not want it forgotten what kind of championship he held, or that he had won it by hard work.

Plimpton's questions were more specific and more penetrating. He wanted to know about such things as style and the relationship of art to experience and what a writer learns from another writer. These are difficult matters to speak of at any time, but it was not entirely their difficulty that made Hemingway balk. He had a long-standing apprehension of being thought a highbrow, and Plimpton's questions might make him seem one. He could maintain his credibility only by adopting an attitude of grouchy taciturnity, and especially by insisting on his reluctance to answer the questions at all. His misgivings were manifest in his insistence on working out many answers on paper rather than responding orally; this wariness contrasted with his expansiveness in interviews with, say, Earl Wilson or Leonard Lyons, neither of whom ever noted that he felt the need to write out answers to their questions. Plimpton later said that he thought the reason Hemingway agreed to the interview in the first place was that he had himself started out writing for little magazines like the *Paris Review* and now felt nostalgic.[52] That seems as good an explanation as any, but the *Paris Review* audience was no longer the one Hemingway depended upon, and was just the kind of elite he most distrusted.

VI

The nostalgia which may have made him grant Plimpton the interview showed in his writing, too. His return to Africa in 1953 was an excursion into the past, and the journal he kept of the safari—not published until ten years after his death—was clearly meant to be a companion piece to *Green Hills of Africa*. In 1957 he began a series of autobiographical sketches about Paris in the 1920s; these would become *A Moveable Feast*. He also spoke of writing an appendix which would bring *Death in the Afternoon* up to date. This was never completed, but his account of the 1959 *mano a mano* between Antonio Ordonez and Luis Miguel Dominguin, Spain's greatest matadors, served the same purpose. These reversions to the past were understandable in a man of advancing years, but one is tempted to see them as willed acts of confirmation that their author was still the man he once had been.

A competition between rival bullfighters would not ordinarily have attracted much attention in America, but the Ordonez-Dominguin rivalry received considerable coverage in the American press because of Hemingway's involvement. He went to Spain in 1959 to report the *mano a mano* for *Life*, and journalists and photographers followed him as eagerly as they did the bullfights. American readers were treated to several photographs of him at ringside as well as to his impromptu assessments of the matadors.[53] These reports made clear that he was no mere spectator: he was Ordonez's closest confidant, prescribing his training regimen and giving him valuable advice.[54] His involvement was so complete, *Newsweek* reported, that he turned down an invitation to accompany President Eisenhower to the Soviet Union.[55]

His contract with *Life* called for an essay of 5,000 words, to be published shortly after the bullfight season while the *mano a mano* was still news. He was unable to confine himself to that length, and he was unable to submit the piece in the fall of 1959. He continued with it through the winter and spring, and when he finally finished in late May it totalled 120,000 words and had become a book. This was much too long for *Life*, so he cut it by 50,000 words, and *Life* made further excisions; when it finally appeared in three installments late in the summer of 1960, "The Dangerous Summer" ran to about 40,000 words.[56] He explained why the manuscript was so long. "Various vultures and large-bellied crows" had already "picked over" the *mano a mano*, he wrote a friend at *Life*, and the fights deserved more attention than these cursory and amateurish accounts provided; anyway, he could "write only one way; the best I can."[57]

Another explanation seems more compelling. In the *Look* pieces on his 1954 airplane crashes and his "Situation Report" two years later, he had focused exclusively on himself. This was not possible in "The Dangerous Summer," where he had to share the stage with Dominguin and Ordonez. And yet because he had not published a book in seven years and was having ill-success with writing fiction at all, his standing with the audience which read *Look* and *Life* was more important than ever to maintaining his claim to be the champion writer of his time. Thus, in "The Dangerous Summer" he never relinquished the spotlight for long, including more about himself than about the bullfights, and what had begun as a short feature ballooned into a full-length book.

In "The Dangerous Summer" his ability to convey the drama of a sporting event did not desert him. He was always at his best when describing a process; and his accounts of the fights, and of Ordonez's eventual triumph, had his characteristic feel for the tone and texture of an event, produced by keen selection of significant detail. If on occasion he directed the reader's attention from the matadors to himself, and then back again, thus diminishing a moment's intensity, the shift was not fatal: the rhythm of his description was only slowed, not destroyed. But the fights and the bullfighters were subordinate to events in the author's life. The editors of *Life*, aware anyway that their readers were more interested in Hemingway than in bullfights, seemed to recognize his centrality in the narrative by putting his picture, not the matadors', on the cover of the first installment. And Hemingway appeared in more of the photographs than did either bullfighter.

"The Dangerous Summer" recounted a sentimental journey, the return of an aging man to the scene of youthful triumphs. It began with his 1953 visit to Spain, his first since the civil war—a visit he felt might end before it began, with him barred from the country or even arrested and imprisoned. But the border guards and customs officials, when they discovered who he was, passed him through the checkpoints with the respect due a returning hero. Everywhere he went he was treated with deference, from waiters who addressed him as "Don Ernesto" to a customs official who personally paid his liquor duty because he had admired *The Old Man and the Sea*. As *Life* put it, this was "Hemingway's Spain."[58] He still knew and could recommend cities, hotels, restaurants, main courses, wines, and ships. Even more than *Death in the Afternoon*, "The Dangerous Summer" was a guidebook to the pleasures of Spain. During the summer of 1959 he and his friends spent their days attending ferias and bullfights, or they loafed around villas eating leisurely meals, swimming, partying, wing-shooting, or indulging in horseplay. As Hemingway described it, it was a life of good comradeship, rich and satisfying in every detail, free of anxieties except those related to the bullfights.

"Papa" the still robust model of the good life was complemented by "Papa" the aged hero. As the grizzled veteran returning to his Spain, he declined to write about the Pamplona fiesta because he had written about it "once and for keeps" and because the character of the fiesta had changed.[59] The thousands of tourists who now came to Pamplona got only an inferior imitation of the real thing he had known.

From old experience he had sworn not to become friends again with a bullfighter—it was too painful—but he could not resist. He adopted Ordonez, becoming, as he makes clear, the matador's surrogate father. As "Papa" to Ordonez he advised him, supervised his training, kept him relaxed between engagements, steadied him before he entered the arena, and in general performed paternal offices. Ordonez reciprocated by soliciting Hemingway's opinions and submitting to his discipline. This relationship is one of the central threads stitching the fragmentary narrative together; in a certain sense it is the dominant interest of "The Dangerous Summer." Hemingway's long-standing practice of emphasizing his insider status contributed to making this relationship so salient, but the intensity with which he did so suggests that there was more to it than this. By publicizing in *Life* his standing as Ordonez's surrogate father, he was displaying to readers his absolute competence as "Papa," a man ripe in the wisdom of years and a citadel of steadfast integrity. If this skilled and confident young man deferred to his authority, who could gainsay his patriarchal eminence?

He struck, however, another note in the piece which, muted as it was, suggested something more ominous. Contempt and loathing for the stupidity of the bullfighting public runs throughout "The Dangerous Summer." Manolete used "cheap tricks" to gain his fame because the "ignorant public" demanded them and "enjoyed being defrauded"; Chicuelo II, a canny fighter, cynically manipulated his public; Dominguin's "telephone stunt" with the bull excited spectators but was easy and had nothing to do with true bullfighting; even Ordonez performed some flashy tricks in the ring which the crowd loved, but as Hemingway commented, "He's making fun of them but they don't know it."[60] At one point he chides Ordonez for dedicating a bull to Jean Cocteau in France, and Ordonez replies that the torero not the man dedicated the bull. As a public artist, he had to do things which otherwise he would not do.

Hemingway, embracing this distinction, then explains to Ordonez why "the writer" signed "your friend" in books brought to him for autographs; he too had to perform disagreeable public acts.[61] Like the bullfighter, on whom he had modeled his conception of the heroic artist, he depended upon a heterogeneous audience. That audience was sometimes ignorant, applauded the wrong things, and "enjoyed being defrauded," but it had to be appeased. Hemingway had never openly made so strict a distinction between public writer and private man. That he did so in "The Dangerous Summer" and juxtaposed it with his relentless ridicule of the bullfighting audience suggests that the resentment about being a public writer indicated in "A Situation Report" was still with him. The "man" had integrity and the "writer" compromised, and the division was unhealthy despite that reserve of integrity. It was a division becoming intolerable. Hemingway knew that "The Dangerous Summer" was one of the worst things he ever published—when it appeared he called it a "mess" and said he was "ashamed and sick" at having written it[62]—and it was an expression of the public writer exploiting his personality for one of the largest magazines in the world. "The Dangerous Summer" was not what he had promised to work at in the *Look* article four years earlier.

Less than a year after publication of "The Dangerous Summer" Hemingway committed suicide. What combination of physiological impairments and psychological maladjustments led him to this end is unclear, but his inability to continue writing was a factor. The right words simply would not come. When he died he was the most famous writer in the world, among the most celebrated of all men, yet he had come to feel himself the captive of his public personality and reputation. The persona he had created years before had a life of its own, and he had to sustain it so that it could sustain him. When he could no longer write well enough to satisfy his own high standards, his fame, instead of sustaining him, mocked him, and the disparity between what he was to his public and what he was to himself may have been finally too great to bear.

11

"The Most Difficult Death in America since Roosevelt"

1961–1969

I

For many Americans the announcement of Hemingway's death in Ketchum, Idaho, on July 2, 1961, had the same impact as the news of President Roosevelt's fatal stroke sixteen years earlier. Like FDR, Hemingway seemed such a familiar and immutable presence, such a fixed part of the emotional landscape, that his mourners could remember what they were doing and where they were when they learned he was dead. As the public tributes in subsequent days and weeks would illustrate, his death signified more to his culture than the passing of a distinguished writer. It was the demise of a national institution.

His passing did not end his hold as public writer upon the imagination of his countrymen. If anything, his public personality was more in the public eye in the eight years after his death than before. During this period, which concluded with the publication of Carlos Baker's authorized biography, he was the subject of six other biographies, scores of reminiscences, many poems and short stories, dozens of appreciations, even a syndicated comic strip which purported to tell the story of his life. And in his posthumous memoir, *A Moveable Feast*, he continued to influence the public's perception of his character, adding lustre to his already fulgent Paris years.

The effect of his death on the public consciousness may be measured by the prominence of the announcement in newspapers across the country and around the world. Everywhere it was front-page news, in most papers the day's lead story. Many papers responded editorially as well. The New York *Times* apotheosized him as "a long-enduring figure on America's literary Mt. Rushmore"; *Figaro* believed his death by gunshot was an end "worthy of him"; and the New York *Herald Tribune* eulogized him as a man who "lived as he wrote: he was strongly built and hardily constituted, always ready for a fight. . . ."[1] President Kennedy issued a public statement mourning his death and calling him one of the world's great citizens; the state-operated radio networks of the Soviet Union, France, and Sweden offered special memorial programs; and the matador Antonio Ordonez wept openly while he and thousands of bullfight fans at the Jerez de la Frontera *plaza de toros* stood silently to honor the writer's memory, after which Ordonez killed two bulls dedicated to him.[2] The Louisville *Courier-Journal* expressed the sense of loss and bereavement felt throughout the culture: "It is almost as though the Twentieth Century itself has come to a sudden, violent, and premature end."[3]

Hemingway's general significance was evident also from the broad range of the tributes. Syndicated newspaper columnists as diverse as Walter Winchell, Joseph Alsop, Jim Bishop, and William S. White devoted entire columns to him. The *Reporter, Partisan Review*, and *Commonweal* assessed him as, at some remove from these journals, did *Look, Sports Illustrated*, and *Newsweek*. *Saturday Review* and *Life* featured him on their covers and published photographic reprises of his life. A periodical entitled *Astrology: Your Daily Horoscope* put his portrait on its cover, and inside a three-page description of his star chart ("In Hemingway's horoscope, the Planet Saturn is posited in the Sign Sagittarius. Saturn rules deep and profound thought; Sagittarius rules far off places and adventure. . . . Nothing could stop him from the eternal search for thrills").[4] The "DuPont Show of the Week" on the NBC television network offered an hour-long biography narrated by Chet Huntley.

The tributes took many forms, some familiar from earlier years, but now they were in the past tense and became resumés. Leonard Lyons, Earl Wilson, and Walter Winchell eulogized him with columns of anecdotes and personal reminiscences.[5] These gossip columnists, who usually trafficked in news of Broadway and Hollywood, fondly recalled him as a man of enormous gusto whose life overshadowed his art and who represented the possibilities for heroism in the modern world. Perhaps inspired by Ordonez's example, dedications were also popular. In his syndicated column Robert Ruark paid tribute to his "old friend" by dedicating his upcoming safari to him, and another friend, Robert Cantwell, set out on a trip of homage to the Two Hearted River in upper Michigan, which he reported in a long article for *Sports Illustrated*.[6] Ruark wrote twice more about Hemingway in the months after his death, once in his newspaper column and again in a monthly column for *Field and Stream*. In both instances he explained why he felt Hemingway was such a compelling and significant figure, and those explanations indicated again how little Hemingway's fiction affected his public reputation. Hemingway "was really a very simple fellow," said Ruark, and he hunted dangerous big game not because of any recondite existential necessity, but simply "because he bloody well liked to hunt and shoot." His fictional heroes reflected this simplicity; their instincts and behavior were always "direct and uncomplicated."[7] As literary analysis this was patently ridiculous, and Hemingway was hardly in private the simple man Ruark claimed, but as a public personage he did represent an uncomplicated heroism, and it was this culture hero Ruark was eulogizing. Ruark was not alone in confusing the man and the artist with the public personage; the assumption that they were all one characterized many posthumous reviews of Hemingway's achievement.

In his *Field and Stream* column Ruark reprinted a letter from an unnamed reader who lamented, "the loss of Papa hit me much deeper [than a relative's]." Hemingway had given him the "whole world," allowing vicarious adventures to a man who had no real ones because he lacked the money and courage to pursue them. Hemingway had taught him a standard of manliness and given him the knowledge that "men aren't made at Yale or Harvard, but at the end of a .303, fly rod, or behind a dirty red cape."[8]

Much the same sentiments were expressed by Joseph Alsop, the syndicated Washington columnist. Alsop recalled a memorable afternoon with Hemingway in Cuba in the company of peasants and soldiers of Fidel Castro's revolutionary army, and he speculated about what had made Hemingway such a compelling and unique figure. It was, Alsop thought, his wish that all experi-

ence be "vivid and real and intense," a feeling considered anachron-
istic and even antisocial "in our security-minded, suburbanized,
televised, homogenized, sanitized, endlessly bland era."⁹ Eulogists
often suggest that the deceased was a rare individual whose like the
world will not see again, so it is perhaps not entirely unexpected
that this was true of eulogies of Hemingway. But the frequency of
these laments, and the consistency with which something like Alsop's sentiments were expressed, suggest that the sense of loss
among Hemingway's eulogists was more than conventional piety.
It bespoke a feeling of irremediable cultural diminishment at the
passing of a hero who had represented as no one else the possibilities for rich and fulfilling personal experience. This feeling
was intensified, as Alsop suggested, by the contrast of Hemingway's vitality and adventurousness with the emphasis on security
and conformity identified by many commentators as dominant
values in postwar American society. The death of any writer might
plausibly bring forth such sentiments—heightened consciousness is
what literature is all about—but it was not Hemingway the artist
who was so widely mourned. His fiction examined again and again
the high price paid for heightened consciousness and emphasized
the painful complications it brought in its wake; in the saga of his
life, chronicled by himself and the mass media, it was a less costly
emotion, available to anyone willing to follow his example and his
precepts. It was in large measure this public man whose loss was
felt so universally.

Glossed over in many of the first obituaries and eulogies were the
circumstances of his death. It was certainly self-inflicted, but
whether it was suicide or accident was unclear. Mrs. Hemingway's
insistence that it was "in some inexplicable way an accident" spiked
some of the speculation, at least at first. The family's position was
that he was cleaning his shotgun when it accidentally discharged,
and this explanation was reported in all the newspapers, frequently
in the headline to the story. But less than a week later newspapers
reported that the muzzle of the gun had been in his mouth, and
then *Time* and *Newsweek* revealed that he had been hospitalized at
the Mayo Clinic not for hypertension, as had been reported at the
time and repeated in the first obituaries, but for psychiatric treatment and shock therapy. There could be no question, said *Time*, he
had killed himself, and no doubt, *Life* added, why he did so: he was

in poor health and unable to write any longer.[10] Mrs. Hemingway did not publicly retreat from her claim of an accident until five years later, but within two weeks after his death almost everyone else accepted it as a suicide.

Norman Mailer called it "the most difficult death in America since Roosevelt."[11] Hemingway's death was "difficult" because, by taking his life, he seemed to call into question all that he had represented. He had consistently brought himself forward as champion in everything he undertook, compiling a public record of uninterrupted triumphs, and the problem was how to reconcile his death with his victories.

Irving Howe in the *New Republic*, Wright Morris in the *Partisan Review*, and later Alfred Kazin in the *Reporter*, all suggested that his "panic at the end" stemmed from the contrast between his overblown public reputation and his inability in the last half of his life to do anything but parody his earlier work. This disparity between fame and achievement finally became too great for him to bear.[12] Much the same argument was adopted by Dwight Macdonald, whose satiric biography of Hemingway in *Encounter* almost gloated. "After 1930, he just didn't have it any more," Macdonald wrote, although few people noticed his decline because he was so much in the public prints. But by 1961, "the position is outflanked the lion can't be stopped the sword won't go into the bull's neck the great fish is breaking the line and it is the fifteenth round and the champion looks bad," and the only way out was to destroy himself. His private life, his writing, and his public personality were all of a piece, Macdonald argued, so when his professional career faltered he was left with nothing.[13]

In these analyses (save Morris's) there was more than a hint of satisfaction that Hemingway's suicide confirmed what critics had said about him for years, that his public personality was dishonest and self-destructive. Leslie Fiedler's account of a visit he paid Hemingway in November 1960 echoed this judgment, although in a more complex and less patronizing way. Fiedler found Hemingway aged beyond his years, inarticulate, unsure of himself, and "obviously flirting with despair." He "had worn himself out" selling his legend, and had failed to grow as an artist after his first great books; now at the end of his life he was a pathetic figure uncertain whether anything he had done was of lasting consequence. Fiedler

saw Hemingway's misgivings as a personal tragedy and symptomatic of a national malaise. His uncertainty had been a lifelong
personal affliction—turned into a literary strength in *The Sun Also
Rises*, his truest and best book—which had been hidden only by his
exertions in behalf of his public personality; and his distrust of his
own achievement signified something unhealthy about a culture in
which no amount of honors could allay feelings of inadequacy.[14]
Some years later Fiedler regretted that his article appeared in *Partisan Review*, the "wrong context" for it. He had sold it to someone
who proposed to issue it separately but the project had fallen
through and the essay was sold to *Partisan Review* without Fiedler's
knowledge.[15] Why he felt *Partisan Review* was the wrong context
Fiedler did not say, but he may have wished to dissociate himself
from the smugness of so many responses by the intellectual elite to
Hemingway's suicide.

Popular periodicals, which had not regarded Hemingway's
public personality as empty posturing, found a different meaning
in his death. *Life* was typical. All his life, the magazine explained,
he had been driven by "his incredible energy, his love of bravery
and danger," but "the uncertainty, pain and corrosive indignity of
ill health" began to wear the "gigantic man" down. He had always
reserved special contempt for animals and men who died badly, so
with the prospect of a slow and humiliating death before him it was
not surprising that "the writer, as always in control of his material. . . , had written the deliberate last chapter by shooting himself
with a double-barreled shotgun."[16]

As A. Alvarez has pointed out in *The Savage God*, taking one's life
is usually regarded in modern western societies as an act of cowardice and an admission of failure (and/or as a psychopathological act),
with the frequent result that the suicide's memory is scorned.
Hemingway's suicide did not provoke any such public reaction.
There were at least three reasons why this was so, all of them
explicit in the *Life* feature. His ill health and mental depression
were widely publicized, making his act comprehensible and not
irrational. Second, he had written so frequently about the meaning
of death, and had risked it so often, that it seemed somehow appropriate he embrace it by an act of will. Last, there was an air of
tragedy about his death which ennobled it. He was a heroic figure
brought low in what ought to have been the prime of life. His

energy and his capacity for intense experience had not been proof against the vicissitudes of physical and mental deterioration. Thus his decision to die rather than play out a deprived life evoked admiration rather than condemnation.

The cover photograph *Life* used on the memorial occasion suggested these views. One year earlier, when the magazine was serializing "The Dangerous Summer," its cover photograph showed him against a mottled but colorful background, looking directly at the camera and smiling broadly, the very image of a man whose life was satisfactory. In the later cover the background was a brownish-black, and he was looking to the left and beyond the viewer, as if he were contemplating something profoundly disquieting. His deep-brown eyes, the focal point, were alert but resigned, their depth emphasized by the soft focus along the edges of his hair and beard. The later cover assimilated his suicide into the legend, making him a tragic hero. If it was a naive kind of tragedy which *Life* and other popular periodicals purveyed, it nevertheless gave his death a meaning consonant with his public life.

Ultimately this attempt to make consistent the Hemingway legend had to be modified. Early in 1965 *Life* featured a short story by Ray Bradbury, "The Kilimanjaro Machine," only the twelfth work of fiction the magazine had published (two of the previous eleven had been by Hemingway), which suggested the direction this modification would take. The narrator arrives in Ketchum in 1964 driving a Land Rover purchased with contributions from his friends who, like him, were "readers." He looks for a hunter quoted in the newspapers as remembering "that poor old man on the road," namely Hemingway in his last year of life, and when he finds the hunter he tells him that the Land Rover is really a time machine. There is a right and a wrong time to die, the narrator says, and the grave in the Ketchum cemetery is "a wrong grave for a right man." He leaves the hunter and drives along the roads near Ketchum, challenging death by closing his eyes as he wheels around the hairpin mountain turns. This gamble succeeds: when he opens his eyes the grave in the cemetery is gone and the old man is walking along the road. The driver stops and offers him a ride, telling him the Land Rover will become an airplane and that he is going backward in time to January 24, 1954 (the date of Hemingway's first African airplane crash). "That's a good day you're talking about," says the old man, and he accepts the ride after assurances that the landing will be different this time. Once seated in the Land Rover the old man starts to mention a mountain, then stops himself; but the narrator, knowing what the old man is thinking, recites to himself the epigraph from "The Snows of Kilimanjaro," and thinks how he will put the old man up on the slope near the leopard, and "write your name and under it say, nobody knew what he was doing here so high, but here he is." The story closes with the old man's elated announcement that they are flying.[17]

The story was Bradbury's attempt "to throw off the pall" which had oppressed him since Hemingway's death, a death which had left him "with a mystery and a sense of unease."[18] *Life*'s publication of "The Kilimanjaro Machine" made this private act public and implied that the magazine, and presumably its readers, shared Bradbury's unease. In an age characterized by the transience of fame and the rapid replacement of one celebrity by another, moreover, the lapse of nearly four years between Hemingway's suicide and Bradbury's story in *Life* testified to how shattering his death had been.

By publishing Bradbury *Life* retreated from its position that Hemingway's death had been consonant with the version of his personality the magazine had extolled in earlier years. He had been a tired and sick old man in the last year of his life, and his suicide had been more a desperate defeat than a grim but ennobling victory. Had he been killed in 1954, as the world for twenty-four hours once assumed, and as Bradbury imagined in this story, his death would have been a fitting epitaph to his heroic life. But he had not been killed, his true end had been ignominious, and Bradbury's story could not change that truth, only voice a sense of profound regret.

Because of its reference to "The Snows of Kilimanjaro," Bradbury's story embodied another, and more transcendent, meaning. Hemingway's ability to play for high stakes and to be a perennial winner had been one of the most attractive things about him to a culture which prized individual achievement, and clearly that aspect of his fame had to be reconstituted in the light of his suicide. *Life* did not address itself to how this might be done, but implicit in Bradbury's story was an answer, the simplicity of which was surpassed only by the irony that the answer appeared in *Life*. It was to turn to the fiction, in which Hemingway had demonstrated his real heroism. By directing attention to one of his finest stories, and the one in which he expressed most directly the heroic qualities the serious artist must possess, Bradbury implied that the true measure of Hemingway's greatness might be found not in tales of derring-do, but in his ability to transmute his own fears and maladies into the stuff of art. That was his greatest triumph, and one not altered by the circumstances of his death. If anything, his suicide—which indicated how radical were those anxieties which had afflicted him all his life—retrospectively made his literary achievement all the more a victory.

II

Besides implying that Hemingway's heroism could most genuinely be seen in his art, thus anticipating the direction his reputation would take in the future, "The Kilimanjaro Machine" also looked backward to his fame as a daring adventurer who had survived two plane crashes in as many days. And in the seven years after his death, as in the thirty years before it, it was the man of action rather than the artist who held the public imagination. This legendary figure dominated most of the posthumous accounts of his career, but nowhere more so than in three biographies which appeared in the months after his death.

These "vulture biographies," as Phillip Young dubbed them, were "paperback originals," hurried into print as soon after Hemingway's death as possible. They were vulturous not only because they rushed to cash in on the publicity generated by his suicide, but also because they borrowed copiously from earlier serious works about him, notably those by Charles Fenton, Phillip Young, and Carlos Baker, and more generously from the columns of *Time*, *Look*, Earl Wilson, Leonard Lyons, and all the other chroniclers of the legend. Their controlling principle was that Hemingway's life was more fascinating than his fiction; therefore the Hemingway they presented was quintessentially the public man, little more than the sum of all the shopworn anecdotes which had been circulating during the previous thirty years.

The best of the lot was *Ernest Hemingway: The Life and Death of a Man*, by Alfred G. Aronowitz and Peter Hamill, two New York *Post* journalists (much of their book first appeared serially in the *Post*). Its relative superiority was due to its avoidance of the excesses of its two competitors. In a workmanlike journalistic style it strung together all the best-known Hemingway anecdotes: a chapter on the "real story" behind *The Sun Also Rises* (mostly culled from Harold Loeb's autobiography, *The Way It Was*); a paragraph or two on his KO of a taunter in the Stork Club; six pages on his scrap with Max Eastman; a couple of pages on his friendship with Marlene Dietrich; and so on, for over two hundred pages. The authors apparently interviewed Mrs. Hadley Mower, Hemingway's first wife, who said her husband had not had an affair with Lady Duff Twysden (the model for Brett Ashley), and his first son, John, who expressed regret that the priest at his father's funeral had failed to read the entire passage from *Ecclesiastes* that formed part of the epigraph to *The Sun Also Rises*, but aside from a few such scant revelations everything else in the biography derived from published books and the back numbers of newspapers and magazines.[19]

Milt Machlin, the managing editor of *Argosy* and a previous contributor of articles on Hemingway to that magazine, adopted in his *The Private Hell of Hemingway* much the same patchwork strategy as Aronowitz and Hamill. His celebration of Hemingway as "the adventurer of his age" and the description of the book's contents on its cover, "The brawling, boozing, battling years of America's greatest writer," left no doubt in the reader's mind that this was to be the Heroic Hemingway. The anecdotes Machlin rehashed were the familiar ones Aronowitz and Hamill had used, rendered in a more pedestrian style, but the difference between the books was Machlin's casual use of Hemingway's fiction as autobiographical fact. Thus it was Hemingway himself as a boy hobo who was knocked off a freight train by a brakeman and later challenged by an ex-prizefighter named Ad Francis (Machlin never mentions "The Battler," in which these things happen to Nick Adams), and it was Hemingway who while convalescing from his war injuries had an affair with an English Red Cross nurse during which "they made love, such as his condition permitted, in the actual hospital room and in whatever places they could get in Milan." Machlin could so easily dissolve the line between fact and fiction because for his purposes Hemingway the artist was irrelevant, and what he had written subsidiary to his real achievement of bringing "a more vivid kind of living to the world."[20]

Machlin's free and easy way with Hemingway's fiction paled before the inventiveness of Kurt Singer, author of *Hemingway: Life and Death of a Giant*. Singer did not trifle with the half-measure of using the novelist's fiction as fact; he invented episodes in Hemingway's life out of whole cloth. Readers learned, for example, about "Mrs. X," a thirtyish "ex-Oak Park socialite" who tutored the high school youth in the arts of love; about Maria, an Italian slum girl in Chicago with a body "pathetically thin but strong like steel wire" which she used to help him forget the terror of his war experiences; and about Heloise, a Parisian sculptor with whom he shared a studio, and who one evening after work "slid out of her dusky smock and stood naked, pushing her body against his." Even when Singer reproduced the familiar Hemingway anecdotes, he could not resist embroidering. Thus, according to Singer, when the *Pilar* was scouring the Caribbean for German U-Boats during World War Two, Hemingway's plan had not been to drop grenades down the submarine's conning tower, as widely reported elsewhere, but kamikaze-style to ram the *Pilar*, whose bow was loaded with high explosives, directly into the enemy ship. Before impact Hemingway and his crew would jump overboard and save themselves as best they could.

Singer also showed greater temerity than either Machlin or Aronowitz and Hamill in venturing into literary discussion, but he seems not to have read Hemingway's works. *The Sun Also Rises* (his first "story book") was the love story of the "traditional" Brett Ashley (also described as a "nymphomaniac"), and a "variation on the theme of *Lady Chatterly's Lover*"; in *For Whom the Bell Tolls* "Hemingway was saying the Commies had not come to Spain to save its people, but to push the country into the Soviet Satellite world"; *Across the River and into the Trees* was "a love fantasy about a middle-aged couple"; and so on. Singer's discussions of more general artistic matters were no more successful. On one page he suggests that Hemingway's early work had things in common with the "realistic painting" characteristic of the Paris art world of the 1920s; a few pages later he solemnly says that the early stories used a technique of "stream of consciousness."[21]

Singer's book was hardly informed. When he quoted Hemingway as saying in conversation, "When I write about suicide, castration, shell-shock, homosexuality, it is because I know the people who have experienced these things. But when you flip through the American books and magazines you see that they have been written by weaklings who have never experienced real sex, never seen a killing, never seen the blood and guts of death. It makes me laugh,"[22] he made him sound like a character who has just stepped from the pages of Mickey Spillane. Singer's book—and Machlin's and Aronowitz and Hamill's—were biographies only in name; they were truly pulp adventure stories, and were published by houses specializing in such literature. Their authors could disregard Hemingway's literary career—or disfigure it beyond recognition—because the introspection through which he had transformed experience into fiction was foreign to the story they wished to tell. That story was of deeds not thought, of the thrilling adventures of a larger-than-life hero, and it was calculated to amuse and titillate as well as to point to an easily grasped "moral." Singer's hope for his book represented the attitude of all three biographers:

> May this book help to describe for the young and old generation the great individualist—one of the last men with guts and courage; a human being who was *all man* in a world where automation, luxuries, and wealth shine brightly in a gutter of hunger and confusion; a world which, without Ernest Hemingway, will never be the same.[23]

Similar hero worship pervaded Leo Lania's *Hemingway: A Pictorial Biography*, published in hardcovers by the Viking Press just a week or two before Hemingway's death. With its glossy cover and tweedy binding it was more impressive in appearance than any of the vulture biographies, but its contents were every bit as vulgar and tired. Its premise was that "no aesthetic research into or analysis of his creations can say so much about them or their creator as the story of his life," and so the life it chronicled was that of the public Hemingway. The text was a pastiche of the most obvious biographical facts ("During the Civil War he travelled to Spain four times. He was always to be found where the fighting was at its height") and superficial, frequently erroneous summaries of his books (*Green Hills of Africa* was about "a hunting expedition for lions and elephants"). The photographs which were the main reason for the book were familiar, illustrating him in most of his public guises, as sportsman, world traveler, soldier, and *bon vivant*. Only one of the 113 photographs showed him at work; but a writer at his type-writer was not a dramatic pictorial subject, and Lania was inter-ested only in Hemingway as a heroic adventurer whose life "firmly demonstrates his male ideals."[24]

If the vulture biographies resembled pulp adventure stories, Lania's pictorial history was more like a comic strip. Suggesting a law of devolving forms which seems to characterize the mass media, a syndicated comic strip eventually appeared. "The Giants: Ernest Hemingway" sketched the story of his life in fifteen panels of three frames each, a whirlwind tour through the Latin Quarter, the bullrings of Spain, the African bush, and the ravaged country-side of war-torn France.[25] Because of his fame as an adventurer, it was not surprising that the story of his life appealed to an audience whose fare had been the comic-strip exploits of Steve Canyon and similar heroes. His heroism, "The Giants" made clear, was com-pounded of the same stuff as these fictional heroes: a taste for action, fearlessness, and self-reliance.

These same heroic qualities made Hemingway a favorite of the slick men's magazines which were multiplying during the 1960s. Although these magazines, which had names like *Rogue, Dude*, and *Sir*, ordinarily showed little interest in art or artists—their stock in trade was pictures of girls, spicy stories, and advice on consump-tion—they were enamored of Hemingway. His history could gen-erate richly dramatic, "masculine" copy. Of equal importance was his fame as model of the good life. These magazines were com-mitted to instruction in proper style and taste.

Playboy's first celebration of the Hemingway legend preceded its three selections from his wisdom literature in the eight installments of Jed Kiley's memoir, "Hemingway: A Title Fight in Ten Rounds." The exaggerations and inaccuracies in Kiley's account of his friendship with Hemingway over three decades are numerous, and they all serve his hero worship of "The Champ." In Kiley's gaudy account, Hemingway drinks stronger whiskey, punches harder, fishes better, and makes more money than anyone else. Kiley professes ignorance of and indifference to his friend's literary achievement, arguing that however great the writer was, the man was even greater, unique and yet deserving imitation.[26] *Playboy* readers, whose fantasy life the magazine fed in a number of ways, could not miss the message: here was a man's man, skilled in sports, self-reliant and tough, full of gusto, admired by beautiful women, a hero for our time.

Playboy continued to dwell on Hemingway after his death. Four large installments of Leicester Hemingway's memoir appeared in the magazine, as did "My Papa, Papa," a reminiscence by the novelist's son Patrick. Arnold Gingrich, *Esquire*'s publisher, wrote about fishing with Hemingway in the 1930s, and Kenneth Tynan recounted a meeting between Hemingway and Tennessee Williams in Havana. *Playboy* even published a story about "Papa's Planet," a future world "dominated by one of the most fascinating men who ever lived," in which dozens of humanoid Hemingways of different ages live side-by-side in recreations of Pamplona, Paris, Key West, and so forth.[27]

Playboy's imitators were no less assiduous. Articles ranging from a reminiscence by the white hunter of Hemingway's last African safari to an account of the novelist's use of his head to break in half a shillelagh belonging to John O'Hara to a taxonomy of his drinking habits became almost a staple in these magazines in the half-dozen years after his death. Most of these pieces were by persons who knew him, or claimed to, such as Robert Bell Craneston, a volunteer ambulance driver in World War One, and Jay Robert Nash, a young writer who finagled an interview with the aging master. None of these pieces was modestly billed: they usually promised to "set the record straight on Papa," and they often ran under titles like "Ernest Hemingway—The Truth."[28]

There was more heat than light in such claims. None of these pieces—except perhaps those by Hemingway's brother and son—contained any significant new information, only the same old anecdotes, and they offered up the same adorations his public personality usually elicited from the mass media. The closing lines in *Dapper*'s story, "The Man Who Looked Like Hemingway," about the transformation of a man who suddenly realizes he resembles Hemingway, could characterize the tone in most of these men's magazines: "Something ended when he died, Stella. He . . . he was so much more than other men. Most of us are just clods, you know?"[29]

If the men's magazines continued to reflect the monochromatic view of the Heroic Hemingway which had been a staple of popular journalism for a generation, general interest magazines presented slightly more mixed reports. Reminiscences by visitors to the Finca Vigia illustrate this modest shift. Robert Emmett Ginna's memoir in *Esquire*, "Life in the Afternoon," presents a shy but warm and thoughtful Hemingway at variance with the rude, belligerent, and profane vulgarian in Howard Nelson's "Hemingway without Tears," published in *Fact*.[30] Both versions of Hemingway's personality were no doubt "true"—other informants corroborated them, and Hemingway surely presented different faces on different occasions—but the significant point is that neither version matches the public Hemingway, in that each makes him more human than legendary. He is not the heroic adventurer and freewheeling *bon vivant* of past magazine treatment.

John Dos Passos's bittersweet reminiscence of Key West during the 1930s, "Old Hem was a Sport," in *Sports Illustrated*, recalls the time before Hemingway began to take his legend too seriously. In those days he "was still a barrel of monkeys to be with," and Dos Passos fondly talks about fishing, drinking, and conversation with "Old Hem." "What made his company so delightful in his younger days was that outside of his literary gifts—being able to write doesn't mean that a man's fun to be with—he had real talents," Dos Passos reminisced, including sporting skill, patience, good humor, and "a warm-hearted understanding of many different kinds of people." When Hemingway became a "famous writer," according to Dos Passos, "life became less free and easy." On one of his last visits to Key West, Dos Passos found a bust of Hemingway in the front hall of his house. The irreverent Dos Passos tried to ring it with his panama hat when he entered the door. Hemingway took umbrage at this disrespect, and "after that things were never so good."[31] As with the Ginna and Nelson pieces, Dos Passos's memoir portrayed a man with human rather than superhuman features, his comradeliness and easy geniality finally giving way to self-regard and solemnity.

Arnold Gingrich's *Playboy* article examined some of these moments in Hemingway's and Dos Passos's lives, but without Dos Passos's nostalgia. His Hemingway is all warts: he is foul-tempered, a show-off, unbearably competitive, "and a very poor sport."[32] Perhaps he was responding to Dos Passos's characterization of him in *Sports Illustrated* as "in a trance" around Hemingway, unable to take "his fascinated eyes off Old Hem," but be this as it may, he did not flatter him, unlike the other articles in men's magazines. Gingrich was no more complimentary in his reminiscence of Fitzgerald and Hemingway for *Esquire*. Once again Hemingway is egotistical and competitive—"always the sore loser, blustering when he couldn't be first in anything and everything"— and he behaves shabbily toward Fitzgerald. A Levine caricature accompanying the memoir sums up Gingrich's analysis: Hemingway and Fitzgerald are tricked out as dancing vaudevillians, with bow ties, straw hats, and pens instead of canes. The point of Hemingway's pen is planted squarely in the middle of Fitzgerald's chest.[33]

Yet popular magazines still published articles which assumed Hemingway's unqualified heroism, just as before 1961. Kenneth Crawford eulogized him in *Newsweek* as a "good man in a fight," who would rather be remembered as such than as a great writer.[34] *True* published a largely spurious account of his D-Day landing on Omaha Beach, and S. L. A. Marshall reminisced in *American Heritage* about Hemingway's triumphant entry into Paris in 1944.[35] Robert Manning, who gathered much of the material for *Time*'s 1954 cover story after the Nobel Prize, and who visited Hemingway in Cuba, recalled his visit for the *Atlantic*. His reminiscence was in the manner of *Time*'s hagiographic cover story.[36] Both *This Week* and *Esquire* sent a correspondent and a photographer to the Finca Vigia to report on changes after Hemingway's death, and their articles and especially their pictures evoked the master of the good life who used to live there.[37] And Hemingway the sportsman was recalled again in *Sports Afield* and *Motor Boating*, which agreed that had he never been a writer, he "would have become famous as a big-game hunter and fisherman and applauded for the very real contributions he made to these sports." In these articles, as in so many others of past years, there were photographs of him fishing and hunting.[38]

These journalistic features indicate a slight shift toward a demythologization of Hemingway, if only because some of them employ categories of description and explanation he did not use in developing his public personality. What is most remarkable even in these later items is his lasting hold on the public imagination. In the 1960s, when celebrities quickly came and rapidly went, Heming-

way continued to be scrutinized, analyzed, and celebrated. That he
went unreplaced as the American public writer for more than half a
decade after his death, despite serious attempts at that title by
Truman Capote and Norman Mailer, testified to how profoundly
he had impressed his public personality upon his culture,
confirmed its appeal to enduring values, and demonstrated the cultural conservatism of the mass media and their followers.

III

Mary Hemingway, the novelist's widow, played a significant role
in keeping her husband's fame alive. In articles for half a dozen
magazines, she revisited old haunts where she had spent time with
him—Africa, Cuba, Spain, Venice. In *Look* two months after his
death she reminisced about their safari to Africa and about fishing
in the Gulf Stream; two years later in *Life*, she reported on a "sentimental safari" to the east African highlands she had hunted with
him in 1953, and in *Harper's Bazaar* a few months later she explained why she loved Africa. For *Saturday Review* and *Sports Illustrated* she recalled Cuba in the 1950s and described an idyllic fishing
trip with Hemingway to a small, uninhabited island off the Cuban
coast. "Hemingway's Spain" was her subject in the *Saturday Review*
in 1967, and the next year she described the atmosphere and cuisine
of Harry's Bar in Venice for *Holiday*.[39]

All these pieces were strongly nostalgic. Mrs. Hemingway did
not go into intimacies of life with Hemingway, although she made
clear the camaraderie and affection of their relationship. "We felt
not merely male and female," she wrote, "but friends and brothers.
Papa was my only brother and the best friend I ever had."[40] Even
though Mrs. Hemingway comes through in these articles as a
woman of strong convictions and cultivated tastes, as well as a
capable journalist in her own right, their central feature is the
presence of her husband. And, for the most part, it is the public
Hemingway—sportsman, world traveller, and *bon vivant*—whom
she evoked. In her reminiscences he was an expert hunter and
fisherman, a boon companion, a discriminating although casual
connoisseur of the good life, a man of extraordinary energy and
vitality. In short, her portrait reflected the version of his personal-

ity he promulgated and the mass media circulated during his lifetime. Theirs was a happy marriage, although, as her later auto-biography *How It Was*[41] suggests, not without tensions and difficulties. They were married in 1946, and so their life together matched the years in which Hemingway's fame was at its height and in which the roles of world traveler, sportsman, and *bon vivant* were especially prominent. The articles were homage to a great and dearly loved man, and they helped sustain his cultural stature by recommending his personality to his old audience.

Other family members also reminisced in print. His son Patrick, in addition to his *Playboy* memoir, told "The Truth about My Old Man" in *Climax*, an action magazine for men.[42] His were affection-ate memoirs, acts of filial piety to a man he says he was "hard pressed to find fault with . . . as a father." Their form was anec-dotal, with many of the stories drawn from the Key West years when Patrick spent the most time with his father. Hemingway as a tender and loving father had not been more than a possibility in the public personality, but many of Patrick's anecdotes concerned his father's fishing and hunting feats, boxing prowess, and drinking and eating preferences—familiar information about the public man. "What an overwhelming vitality he had!" Patrick exclaims, and his stories corroborate the familiar view of Hemingway as primarily a man of action and devotee of the good life who happened also to be a writer.

Nor was Hemingway's older sister, Marcelline, or his younger brother, Leicester, much concerned with Hemingway as a literary man. Leicester was sixteen years Ernest's junior, and his account of the novelist's early years is necessarily based on the recollections of other family members and occasional letters which their mother preserved. His first-hand experience with his brother came in the 1930s, when as an adolescent he visited the already famous novelist in Key West; after World War Two they apparently saw little of one another. His book is worshipful and awestruck; he is the kid brother sitting at the feet of the successful big brother. Marcelline was a year older than Ernest and less inclined to hero worship—she could also draw largely on her own recollections. Her account is not so directly focused on her famous brother; as her title indicates, *At the Hemingways* recounts family life before the children left home, with postscript chapters describing events leading up to her father's suicide in 1928 and her mother's death in 1951. In their chronological coverage these two books complement one another, although they leave the final fifteen years of Hemingway's life only cursorily treated, but they pursue such different tangents as to demand separate discussions.

Leicester's memoir aspires to biography in its scope, and some of the information from family records and from his brother's friends either corrected old misapprehensions (often given currency by Ernest) or enlarged understanding of certain events in his brother's life. He provides details, for example, of the vexed relationship between Ernest and his parents, which reached its first major crisis when Ernest "got formally drummed out of the house just after his twenty-first birthday" because his parents felt that writing was not proper work for a young man and that he was too willing to live off them. This rift was eventually patched but never closed, opening again when they were dismayed by what they thought was his salacious writing, and especially by his divorce from his first wife.[43] Leicester also corrects some old canards: Ernest injured his eye boxing at home, not at a Chicago gymnasium in a bout against a professional; he did not run away from home, as had been widely reported; and the revolver with which his father killed himself was sent to him at his own request and not gratuitously by his mother, as he later claimed.[44]

Most of Leicester's book recapitulates well-known anecdotes— such as the one about Hemingway's fistfight in Bimini with Joseph Knapp, the magazine publisher—or draws upon his brother's nonfiction to account for his activities during the Spanish civil war, or relates his impressions of Ernest's behavior during visits to Key West. The stories Leicester tells are of a piece with the public Hemingway. Leicester barely alludes to his brother's writing; more space is given to the movie of *For Whom the Bell Tolls* than to the novel.

Marcelline's memoir, on the other hand, scants her brother's public personality. It ends just as Hemingway was achieving his first success as a writer, and her purpose was to write a chronicle with equal attention to all the permutations of the family relationships. She succeeded, and her book is a valuable account of the earliest years of a writer on whom family influences had an important, although often covert, impact. In its large patterns, her view of family life at the Hemingways agrees with Leicester's. But he is inclined to take Ernest's view that their parents were stiff-necked prigs and Victorian in the worse sense, while she recalls an appropriately strict family regimen softened and humanized by the genuine love of her parents, as well as by their zest for family fun. In her view, life at the Hemingway homes in Oak Park and Walloon Lake was fulfilling for both children and parents. The Ernest of her memoir shows nothing in his early years that foreshadows his career. His boyhood is normal: he has his paper route; he mildly transgresses parental rules and is mildly reproved; he tramps the woods with chums; he manages the high school track team and plays on the football team; he participates in the young people's group at the Congregational church. He becomes exceptional with wounding in Italy and his return home as a nineteen-year-old veteran, about which Marcelline reflects that "for Ernest it must have been something like being put in a box with the cover nailed down to come home to conventional, suburban Oak Park living, after his vivid experiences," and this makes her wonder if he would ever again be happy living at home.[45]

Marcelline's memoir was a corrective to the Hemingway legend, and it is instructive to compare the publishing history of her work with Leicester's. Marcelline's book was first serialized in the *Atlantic*, then issued in hard covers. No paperback edition appeared. Leicester's book was serialized in *Playboy*, with a readership five or six times larger than the *Atlantic*'s, then published in hard covers, and finally reissued in a paperback to sell on newsstands and supermarket book racks. Until Carlos Baker's biography appeared in 1969, Leicester Hemingway's book was the standard biographical reference, and its story, available to millions more readers than Marcelline's, was, as the publisher's jacket copy promised, "as real, as exciting as the man himself," by which was meant that readers looking for vivid tales of derring-do and high life would find them here.

As had been the case after the negative reviews of *Across the River and into the Trees* and especially after the 1954 airplane crashes, an absurd journalistic feature again implied the compelling interest in Hemingway for an audience usually indifferent to writers. The *National Insider*, a tabloid featuring celebrity gossip and accounts of bizarre crimes, presented in its February 3, 1963, number an "Insider Exclusive" supposedly by Mrs. Grace Hemingway about her son. She is made to tell how after Ernest was found alive following the 1954 crashes, the newspapers wanted a photograph of him beside the wrecked plane, so he came back to Africa from Paris, "where he was discussing rights on a new picture," and marched through the same nearly impenetrable jungle parties had searched, so that the photograph might be taken.[46] This story was a fabrication, but the fabrication was not Mrs. Hemingway's. She had died in 1951. The *National Insider* shared the impulse of more respectable periodicals to cash in on the unabated public interest in Hemingway's life.

IV

Because celebrity depends upon a mass audience and is nourished more by repetition than by novelty, hardcover books are usually less important to it than more transient but widely distributed forms of writing (and electronic communication). Hardcover books serve popular journalists who draw upon them for information and opinion, but their immediate influence is less significant than that of magazines and newspapers. These observations hold, with one notable exception, for the books about Hemingway published after his death.

The exception was A. E. Hotchner's *Papa Hemingway*. Three large segments first appeared in the *Saturday Evening Post*, giving them a wider readership than a whole book could get; in a well-publicized suit Mrs. Hemingway tried to enjoin its publication; and it became an overwhelming commercial success. It was a Book-of-the-Month Club selection and remained on the New York *Times* best-seller list for twenty-five weeks, unprecedented for a work *about* a novelist.

Hotchner became acquainted with Hemingway in 1948, when as a staff member at *Cosmopolitan* he was assigned to try to persuade Hemingway to contribute an article on "The Future of Literature." Hemingway did not write the article, but he and Hotchner remained friends until Hemingway's death. During the fourteen years of their friendship Hotchner visited Hemingway in Cuba and Idaho at least a dozen times, and traveled with him in Italy, France, and Spain on several occasions. *Papa Hemingway* recounts these times.

Hotchner was in his twenties when he met Hemingway, who was nearing fifty, and he had an admitted case of "Hemingway Awe" which he never lost as the two men became more intimate. He was the last, and perhaps the most consummate, of those spiritual kid brothers Leicester said his brother always needed nearby. Hotchner never seemed to resent this role or find it uncomfortable; on the contrary, he writes again and again of his pleasure in the older man's company. As a kid brother, Hotchner heard hundreds of Hemingway's anecdotes and reminiscences, and these, along with narratives of their activities together, make up about four-fifths of his book. Hotchner's own presence is largely limited to asking leading questions and expressing sufficient awe at the stories he hears.

The pattern set in the first chapter holds for most of the book, although the locales change and the cast of characters increases. Hemingway meets Hotchner for the first time in La Floridita, his favorite Cuban bar, and begins their acquaintance by bragging about holding the house record for drinking in one night sixteen "Papa Dobles," a powerful daiquiri named after him of which the principal ingredient was two and a half jiggers of Bacardi White Label Rum. He then proceeds to expatiate on the pleasures of living in Cuba, the nearby fishing, cockfighting, pigeon shooting with members of the Brooklyn Dodgers, and the ease with which one can "get away from yourself" in Havana with its girls with "hot sunlight" in their eyes. The next day Hemingway takes Hotchner fishing on the *Pilar*, which provides him the occasion for talking about his submarine hunting mission during World War Two. None of this does anything to reduce Hotchner's awe. The anecdotes continue when Hotchner returns to Cuba a few months later: stories about visits to the Finca Vigia by Jean-Paul Sartre and the Duke and Duchess of Windsor; about Hemingway's lion-taming at a nearby circus; about his first meeting with Marlene Dietrich on board the *Ile de France;* about a "young Irish beauty," the wife of an English lord, who came discreetly and unasked to Hemingway's hotel room in Nairobi; and about his ability to talk to bears.[47] And so it goes through most of the book, anecdote following anecdote in random order.

Hemingway was almost always "on" when Hotchner was around, and Hotchner was sometimes extraordinarily credulous as well as worshipful. Thus, he passes along without comment some fabulous Hemingway tales, such as the one about his making love to the girlfriend of Legs Diamond in the kitchen and entrance landing of Club 21, receiving from her $300 for his services; or the one in which he bodily removed a welterweight prizefighter and his pet lion from Harry's New York Bar in Venice.[48] Only once does Hotchner express a reservation about any of Hemingway's stories. This one involved his supposed liaison during World War One with the famous spy Mata Hari, whose sexual capacities Hemingway carefully appraised. Hotchner belatedly realizes she was executed the year before Hemingway landed in Europe.[49] Hotchner's ascription of this deceit to Hemingway's "practical joke fantasy," rather than to anything more ominous or self-serving, only confirms his gullible reverence.

Anecdotes by and about Hemingway which had previously appeared in print show up in Hotchner's book as conversation, as Phillip Young pointed out in a review.[50] Hotchner has Hemingway and the movie star Ava Gardner chatting amiably in her Madrid hospital room; she expresses incredulity that he has never used a psychoanalyst. He replies to her that his typewriter is his analyst, that he kills animals so he will not kill himself, and that when a man is in rebellion against death as he is, "he takes pleasure out of taking to himself one of the godlike attributes, that of giving it." After this pontification, all Miss Gardner could say was, "That's too deep for me, Papa."[51] As Young points out, Hemingway's "response" to Miss Gardner's question is a pastiche of something he once said to Earl Wilson which Wilson repeated in his column, a variation on what Hemingway had written about himself in 1936, and a well-known *bon mot* from *Death in the Afternoon*. There is no question that Hotchner, Hemingway, and Ava Gardner were together in Madrid in 1954—Hotchner did a piece for *This Week* on the mutual admiration of movie star and novelist, illustrated with his own photographs—but his report of this conversation does not breed confidence in his capacity to "tell the reader the way it truly happened," which he claims to be the guiding principle of his memoir.

In Venice, after his 1954 airplane crashes, Hemingway told Hotchner that he wanted to inform him about things he hoped to write about and had been holding back, "so that if I never actually get around to it, then someone would know."[52] What these revelations might have been remains a mystery: the stories Hemingway tells about himself were already well known or, if not familiar in specifics, were consonant with the image of himself he consistently advertised. If Hemingway thought of Hotchner as a Boswell, as this conversation seems to imply, it was the Heroic Hemingway he was to immortalize, the man who could drink sixteen Papa Dobles in a single evening, the next day tame lions and talk to bears, and the day after that charm Marlene Dietrich. If that was what Hemingway had in mind, Hotchner's book would not have disappointed him. Most of it is different only in degree from the vulture biographies published a few years earlier. It is better written than they, and Hotchner had the advantage at least of some first-hand observation, but like these earlier books it is a jumble of anecdotes which does nothing more than elaborate the well-known public man. Hotchner's first impression of Hemingway—that he had "never seen anyone with such an aura of fun and well-being"[53]—is confirmed throughout in repetitions of stories about Hemingway the discriminating gourmet and connoisseur of drinks, world traveler *par excellence*, champion sportsman, heroic man of action, and so forth.

There is a signal difference between Hotchner's memoir and the vulture biographies, however, in its account of Hemingway's final years. The tone of *Papa Hemingway* changes markedly in the last one-fifth of the book, as the spirited man of action is replaced by the beaten man descending into madness and suicide. The stories of good times and past heroics come to an end, yielding to others about paranoiac delusions and physical debilities. This change is not entirely unprepared for: in earlier parts of the book Hotchner now and again portrays Hemingway as driven by physical infirmities to irrational behavior, but his powers of recuperation are strong and the flow of anecdotes resumes. But after what he called "the best summer of my life," in Spain following the *mano-a-mano* of 1959, Hemingway's recuperative powers fail, and his last two years are a hell of fears about being pursued by the FBI, imagined betrayals by friends, an inability to write, physical decline, hospitalization and electrical shock treatments which cause loss of memory, and ultimately several suicide attempts.

It was this portion of *Papa Hemingway* that made the book sensational, and that apparently caused Mary Hemingway's attempt to block publication, although she chose to press her suit on broader grounds. She charged that the conversations between Hotchner and her husband were her literary property, just as letters were, and were thus protected by common-law copyright and could not be reproduced by Hotchner; that his book would compete unfairly with other books by and about Hemingway; that Hotchner had breached her husband's trust and confidence, and was trying to make public matters which he would have regarded as confidential; and that his book violated her own right of privacy. Justice Harry B. Frank of the New York Supreme Court decided against her, rejecting all four of her charges, and his decision was upheld unanimously on appeal.[54]

Because her suit was widely reported in the press, Mrs. Hemingway's attempt to suppress Hotchner's book stimulated public interest in it. But it would have had a large audience without her suit because it conflated an extended account of the public Hemingway with sensationally intimate details about his decline. There are grounds for reservation about fact and interpretation in Hotchner, yet his account of Hemingway's final illness seems authentic. (It is confirmed for the most part in Carlos Baker's scrupulously researched biography, published three years later.) Readers of Hotchner got two different Hemingways. One, the public man they already knew, radiated self-confidence and lived his life all the way up; the other, unknown before (except obliquely in Hemingway's fiction), was frail in mind and body, and caught in an unrelenting descent into despairing morbidity. Because of his idolatry of the public Hemingway, Hotchner is not able to relate these two figures satisfactorily; to him they are equally substantial and separate integrities. Lacking some such integration, Hotchner's portrait is more pathetic than tragic. Perforce, though, there is poignance in Hotchner's treatment of Hemingway's decline. After enthusiastically celebrating Hemingway's *joie de vivre* for over two hundred pages, the only convincing reason Hotchner can put forward for Hemingway's growing despair is that he is no longer capable of writing, whether well or badly. Near the end of the book, after hundreds of anecdotes and scores of high times, Hotchner remembers that what mattered most for Hemingway was that he was a writer.

Hemingway's fame as a man whose life was bountiful and satisfying could hardly withstand Hotchner's revelations in the final pages of *Papa Hemingway*. Three years after Hotchner, Carlos Baker's authorized biography confirmed him and otherwise weakened the Heroic Hemingway. *Ernest Hemingway: A Life Story* was no foray into debunking, but it was ineluctably revisionist. Baker's intended audience was more scholarly than popular, although his book found thousands of readers among the general public. It was not a critical biography, but Baker shows throughout that he thinks Hemingway important primarily because he was a writer. While Baker tells many tales about Hemingway the man of action, these are always subordinated to his literary career. Baker tried to gather details of a sort lost forever with the passing of contemporaries, and he concludes with four pages of closely printed acknowledgments to persons who supplied him with reminiscences and correspondence. This information sometimes puts Hemingway in a bad light, and the man of this book has his full share of deceits, foibles, and vanities, his acts and enterprises no longer easily interpreted as manifestations of a heroic will. Rather, he is a man riven by contradictions: by turns diffident and full of braggadocio; generous and mean; courageous and timid; a sentimentalist and a bully; a loyal friend capable of extreme cruelties to those who loved him; a dedicated artist and a potboiler.

Whether Baker's biography *qua* biography is ultimately satisfying or not is beside the point here. He himself makes only modest claims for it, and foresees future studies by other hands which will employ the materials he has gathered in the service of more speculative and interpretive analyses of Hemingway's life and work. What is more relevant is that his biography rendered obsolete all prior biographical studies. The public personality Hemingway imposed upon his culture, which continued to have currency in the half-dozen years after his death, could not maintain credibility after Baker's authoritative portrait of a more complex—and ultimately more interesting—human being.

By 1969 Hemingway was no longer so important to his culture as he had been. That he remained an important object of public attention for over half a decade after his death represents the momentum of his fame among people who had followed his life for years. A generation that did not remember him, that could only learn about him, had its own celebrities, and his name and face appeared less and less in magazines and newspapers. His literary reputation seemed stable—although at what level was conjectural—but with the 1970s Hemingway the public writer was becoming matter for history.

V

Hemingway was not without influence in shaping his posthumous reputation. In *A Moveable Feast*, published in 1964, he imposed a version of his personality on the 1960s just as indelibly as he had when he was bagging big game in Africa or battling the fascist menace or dispensing ageless wisdom as Papa. In *A Moveable Feast* he put forward the version of himself which would somewhat neutralize revaluations which argued that he had not taken his art seriously and had misused his talents by putting so much energy into his performance as a public figure.

Gertrude Stein had said in *The Autobiography of Alice B. Toklas* that "the confessions of the real Ernest Hemingway" would be "very wonderful" and would make quite a book, but she was sure he would never write it because of his protectiveness about his reputation.[55] Had she lived to read *A Moveable Feast*, it would not have changed her view, but Hemingway's memoir of Paris in the 1920s was nonetheless a confession of sorts. Hemingway had written about his life in Paris before—notably in *Green Hills of Africa*— and as late as 1958 he professed to be disgusted by "backyard literary gossip while washing out the dirty clothes of thirty-five years ago," adding however that there would be some value to it "if one had tried to tell the whole truth."[56] He did not reveal with that statement that he was even then working on what would become *A Moveable Feast*, a book which we can assume he felt told the truth, if not all the truths. His preface implies that another volume might be forthcoming, because "for reasons sufficient to the writer" he had been forced to leave out many things, and he suggests that if readers prefer they can regard the book as fiction. *A Moveable Feast* employed fictional strategies, as autobiography commonly does, but Hemingway felt that it contained "the true gen [intelligence] on what everybody has written about and no-one knows but me."[57]

A Moveable Feast was in the style without "scrollwork or orna-

ment" which Hemingway made famous as a young man, and his
dialogue was his best since 1940. The book was made up of twenty
sketches, which constituted Hemingway's portrait of himself as a
young artist in much the same way the Nick Adams stories when
grouped together caused each to resonate more fully. In choosing
this arrangement, he was not only returning to the form of some of
his best work, but also nostalgically measuring the distance he had
traveled and marking the success he had achieved. In *Green Hills of
Africa* he looked back to his Paris years and remembered living on
leeks and water because his stories were rejected by editors who
always called them sketches, *contes*, and anecdotes; no such danger
of incomprehension threatened these sketches because the taut,
understated Hemingway manner had been fully assimilated by the
consciousness of readers everywhere.

The sequence is roughly chronological, beginning with the
young writer composing "The Three Day Blow" and concluding
with his final revision of *The Sun Also Rises*, although there are
excursuses. This chronology relates a success story in which a
young man, by dint of discipline, hard work, determination, and
the force of talent, makes his way in the world. But other patterns
also inform the arrangement of the sketches. There is a movement
through several seasons, beginning with the cold rains of late fall
and concluding with the crisp winter of the Austrian Voralberg; a
related pattern involves images of warmth and cold; yet another
employs imagery of hunger and satiety. But the most important
structural arrangement breaks the book into two parts. One, com-
prising the first eight sketches, stresses Hemingway's artistic discipline, together with celebrations of his idyllic relationship with
Hadley; the other, the next eleven sketches, concerns the Left Bank
artistic community. In the final sketch, these two parts are brought
together, although the primary locale is Austria and John Dos Passos is the only other artist present.

Two sketches in the first section concern Gertrude Stein; three
sketches in the second section are on F. Scott Fitzgerald and lead to
further treatment of Hadley. These exceptions to the overall struc-
ture neatly balance one another. Stein and Fitzgerald contrast with
Hemingway. Stein lacks Hemingway's artistic discipline, and her
advocacy of homosexuality clashes with Hemingway's heterosex-
uality, frequently mentioned early in the book. Hemingway im-

plies that his sexual normality, of which his intimacy with his wife is the manifest, enforces his integrity and his artistic power, an integrity and power unavailable to Stein because of her sexual orientation. Fitzgerald likewise lacks discipline, and again in some measure because of sexual dislocation. Fitzgerald's dislocation is caused by his wife Zelda's destructiveness, sexual and otherwise, and their blighted relationship Hemingway contrasts with his own happy marriage. Thus, these two groups of sketches parallel one another and subtly link Stein and Fitzgerald as similarly undisciplined artists whose warped personal lives diminished their writing. It is significant that Stein and Fitzgerald, after the author, are the most prominent individuals in the book. Their stock as literary figures was rising in the 1950s (especially Fitzgerald's), and Hemingway, as always competitive, seems to have felt they needed deflation. They were perhaps the two persons in the 1920s Hemingway had depended upon most for advice and help (although he denied this in the sketches), and so exposing their weaknesses exorcised his sense of obligation. In Stein's case he was also settling the old grievance of her autobiography.

When Mary Hemingway read a few of the early sketches, she complained that they did not seem like autobiography because they were not so much about Hemingway as about others. "It's biography by *remate*," he replied, using the jai-alai term denoting a two-wall shot, by which he meant that his own character was illuminated "by reflection."[58] The *remates* occur mostly in the second part of the book; the first part centers on the young artist, providing the basis for later comparisons. Even the two sketches of Gertrude Stein begin and end with Hemingway alone, walking in the Luxembourg gardens and drinking a cold beer at the Closerie des Lilas, his favorite cafe, and then going home to his wife, their nominal subject giving way, as in the Nick Adams stories, to an invocation of the protagonist's sensibility.

In *A Moveable Feast* Hemingway made himself less a man of action than he had been in his earlier nonfiction, and more a reflective hero. He assumes many of his familiar roles—the discriminating connoisseur of food and drink, the habitué whose intimate knowledge guaranteed he would never be mistaken for a tourist, the hard-boiled and experienced man who saw through pretense, the expert sportsman—but these are subordinate to himself as heroic artist. In the first section of the book he represents his efforts to forge a new aesthetics with his fiction, and he fondly recreates the difficulties of that enterprise. These difficulties included poverty and a lack of recognition, especially poverty, but they did not include any self-doubt about the importance or ultimate success of the stories he was writing: "Well, I thought, now I have them so they do not understand them. There cannot be much doubt about that. There is most certainly no demand for them. But they will understand the same way that they always do in painting. It only takes time and it only needs confidence" (*AMF*, 75).

If he had plenty of confidence the same was not true of money, and the poverty he endures for the sake of his art is a dominant theme of these sketches. In cold weather when the wind is wrong he cannot use his workroom in the hotel where Verlaine died because the fireplace will not draw properly and fills the room with smoke; his flat in the rue Cardinal Lemoine has no hot water or inside plumbing, and the odor of the nearby cesspools is strong in the summer; his weatherproof is "old" and his felt hat "worn and weathered"; he has no money to buy books, although Sylvia Beach extends lending privileges to him at her bookstore; he always travels third class on the train; and so on. But rather than being oppressive, this poverty is exhilarating. He and his wife exult in it: "We thought we were superior people and other people that we looked down on and rightly mistrusted were rich. . . . We ate well and cheaply and drank well and cheaply and slept well and warm together and loved each other" (*AMF*, 51). Hemingway emphasizes his happiness and his satisfaction with the simple pleasures Paris afforded, but he makes clear that his "good luck" with his writing and his confidence in it are the enabling conditions which allow him to enjoy other parts of his life so fully.

His poverty, moreover, is the warrant of his artistic integrity. The final sketch in the first section of *A Moveable Feast* is "Hunger Was Good Discipline," which could be the subtitle of the entire opening group of sketches. In it, after describing his feeling of being "belly-empty, hollow-hungry" and his carefully planned efforts to avoid walking by restaurants and bakeries, and then his pleasure in a meal of sausage, potato salad, and beer at Lipp's bought with an unexpected check from *Der Querschnitt*, he concludes with an account of his beginning to write "Big Two-Hearted

River." The paring down of his life to essentials, the personal discipline imposed by his dedication to his work, make possible the true art he knows he is creating. His willingness to endure hunger was the price he gladly paid for his art, even if it was not yet understood, because "no other thing mattered" (*AMF*, 69–77).

The second section of *A Moveable Feast* elaborates his portrait of himself as a heroic artist by *remate*, by contrasting his discipline with the laxity of others in the Parisian artistic community. None possesses his integrity, high standards, and clearsightedness, and many have more severe liabilities. Wyndham Lewis had the eyes "of an unsuccessful rapist" and was both derivative and incompetent as an artist; Ernest Walsh was a poseur and incurably dishonest; Harold Acton was a whining homosexual whose writer's block was a blessing because it meant he could no longer inflict his wretched prose on the world; Ralph Cheever Dunning was an indifferent poet whose opium addiction did not improve his work. More significant figures do not fare much better. Ford Madox Ford was personally offensive, but more important was an inveterate liar and a fool. John Dos Passos had "the irreplaceable early training of the bastard and a latent and long denied love of mony" (*AMF*, 208), and betrayed those who trusted him. Gertrude Stein, whom Hemingway finishes off with a final sketch in the second section, besides being a lesbian, is afflicted with a megalomaniacal ambition far in excess of her talents and her capacity for artistic discipline. Scott Fitzgerald, although a good writer, was a bad drunk, too willing to compromise his art, and fated by a destructive marriage to squander his talents. Even Ezra Pound, whom Hemingway calls "a sort of saint" for his kindliness and helpfulness to other writers, lacked clear judgment about his own work and the work of his friends (*AMF*, 107–108).

What is most striking about *A Moveable Feast* is just how "literary" a book it is, unlike anything else Hemingway had written. He was never in practice so unwilling to speak of literary subjects as he sometimes liked to claim, but he usually managed to put such discussions in a context which made his comments seem grudging, and he almost always intimated that he would rather talk about fishing or hunting. There was none of this bluff quality in *A Moveable Feast*. Paris may have been the city where one could live and love better than anywhere else, but more than that it was a place

where one could write well, at least if one were Ernest Hemingway. Each section contributed to emphasizing his distinctive artistic heroism. The first section portrayed him at work in splendid
isolation, writing the stories which would make him famous; the
second, by enlarging the scope, developed the thesis that no contemporary even approached his talent, dedication, and discipline.

It is not entirely accurate, however, to say that we see Hemingway in isolation in the first section, because he makes his relationship with his wife a recurrent feature in it, and it is in his
remembering this relationship that the confessional aspect of the
book comes in. *A Moveable Feast* is an expression of remorse for the
breakdown of his first marriage, and if others bore blame for his
divorce he also takes responsibility. For all that she is the heroine of
this memoir, however, Hadley Hemingway is never much more
than a one-dimensional figure. Her major virtues seem to have been
that she adored her husband, encouraged him in his work, and
enjoyed most of the same things he did. Hemingway's *mea culpa*
about her is genuine, but his remorse for the dissolution of his
marriage is also a synecdochical expression of regret for the loss of
the young man he had been, a young man innocent of fame who
was writing better than he ever would again.

The actual breakdown of the marriage occurs late in the book,
although no reader could be surprised, because of the frequent
foreshadowings of loss Hemingway inserts in several sketches in
the first section. These prophecies of doom look forward to the time
"when the first part of Paris was broken up" (*AMF*, 64). When that
time arrives, it is after the success of *The Sun Also Rises*, and is the
consequence of that success. Attracted by Hemingway's new-
found fame, "the rich came led by the pilot fish," John Dos Passos,
as they would never have done in earlier years because "they never
wasted their time nor their charm on something that was not sure"
(*AMF*, 208). Although Hemingway accuses himself of complicity
by being "as stupid as a bird dog" who "wagged my tail with
pleasure," these unnamed rich in some insidious way destroyed his
marriage and ended the most fruitful period of his life.

A Moveable Feast is thus in part about the failure of success, and
this theme links it with nonfiction Hemingway wrote in the five
years preceding his death. In "A Situation Report" and "The
Dangerous Summer" he had suggested that he was a captive of his

fame and that the demands of it were destroying his ability to lead his personal life as he chose and his capacity to continue serious writing. In *A Moveable Feast* the rich are the destroyers, but they are so generalized in his treatment that it is difficult to see them as the villains they are meant to be. It is not so difficult, though, to see the success of *The Sun Also Rises* and the fame it brought its author, which caused the rich to gravitate to him, as the force which altered his life, and not for the better.

But the dominant motif of *a Moveable Feast* is not failure but triumph, the triumph of a writer who learns to write "the truest sentence that you know" (*AMF*, 12), and by so doing creates a new literary idiom. The epiphanies of the book all center on the act of creation, on the solitary writer who "belong[s] to this notebook and pencil" discovering what miracles he can perform with language, a discovery so profound that "after writing a story I was always empty and both sad and happy, as though I had made love . . ." (*AMF*, 6). The details of this triumph are all Hemingway's own, but the story he tells is the old one of the unknown artist already in the fullness of his talent, who by unstinting allegiance to his art and willingness to suffer deprivation makes it new and alters the consciousness of his time.

In *A Moveable Feast* Hemingway returned to his first fame, that of the artist unaffected by fashion, impervious to temptation, dedicated to his work. This was the fame he had enjoyed in the 1920s, and he meant to have it again. This final representation may signify that he regretted his development of the later public personality, but he was writing for roughly the same audience which had accepted that personality. In 1929 he could not have generated much interest outside the intellectual elite in his role as heroic artist, but thirty years later, after making himself a major American celebrity, he knew that the public personality would ironically sanction the heroic artist.

He was probably right. *A Moveable Feast* was a Book-of-the-Month Club selection, and remained on the New York *Times* bestseller list for twenty-nine weeks, nineteen of them in the top position; later it appeared as a mass-market paperback. Hundreds of thousands of readers bought the book. Earlier, millions more read generous excerpts in *Life*, embellished with a dozen stunning color photographs of Paris by Gordon Parks as well as with seventeen contemporary black-and-white snapshots of Hemingway, Hadley, the Fitzgeralds, and other figures, the whole feature running to twenty-eight oversized pages, about one-fourth the entire issue.[59] But with *A Moveable Feast* Hemingway was also looking beyond to a later audience that would judge him by his art rather than by his standing as a celebrity. Readers learning about the young artist who wrote the Nick Adams stories and *The Sun Also Rises* would be reminded that he had instilled these works with his original virtue, whatever may have happened to the older man. "No other thing mattered," he had written of his work, and if this dictum wrongly denied the interest of cultural history in recovering and understanding the past, it was still more than a half-truth. The great work was there—would *always* be there—and the pride he felt in it was not misplaced.

"He Had Sold Vitality . . . All His Life"

At the end, then, Hemingway came to know, if he did not always know, that history would judge his importance by his books and not by the number of times he had appeared on the cover of *Life*. Although for most of his career he insisted that his life and his art were of a piece, the eagerness with which in "The Dangerous Summer" he distinguished between the "man" and the "writer," the former forced to behave in ways the latter found repugnant, betrayed his uneasiness that somewhere along the way he had become divided. From this it was only a short step in *A Moveable Feast* to the bittersweet evocation of a golden moment when the man and the writer were congruent.

From the standpoint of literary criticism, the major question regarding Hemingway's celebrity is what consequences it had for his fiction. The interests of cultural history are different, but for it too this question is relevant. There seems to have been an inverse relationship between the growth of Hemingway's celebrity and the quality and even quantity of his fiction. His best work came early, during the 1920s and early 1930s, with *The Sun Also Rises*, *A Farewell to Arms*, and some of the stories in *In Our Time*, *Men Without Women*, and *Winner Take Nothing*, all of them written before he achieved his full standing as public writer. In the middle and late 1930s, when he first won a large public reputation, the quality of his imaginative writing was mixed. *To Have and Have Not* and *The Fifth Column* were interesting failures, not up to the standard of the earlier work, but "The Short Happy Life of Francis Macomber" and especially "The Snows of Kilimanjaro" rank among his finest stories. And *For Whom the Bell Tolls*, published in 1940, was certainly his most ambitious work and a powerful and rich novel. After 1940, when he had become the renowned public writer, he published little fiction—only one more novel, one novella, and not a single story of consequence. Most commentators agree that these later works represented a decline from his earlier fiction.

But to find a single-factor explanation for this decline in his pursuit of celebrity would be too easy and would ignore other functional circumstances. From the mid-1930s Hemingway's way of life was seldom congenial with creative work. Two wars usurped nearly a decade of his middle years. After the wars he was often on the move, and even when he was at home guests and hangers-on frequently drove him to sea to find solitude. He had been accident-prone since youth; and lacerations, concussions, infections, broken bones, bouts with hypertension, and other medical disorders were many and frequent. After the African airplane crashes in 1954, ill health plagued him more than ever, and he never fully recovered from his injuries. In view of this medical history, one wonders how he could complete any sustained work. Hemingway's most notable achievements as a writer may also help account for his creative decline. He was not much interested in exploring ideas in his fiction, nor did he fabricate dense social settings. His distinctive achievements were a style and a set of heroes who embodied the moral imperatives implicit in that style, and they limited his development because they fixed him in a narrow range of exemplary characters and situations. Thus Hemingway's fiction might have deteriorated even had he not become a public figure.

But there was a noticeable effect of Hemingway's celebrity on his fictional heroes, and these characterizations suggest additional reasons why his later works declined. A common misapprehension about Hemingway's heroes is that they were all tough guys, dishing it out and taking it with equal stoicism. This notion had currency by the 1940s, and to some extent it was a reading of the heroic Hemingway into his fictional characters. Yet Jake Barnes, Frederic Henry, and Nick Adams had not been tough guys, and their stoicism was tenuous at best. The moral and psychic triumphs Hemingway gave them lay in their gradual recognition of their ultimate vulnerability, a recognition earned through costly and painful disillusion. The alien forces of biological betrayal, societal disorder, and cosmic indifference plagued the later Hemingway heroes, but he does not have them learn much because he posits them from the start as knowing pretty much all they need to know. There are no wise Counts in the later novels because the heroes do not need them. The knowingness and self-confidence of figures like Harry Morgan, Robert Jordan, and Colonel Cantwell make them seem heroic in an exalted sense. They are omnicompetents, and in this respect they resemble the public Hemingway.

The public Hemingway knew just what to do and how to do it and what to feel about it; and rather than need counsel, he could teach others. Beginning with *For Whom the Bell Tolls* Hemingway's heroes always have an adoring secondary character close by who serves as the "spiritual kid brother" Leicester Hemingway said Ernest always needed. Maria sedulously attends to Robert Jordan's ruminations about life and death; the eighteen-year-old Countess Renata's ingenuousness is never more apparent than when she questions Colonel Cantwell about his views; and the boy Manolo occasions some of Santiago's grandfatherly meditations. These later heroes are heroes of action as well as of perception. They can singlehandedly foil the murderous schemes of hotheaded revolutionaries; expertly and against long odds mine and blow up a bridge; make love three times in a single evening while riding in a delicately balanced gondola; and fight and land from a skiff the largest marlin anyone ever saw.

If they are all-capable, they are not all-powerful. Harry Morgan, Robert Jordan, and Colonel Cantwell die, and Santiago's approaching death is indicated by the cruciform position of his sleep after his battle with the sharks. But death confirms their heroic stature. They have largely achieved what they set out to do, they have so lived that the pattern of their actions has the symmetry of art. Their deaths are the warrant of their purity and untarnished heroism. Too noble for a corrupt world, they must die. Nick Adams, Jake Barnes, and Frederic Henry survive the conclusions of their stories; we imagine them living on, using dearly bought knowledge to devise strategies for controlling what kept them awake in the night. The measure of their stature is their painful recognition of how life might be organized so as to offer at least some moments of repose. By providing his later heroes with transcendent deaths, Hemingway made them figures larger than life and as such further like the Hemingway of the public personality.

Hemingway addressed himself in his fiction to the consequences of fame only once, and then obliquely. That one occasion was in "The Snows of Kilimanjaro," first published in 1936, one of his best stories. He liked to boast that it could have generated several novels; he regarded it as a kind of potlatch of his creative vitality. It touches upon many thematic topics—World War One, Parisian artistic life in the 1920s, the dynamics of love and marriage, the glories of the African landscape, the pleasures of hunting, the relationship of a writer's private life to his creative drive, and more—and it does so in a dynamic and sophisticated form. Because of its thematic and formal richness it has attracted more commentary than any other Hemingway story, much of this criticism perceptive as to its multiple meanings. Yet one important feature of the story has been often overlooked. "The Snows of Kilimanjaro" is not exclusively a meditation on the hazards of fame for the writer, perhaps not even centrally that, but that it examines this—for Hemingway in 1936—crucial question is clear enough.

The story is not pure autobiography, but the congruences between Harry's life and Hemingway's are striking enough to convince the most skeptical reader that "The Snows of Kilimanjaro" has significant autobiographical overtones. As a boy Harry had summered at a cottage along a northern lake; fought as a young man on the Italian front; worked as a newspaper correspondent during the Greco-Turkish conflict; lived in joyous poverty in Paris where to have a place to write he rented a room in the hotel where Verlaine died; wintered in Austria because the skiing was good; spent much time in the mountains of the American West; and married twice, the second time to a woman of considerable wealth. While the story does not ascribe to Harry the early achievement or artistic preeminence of Hemingway, it does say that Harry's talent was once so substantial that he felt a "duty" to use it to explain how he had seen the world change.

Hemingway was not much given to the reflexivities of stories about artists, however much he had to say elsewhere about writing and writers. "The Snows of Kilimanjaro" is his only fiction (until *A Moveable Feast*, if regarded as fiction, as Hemingway invites readers to do) in which questions of literary vocation are the central interest. This suggests that when he was writing it in the mid-1930s, the question of what kind of artist he had been, and more important, was going to be, was very much on his mind.

When the story first appeared in *Esquire* in 1936, it was taken for a slap at Scott Fitzgerald, the breakdown of whose career Fitzgerald himself had recently described in "The Crack-Up" articles for *Esquire*. Hemingway had been shocked by Fitzgerald's revelations, and claimed to want to give his old friend a salutary fillip which might help him pull himself together. In the *Esquire* text Fitzgerald was even named—"poor Scott Fitzgerald"; when the story was later collected this was changed to "poor Julian" at Fitzgerald's insistence. This change did not make much difference, however. The writer who failed because he thought the rich were different and who believed that he was merely a spy among them, immune to their blandishments, was still clearly identifiable. It is misleading to regard these allusions to Fitzgerald as merely diversionary, but they are something of a red herring.

Most of Harry's history and character derive rather from Hemingway than from Fitzgerald, and the representation of Harry betrays Hemingway's uneasiness about his success and his fears about what it has cost. Harry has traded his creative passion, his duty as an artist to tell the truth, for the comfort and security his wife's money provide. Something important had been lost in the passage from the cheap hotel where Verlaine died to the Crillon, from the Place Contrescarpe to the luxurious places featured in *Town and Country*. Nominal blame for this loss is placed upon Helen, Harry's wife, yet Harry realizes that if it had not been she it would have been someone else, and Hemingway further exonerates her by making her one of his most complex and interesting female characters. Like the Hemingway heroes, she had been deeply lacerated by traumatic experience, first the death of her husband, and then her child's; and she had taken to drink to anaesthetize her pain and to put herself to sleep. If Helen is the instrument of Harry's decline, she is not the cause of it. More generally, blame is assigned to the corrupting influence of wealth, to "the rich," to whom Harry admits he would have succumbed in any case. Perhaps this alludes to the wealth the second Mrs. Hemingway, Pauline Pfeiffer, brought to the marriage, but if so equally plausible is the suggestion that, as in *A Moveable Feast*, to indict the rich is to deal in metonymy.

"The rich" are associated with fame and success, just as they are in the later memoir of the 1920s. Yet Hemingway does not emphasize so much the distortion of sensibility and values which wealth causes—that was Fitzgerald's great theme—as its deflection of Harry from his true calling to the pursuit of inconsequential ends. Harry's problem is not that he has become morally obtuse like Fitzgerald's Anson Hunter or Tom Buchanan, rather that he has frittered away the best years of his life in irrelevancies. Hemingway does not identify these irrelevancies; we know only that they were wasteful. This vagueness is important if one is examining the story in autobiographical terms. What Hemingway tells us about Harry's life between his period of artistic heroism and the present of the story is that he has "traded" on his talent and "sold vitality" without maintaining an emotional connection with its product. One can fill in the blank of Harry's irrelevancies with Hemingway's development of the public personality and come to similar conclusions.

When he wrote "The Snows of Kilimanjaro," Hemingway had not published a novel in seven years, and what he had thus far done on *To Have and Have Not* was not progressing well and was inferior to his earlier work. On the other hand, he had just written the last of his *Esquire* letters—the third segment in his public personality trilogy consisting of these letters, *Death in the Afternoon*, and *Green Hills of Africa*, all of them appearing between 1932 and 1936. He had reached a crossroads, and "The Snows of Kilimanjaro" reviewed the course which had led him there and, more important, indicated a new direction. It signified Hemingway's determination to avoid Harry's fate, to resist the seductions of the comfort and security his sale of vitality to the unworthy had gotten him, and to devote himself to scaling the peaks of Art, where one might with luck and dedication create something so mysterious and imperishable as the frozen leopard found near the summit of Mount Kilimanjaro.

But Hemingway did not take this new direction after 1936. Habit was strong, the rewards in influence and self-confidence and celebrity were tempting, and the Spanish civil war allowed him to continue exploiting himself, now with the excuse that this cause was more honorable than his past self-advancement. Yet selling vitality to Carnegie Hall and to the readers of *Life* and *Look* and *True* and all the rest reduced the energies Hemingway could devote to his art, and indeed suborned that art. After "The Snows of Kilimanjaro" he never faced in his fiction what he had faced there: the consequences for a writer of pursuing ends other than his art. Had he done so—and no one was in a better position to do so—he might have produced, as his quondam disciple Norman Mailer since has, works that analyzed a culture in which the mass media and the concept of celebrity it feeds upon create extraordinary possibilities and risks for the public writer.

NOTES

CHAPTER 1

1. "Photoquiz," *Look*, 18 (Feb. 23, 1954), 118–119.
2. Quoted in Justin Kaplan, *Mr. Clemens and Mark Twain* (New York: Simon and Schuster, 1966), 381.
3. Daniel Boorstin, *The Image* (New York: Atheneum, 1962), 45–49.
4. William Dean Howells, *Years of My Youth* (New York: Harper, 1916), 204–205.
5. Edward Bok, *The Americanization of Edward Bok* (New York: Scribners, 1920), 40.
6. Quoted in Henry Nash Smith, *Mark Twain: The Development of a Writer* (New York: Atheneum, 1961), 105.
7. Malcolm Cowley and Henry Seidel Canby, "Creating an Audience," in Robert E. Spiller et al., eds., *The Literary History of the United States*, 3rd ed., rev. (New York: Macmillan, 1963), 1130.
8. Leo Lowenthal, *Literature, Popular Culture, and Society* (Englewood Cliffs, N.J.: Prentice Hall, 1961), 137–140.
9. Wallace Stevens ["Art as Establisher of Value"] in Richard Ellmann and Charles Feidelson, Jr., eds., *The Modern Tradition* (New York: Oxford University Press, 1965), 219–220.
10. Gustave Flaubert ["An Aesthetic Mysticism"] in ibid., 194.
11. Carlos Baker, *Ernest Hemingway: A Life Story* (New York: Scribners, 1969), 126.
12. Ibid., 143.
13. EH [Letter to Sidney James], reprinted in *Life*, 51 (July 14, 1961), 71.
14. His first two novels, *The Sun Also Rises* (1926) and *A Farewell to Arms* (1929), had a combined sale of over three million copies between their publication dates and 1965. *For Whom the Bell Tolls* (1940) ranked high on best-seller lists for two consecutive years, and the critical strictures which greeted *Across the River and into the Trees* (1950) did not prevent it from becoming the third most popular book of that year. Even with *Life*'s publication of *The Old Man and the Sea* (1952), estimated by the magazine to have had a circulation of nearly five and a half million copies, the bound book itself still sold well enough to place it seventh among the year's best-selling novels.
15. Morley Callaghan, *That Summer in Paris* (New York: Dell, 1964), 22.
16. Randall Jarrell, "A Sad Heart at the Supermarket," in Norman Jacobs, ed., *Culture for the Millions?* (Boston: Beacon, 1964), 106.
17. Baker, 525–526.

CHAPTER 2

1. All quoted from reviews annotated in Audre Hanneman, *Ernest Hemingway: A Comprehensive Bibliography* (Princeton: Princeton University Press, 1967), 347–365.

2. Morley Callaghan, *That Summer in Paris* (New York: Dell, 1964), 22.

3. "Has 227 Wounds, But Is Looking for Job," New York *Sun* (Jan. 22, 1919), 3.

4. "Worst Shot-up Man in U.S. on Way Home," Chicago *American* (Jan. 21, 1919), 3.

5. Quoted in Edmund Wilson, *The Shores of Light* (New York: Random House, 1961), 123.

6. EH, "And to the United States," *transatlantic review*, 1 (May–June, 1924), 357.

7. EH [Conrad memorial], *transatlantic review*, 2 (Sept., 1924), 341–342.

8. Edmund Wilson, "Mr. Hemingway's Dry Points," *Dial*, 77 (Oct., 1924), 340, reprinted in *The Shores of Light*, 121.

9. Ford Madox Ford, "From a Paris Quay (II)," New York *Evening Post Library Review* (Jan. 3, 1925), 1–2, quoted in David Dow Harvey, *Ford Madox Ford: 1893–1939: A Bibliography of Works and Criticism* (Princeton: Princeton University Press, 1962), 244.

10. Carlos Baker, *Ernest Hemingway: A Life Story* (New York: Scribners, 1969), 132.

11. EH, "Pamplona Letter," *transatlantic review*, 2 (Sept., 1924), 300–301.

12. Ibid.

13. Malcolm Cowley, *Exile's Return*, rev. ed. (New York: Viking, 1956), 223.

14. Robert Forrest Wilson, "Paris for Young Art," *Bookman*, 61 (June, 1925), 408

15. EH, *The Sun Also Rises* (New York: Scribners, 1926), 115.

16. Burton Rascoe, "Contemporary Reminiscences," *Arts and Decoration*, 24 (Nov., 1925), 57, 79.

17. Cleveland B. Chase, "Out of Little, Much," *Saturday Review of Literature*, 3 (Dec. 11, 1926), 420.

18. Robert Littell, "Notes on Hemingway," *New Republic*, 51 (Aug. 10, 1927), 303–304.

19. Cowley, *Exile's Return*, 225–226.

20. Richmond Barrett, "Babes in the Bois," *Harper's*, 66 (May, 1928), 724.

21. "Sad Young Men," *Time*, 8 (Nov. 1, 1926), 48.

22. "Men Without Women," *Time*, 10 (Oct. 24, 1927), 38.

23. Charles W. Ferguson, "Five Rising Stars in American Fiction," *Bookman*, 65 (May, 1927), 254.

24. Malcolm Cowley, ed., *Portable Hemingway* (New York: Viking, 1944), xii.

25. I.M.P., "Turns with a Bookworm," New York *Herald Tribune Books* (March 30, 1927), 23.

26. Baker, 66.

27. A. E. Hotchner, *Papa Hemingway* (New York: Random House, 1966), 89.

28. "Men Without Women," 38.

29. "Bull Gores 2 Yanks Acting as Toreadores," Chicago *Daily Tribune* (July 29, 1924), 1.

30. I.M.P., "Turns with a Bookworm," New York *Herald Tribune Books* (Nov. 28, 1926), 27.

31. Burton Rascoe, "Contemporary Reminiscences," *Arts and Decoration*, 24 (Nov., 1925), 57.

32. Ibid. (March, 1927), 56, 86.

33. "A Bookman's Notes," *Bookman*, 66 (Feb., 1928), 666.

34. Richard Hofstadter, *Anti-Intellectualism in American Life* (New York: Random House, 1963), 18–19.

35. Ibid., 186.

36. "In the *Bookman* Office," *Bookman*, 68 (Feb., 1929), xxiii.

37. Dorothy Parker, "Profiles: The Artist's Reward," *New Yorker*, 5 (Nov. 30, 1929), 28. The photograph referred to appeared in *Vanity Fair*, 31 (Sept., 1928), 79.

38. "The Phoenix Nest," *Saturday Review of Literature*, 9 (Dec. 24, 1932), 348.

39. "Giant of the Storytellers," *Coronet*, 25 (April, 1949), 16.

40. Parker, 28–31.

41. William Troy, "Mr. Hemingway's Opium," *Nation*, 137 (Nov. 15, 1933), 570.

42. I.M.P., "Turns with a Bookworm," New York *Herald Tribune Books* (Nov. 24, 1929), 27.

43. Callaghan, 240.

44. I.M.P., "Turns with a Bookworm," New York *Herald Tribune Books* (Dec. 8, 1929), 29.

45. Callaghan, 209–218, 240–252.

46. Ibid., 250.

CHAPTER 3

1. "Man, Woman, War," *Time*, 14 (Oct. 14, 1929), 80.

2. Carlos Baker, *Ernest Hemingway: A Life Story* (New York: Scribners, 1969), 206.

3. Lillian Ross, "Profiles: How Do You Like It Now, Gentlemen?," *New Yorker*, 26 (May 13, 1950), reprinted as *Portrait of Hemingway* (New York: Avon, 1965), 65, 91.

4. Dorothy Parker, "Profiles: The Artist's Reward," *New Yorker*, 5 (Nov. 30, 1929), 30.

5. Baker, 206.

6. Virginia Woolf, "An Essay in Criticism," New York *Herald Tribune Books* (Oct. 9, 1927), 1, 8.

7. Baker, 187.

8. EH, "Valentine," *Little Review*, 13 (May, 1929), 42, reprinted in Robert F. Weeks, ed., *Hemingway: A Collection of Critical Essays* (Englewood Cliffs, N.J.: Prentice-Hall, 1962), 4.

9. EH, *DIA*, 139.

10. Norman Mailer, *Advertisements for Myself* (New York: Putnam, 1966), 19.

11. Wyndham Lewis, "The Dumb Ox: A Study of Ernest Hemingway," *American Review*, 3 (June, 1934), 290.

12. Quoted in Baker, 120.

13. Leicester Hemingway, *My Brother, Ernest Hemingway* (New York: Fawcett, 1963), 117.

14. John Peale Bishop, "Homage to Hemingway," *New Republic*, 89 (Nov. 11, 1936), 40.

CHAPTER 4

1. EH, *Death in the Afternoon* (New York: Scribners, 1932), 517. Subsequent references will be abbreviated *DIA* and placed in parentheses in the text.
2. Lincoln Kirstein, "The Canon of Death," *Hound and Horn*, 6 (January–March, 1933), reprinted in John K.M. McCaffery, ed., *Ernest Hemingway: The Man and His Work* (Cleveland and New York: World, 1950), 60.
3. E. L. Duffus, "Hemingway Now Writes of Bullfighting as an Art," *New York Times Book Review* (Sept. 25, 1932), 5.
4. George Plimpton [Interview with Hemingway], in *Writers at Work: The Paris Review Interviews, Second Series* (New York: Viking, 1963), 239.
5. Phillip Young, *Ernest Hemingway: A Reconsideration* (University Park, Pa.: Pennsylvania State University Press, 1966), 96.
6. "The Hemingways on Land and Sea," *Vanity Fair*, 42 (July, 1934), 25.
7. Carlos Baker, *Ernest Hemingway: A Life Story* (New York: Scribners, 1969), 211.
8. EH [Letter to Robert M. Coates], "Books," *New Yorker*, 8 (Nov. 5, 1932), 74.
9. [Cover], *Saturday Evening Post*, 239 (March 12, 1966).

CHAPTER 5

1. Arnold Gingrich, *Nothing But People* (New York: Crown, 1971), 80–81.
2. Leicester Hemingway, *My Brother, Ernest Hemingway* (New York: Fawcett, 1963), 119.
3. Gingrich, 106–109, 115.
4. Quoted in ibid., 102.
5. Carlos Baker, *Ernest Hemingway: A Life Story* (New York: Scribners, 1969), 244.
6. EH, "Marlin off the Morro: A Cuban Letter," *Esquire*, 1 (Autumn, 1933), 8–9.
7. EH, "Remembering Shooting-Flying: A Key West Letter," *Esquire*, 3 (Feb., 1935), 21, 152.
8. John W. Aldridge, *After the Lost Generation* (New York: Noonday, 1958), 24–25.
9. C. Wright Mills, *White Collar* (New York: Oxford University Press, 1956), 237–238.
10. "Getting Away From It All," *Vogue*, 81 (May 15, 1933), 32.
11. O. O. McIntyre, [Column], *Philadelphia Record* (June 2, 1936).
12. "The Hemingways on Land and Sea," *Vanity Fair*, 42 (July, 1934), 25.
13. "Transition," *Newsweek*, 3 (April 14, 1934), 34.
14. Sutherland Danlinger, [Column], New York *World-Telegram* (Sept. 25, 1935), 3; Earl Spaulding, [Column], New York *World-Telegram* (Sept. 25, 1935), 2. Both quoted in Sister Mary Richard Grimes, "Hemingway: The Years with *Esquire*," Ph.D. dissertation, Ohio State University, 1965.
15. EH, "a.d. Southern Style: A Key West Letter," *Esquire*, 3 (May, 1935), 25, 156.
16. EH, "On the Blue Water: A Gulf Stream Letter," *Esquire*, 5 (April, 1936), 31, 185.
17. See, for example, EH, "Marlin off the Morro," 8–9, or EH, "Genio after Josie: A Havana Letter," *Esquire*, 2 (Oct., 1934), 21–22.
18. EH, "Genio after Josie," 21–22.

19. EH, "The President Vanquishes: A Bimini Letter," *Esquire*, 3 (July, 1935), 23, 167.

20. EH, "Marlin off the Morro," 8–9.

21. "Prowess in Action," *Time*, 22 (July 24, 1933), 24.

22. "New American and Atlantic Record," *Outdoor Life*, 76 (Oct., 1935), 87.

23. S. Kip Farrington, Jr., "The Greatest Fishing Year—A Review," *Yachting*, 59 (Feb., 1936), 74–75, 160.

24. "Behind the Scenes," *Scribner's*, 97 (May, 1935), 319; "Behind the Scenes," *Scribner's*, 98 (Aug., 1935), 127.

25. Carolyn Marx, "Book Marks for Today," New York *World-Telegram* (June 24, 1936), 33, quoted in Grimes, 331–332.

26. S. Kip Farrington, Jr., "The Big Three," *Pleasure*, 1 (Winter, 1937), 34–35.

27. S. Kip Farrington, Jr., *Atlantic Game Fishing* (New York: Kennedy Brothers, 1937), 4.

28. [Cartoon], *Esquire*, 6 (Sept., 1936), 46.

29. EH, "a.d. in Africa: A Tanganyika Letter," *Esquire*, 1 (April, 1934), 19, 146.

30. EH, "Shootism versus Sport: The Second Tanganyika Letter," *Esquire*, 2 (June, 1934), 19, 150.

31. Cleveland Amory, ed., *International Celebrity Register: U.S. Edition* (New York: Harper and Row, 1959), 338.

32. [Cover], *Saturday Review of Literature*, 12 (Oct. 26, 1935). This was the first of many magazine covers which featured his likeness.

33. Phillip Young, *Ernest Hemingway: A Reconsideration* (University Park, Pa.: Pennsylvania State University Press, 1966), 148–149.

34. John Peale Bishop, "Homage to Hemingway," *New Republic*, 89 (Nov. 11, 1936), 40.

35. Edmund Wilson, "Hemingway: Gauge of Morale," in *The Wound and the Bow* (New York: Oxford University Press, 1947), 226. This essay originally appeared in the *Atlantic*, 164 (July, 1939), 36–46.

36. Marshall Maslin, "All of Us," Philadelphia *Sunday News* (June 10, 1934).

37. EH, "Notes on Dangerous Game: The Third Tanganyika Letter," *Esquire*, 2 (July, 1934), 94.

38. Ibid., 19, 94.

39. Ibid., 19.

40. EH, "On Being Shot Again: A Gulf Stream Letter," *Esquire*, 3 (June, 1935), 156–157.

41. EH, "Million Dollar Fright: A New York Letter," *Esquire*, 4 (Dec., 1935), 35, 190B.

42. EH, "Notes on Life and Letters; Or a Manuscript Found in a Bottle," *Esquire*, 3 (Jan., 1935), 21, 159.

43. EH, "Genio after Josie," 22.

44. "Virile," Philadelphia *Record* (June 10, 1934).

45. Harry Sylvester, "Ernest Hemingway: A Note," *Commonweal*, 25 (Oct. 30, 1936), 12.

46. For EH's account of this scrap, see his letter to Sara Murphy in Carlos Baker, ed., *Ernest Hemingway: Selected Letters* (New York: Scribners, 1981), 438–440.

47. "People," *Time*, 31 (March 21, 1938), 57.

48. Leicester Hemingway, 165–168.

49. "People," *Time*, 33 (Jan. 23, 1939), 31.

50. "Hemingway by K.O. in Big Night Club Card," New York *Sunday Mirror* (Jan. 15, 1939), 3.

51. "Vanity Fair's Own Paper Dolls—No. 5," *Vanity Fair*, 42 (March, 1934), 29.

52. Mitchell Siporin, "Mr. Hemingway Contemplates the Kill," *Ringmaster*, 1 (May, 1936), 10.

53. "Prominent Literati," *American Spectator*, 3 (July, 1935), 1.

54. William Steig, [Cartoon], *Vanity Fair*, 40 (Aug., 1933), 26.

55. S[eward] C[ollins], "Bull Fights and Politics," *Bookman*, 75 (Oct., 1932), 622.

56. Max Eastman, "Bull in the Afternoon," *New Republic*, 75 (June 7, 1933), 96.

57. Max Eastman, *Great Companions* (New York: Farrar, Straus & Cudahy, 1959), 52–58.

58. Baker, 242.

59. Max Eastman, "Red Blood and Hemingway," *New Republic*, 75 (June 28, 1933), 184.

60. [Gertrude Stein], *The Autobiography of Alice B. Toklas* (New York: Harcourt Brace, 1933), 261, 270–271.

61. Ibid., 267–268.

62. Ibid., 265–266.

63. EH, "a.d. in Africa," 19.

64. EH, "The Farm," *Cahiers d'Art*, 9 (1934), 28.

65. Leicester Hemingway, 154.

66. EH, "Introduction" to Morrill Cody, ed., *This Must Be the Place* (London: Herbert Joseph, 1934), 11–13.

67. EH, *For Whom the Bell Tolls* (New York: Scribners, 1940), 289.

68. "All Stories End," *Time*, 30 (Oct. 18, 1937), 84.

69. "Prowess in Action," *Time*, 22 (July 24, 1933), 24.

70. EH, *DIA*, 278.

71. Clifton Fadiman, "Ernest Hemingway: An American Byron," *Nation*, 136 (Jan. 18, 1933), 63–64.

72. Malcolm Cowley, "A Farewell to Spain," *New Republic*, 73 (Nov. 30, 1932), 77.

73. Granville Hicks, "Bulls and Bottles," *Nation*, 135 (Nov. 9, 1932), 461.

74. Baker, 246–247.

75. EH, "Defense of Dirty Words: A Cuban Letter," *Esquire*, 2 (Sept., 1934), 19.

76. Heywood Broun, [Column], Philadelphia *Record* (Aug. 20, 1934).

77. EH, "Old Newsman Writes: A Letter from Cuba," *Esquire*, 2 (Dec., 1934), 25–26.

78. Heywood Broun, "It Seems to Me," New York *World-Telegram* (Nov. 21, 1934), 21.

79. Baker, 280.

80. Robert Forsythe, "In This Corner, Mr. Hemingway," *New Masses*, 13 (Nov. 27, 1934), 26.

81. EH, "a.d. Southern Style: A Key West Letter," 25, 156.

82. EH, "Notes on the Next War: A Serious Topical Letter," *Esquire*, 4 (Sept., 1935), 19, 156.

83. EH, "Wings Always over Africa," *Esquire*, 5 (Jan., 1936), 31, 174–175.

84. EH, "Defense of Dirty Words," 19.

85. "Ole! Ole!," *Time*, 20 (Sept. 26, 1932), 47.

86. Gilbert Seldes, "The Prizefighter and the Bull," *Esquire*, 2 (Nov., 1934), 52.

87. EH, "Notes on Life and Letters," 21.

88. EH, "Monologue to the Maestro: A High Seas Letter," *Esquire*, 4 (Oct., 1935), 21, 174A.

89. Wilson, 226.

90. John V. A. Weaver, "'Touch Hemingway,'" *Ringmaster*, 1 (May, 1936), 11–12, 51.

91. Bishop, 39–40.

92. [Arnold Gingrich], "Reviving the Practice of Salutes to the Living," *Esquire*, 7 (Feb., 1937), 5, 28.

93. Dwight Macdonald, *Against the American Grain* (New York: Random House, 1965), 20.

94. Norman Podhoretz, *Making It* (New York: Bantam, 1969), 39–40.

95. EH, "On the Blue Water," 31.

96. EH, "Remembering Shooting-Flying," 21.

97. Edwin H. Cady, "The Strenuous Life as a Theme in American Cultural History," in Ray Browne, ed., *New Voices in American Studies* (West Lafayette, Ind.: Purdue University Studies, 1966), 59–66.

CHAPTER 6

1. EH, *Green Hills of Africa* (New York: Scribners, 1935), vii. Subsequent references will be abbreviated *GHOA* and placed in parentheses in the text.

2. Carlos Baker, *Ernest Hemingway: A Life Story* (New York: Scribners, 1969), 268.

3. Edmund Wilson, "Letter to the Russians about Hemingway," *New Republic*, 85 (Dec. 11, 1935), 135.

4. Baker, 275.

5. O. O. McIntyre, [Column], Philadelphia *Record* (June 2, 1936).

CHAPTER 7

1. EH, "Who Murdered the Vets?," *New Masses*, 16 (Sept. 17, 1935), 9.

2. Granville Hicks, "Small Game Hunting," *New Masses*, 17 (Nov. 19, 1935), 23.

3. John Chamberlain, "Books of the *Times*," New York *Times* (Oct. 25, 1935), 19; Edmund Wilson, "Letter to the Russians about Hemingway," *New Republic*, 85 (Dec. 11, 1935), 135; T. S. Matthews, "A Hemingway You'll Never Be," *New Republic*, 85 (Nov. 27, 1935), 80; Bernard DeVoto, "Hemingway in the Valley," *Saturday Review of Literature*, 12 (Oct. 26, 1935), 5; Clifton Fadiman, "Books," *New Yorker*, 11 (Nov. 2, 1935), 98.

4. "Hunter's Credo," *Time*, 26 (Nov. 4, 1935), 81.

5. Andrew Kopkind, "Serving Time," *New York Review of Books* (Sept. 12, 1968), 25 fn.

6. Wilson, "Letter to the Russians about Hemingway," 135.

7. Carlos Baker, *Ernest Hemingway: A Life Story* (New York: Scribners, 1969), 296.

8. "Transition," *Newsweek*, 9 (March 6, 1937), 38.

9. "Writer to Aid Loyalists," New York *Times* (Jan. 12, 1937), 4.

10. "Transition," *Newsweek*, 9 (March 6, 1937), 38.

11. Martha Foley, "Emigres All," *Story*, 10 (May, 1937), 96–97.

12. Ira Wolfert, Cable to NANA (Feb. 28, 1937), quoted in Richard Freedman, "Hemingway's Civil War Dispatches," *Texas Studies in Language and Literature*, 1 (Summer, 1959), 172–173.

13. "Transition," *Newsweek*, 9 (March 6, 1937), 38.

14. Robert F. Lucid, "Introduction" to *Norman Mailer: The Man and His Work* (Boston: Little Brown, 1971), 5.

15. Orrin E. Klapp, *Heroes, Villains, and Fools* (Englewood Cliffs, N.J.: Prentice-Hall, 1962), 27–28.

16. Edmund Wilson, "Hemingway and the Wars," *Nation*, 147 (Dec. 10, 1938), 630.

17. EH, "A New Kind of War," NANA dispatch (March 4, 1937), reprinted in William White, ed., *By-Line: EH* (New York: Scribners, 1967), 263.

18. EH, "A Brush with Death," NANA dispatch (Sept. 30, 1937), reprinted in ibid., 275.

19. EH, "Lerida," NANA dispatch (April 29, 1938), reprinted in *New Republic*, 95 (June 8, 1938), 125.

20. EH, "Barcelona," NANA dispatch (April 5, 1938), reprinted in *New Republic*, 94 (April 27, 1938), 350.

21. EH, "Madrid," NANA dispatch (April 10, 1937), reprinted in *New Republic*, 90 (May 5, 1937), 378–379.

22. Claude Bowers, *My Mission to Spain* (New York: Simon and Schuster, 1954), 272–273.

23. Herbert Matthews, *The Education of a Correspondent* (New York: Harcourt Brace, 1946), 95–106.

24. Vincent Sheean, *Not Peace But a Sword* (New York: Doubleday, Doran, 1939), 74–75, 82, 337.

25. Joseph North, "Hemingway: The Man and Writer," *American Dialogue*, 1 (Oct.–Nov., 1964), 7.

26. EH, "On the Guadalajara Front," NANA dispatch (March 3, 1937), reprinted in *New Republic*, 90 (May 5, 1937), 15.

27. "Chewed Up," *Time*, 29 (April 5, 1937), 22; "Abroad: Spain," *Newsweek*, 9 (April 3, 1937), 15.

28. Baker, 324.

29. "Madrid," NANA dispatch (May 12, 1938), reprinted in *New Republic*, 95 (June 8, 1938), 126.

30. Arnold Gingrich, *Nothing But People* (New York: Crown, 1971), 133.

31. Ibid., 145.

32. EH, "United We Fall Upon *Ken*," *Ken*, 1 (June 2, 1938), 38.

33. EH, "A Call for Greatness," *Ken*, 2 (Aug. 25, 1938), 23.

34. EH, "Treachery in Aragon," *Ken*, 1 (June 30, 1938), 26.

35. EH, "Good Generals Hug the Line," *Ken*, 2 (Aug. 25, 1938), 28.

36. EH, "Fresh Air on an Inside Story," *Ken*, 2 (Sept. 22, 1938), 28.

37. EH, "Dying, Well or Badly," *Ken*, 1 (April 21, 1938), 68.

38. EH, "Three Prefaces," to Luis Quintanilla, *All the Brave* (New York: Modern Age, 1939), 7–11.

39. "Hemingway Sees Defeat of Franco," New York *Times* (May 19, 1937), 10.

40. "Creators' Congress," *Time*, 29 (June 21, 1937), 80.

41. EH, "Fascism Is a Lie," *New Masses*, 33 (June 22, 1937), 4.

42. EH, "Who Murdered the Vets?," 10.

43. Baker, 314.

44. Louis Sobol, "Broadway," New York *Evening Journal* (July 9, 1937).

45. "The War in Spain Makes a Movie with Captions by Ernest Hemingway," *Life*, 3 (July 12, 1937), 20–23.

46. Jasper Wood, "Introduction" to EH, *The Spanish Earth* (Cleveland: J. B. Savage, 1938), 13.

47. Ibid., 9–15.

48. Baker, 317.

49. "Pair of Authors Go to Mat over Hair on Chest," New York *Herald Tribune* (Aug. 14, 1937), 15.

50. Max Eastman, *Great Companions* (New York: Farrar, Straus & Cudahy, 1959), 65.

51. "Hemingway Slaps Eastman in the Face," New York *Times* (Aug. 14, 1937), 15.

52. "Pair of Authors Go to Mat over Hair on Chest," 15.

53. "Hemingway Slaps Eastman in the Face," 15.

54. "Hemingway Off to Spain," New York *Times* (Aug. 16, 1937), 21.

55. "He-Man Hemingway Vows to Spank Max," Philadelphia *Inquirer* (Aug. 15, 1937).

56. Walter Winchell, [Column], Philadelphia *Record* (Aug. 17, 1937); Heywood Broun, [Column], Philadelphia *Record* (Aug. 17, 1937); O. O. McIntyre, [Column], Philadelphia *Record* (Sept. 7, 1937); Damon Runyon, [Column], Philadelphia *Inquirer* (Aug. 22, 1937); "Literary Slug Fests," New York *Times* (Aug. 17, 1937), 18; "People," *Time*, 30 (Aug. 23, 1937), 66; "Transition," *Newsweek*, 10 (Aug. 21, 1937), 4.

57. John O'Hara, "Hemingway's Scars," *Time*, 30 (Sept. 6, 1937), 8.

58. "The Talk of the Town," *New Yorker*, 13 (Aug. 28, 1937), 7.

59. [Cartoon], *New Yorker*, 13 (Sept. 4, 1937), 10.

60. Sinclair Lewis, "Glorious Dirt," *Newsweek*, 10 (Oct. 18, 1937), 34; Heywood Broun, [Column], Philadelphia *Record* (Oct. 18, 1937); "Books," *Boulevardier*, no vol. (Nov., 1937), 47; Mary Colum, "Life and Literature," *Forum*, 98 (Dec., 1937), 310.

61. Elliott Paul, "Hemingway and the Critics," *Saturday Review of Literature*, 17 (Nov. 6, 1937), 3.

62. "'All Stories End . . . ,'" *Time*, 30 (Oct. 18, 1937), 79–85.

63. Alfred Kazin, "Hemingway's First Book on His Own People," New York *Herald Tribune* (Oct. 17, 1937), 3.

64. Malcolm Cowley, "Hemingway: Work in Progress," *New Republic*, 92 (Oct. 20, 1937), 305.

65. Edmund Wilson, "Hemingway: Gauge of Morale," in *The Wound and the Bow* (New York: Oxford University Press, 1947), 187.

66. Edward Berry Burgum, [Review of *The Fifth Column and the First Forty-Nine Stories*], *New Masses*, 29 (Nov. 22, 1938), 21–24.

67. "Hemingway Writes Play in Shell-Shocked Madrid," New York *Times* (Nov. 15, 1937), 2.

68. EH, "Preface" to *The Fifth Column and the First Forty-Nine Stories* (New York: Scribners, 1938), v.

69. "Hemingway Play 'The Fifth Column' Brings Madrid Bombing to Broadway," *Life*, 8 (March 25, 1940), 100–101.

70. Lionel Trilling, "Hemingway and His Critics," *Partisan Review*, 6 (Winter, 1939), 52–53.

71. Edmund Wilson, "Ernest Hemingway: Bourdon Gauge of Morale," *Atlantic*, 164 (July, 1939), 36–46.

72. Edmund Wilson, "Books," *New Yorker*, 39 (Feb. 23, 1963), 146–147.

73. Archibald MacLeish, "Post-war Writers and Pre-war Readers," *New Republic*, 102 (June 10, 1940), 789.

74. EH, [Letter], *Life*, 8 (June 24, 1940), 8.

CHAPTER 8

1. Edmund Wilson, "Return of Ernest Hemingway," *New Republic*, 103 (Oct. 28, 1940), 591–592.

2. Louella Parsons, [Column], Philadelphia *Inquirer* (Oct. 15, 1940), 24.

3. "Novel Brings $110,000," New York *Times* (Oct. 25, 1940), 25.

4. Louella Parsons, [Column], New York *Journal-American* (Nov. 13, 1940), 15; Philadelphia *Inquirer* (Nov. 20, 1940), 26; Philadelphia *Inquirer* (Jan. 31, 1941), 19.

5. "People," *Time*, 38 (July 14, 1941), 48.

6. "Ernest Hemingway Meets Ingrid Bergman," *Life*, 10 (Feb. 24, 1941), 48, 51.

7. "*Life* Goes Hunting at Sun Valley with the Gary Coopers and the Ernest Hemingways," *Life*, 11 (Nov. 24, 1941), 116–119.

8. "The Hemingways in Sun Valley: The Novelist Takes a Wife," *Life*, 10 (Jan. 6, 1941), 49.

9. "*Life* Documents His New Novel with War Shots," ibid., 52–57.

10. "*Look* Examines Ernest Hemingway," *Look*, 5 (April 8, 1941), 18, 20–21.

11. "Ernest Hemingway Is Divorced," New York *Times* (Nov. 5, 1940), 13; "Hemingway Weds Magazine Writer," New York *Times* (Nov. 22, 1940), 25; "Hemingways on Way Here," New York *Times* (Nov. 23, 1940), 15; "Transition," *Newsweek*, 16 (Nov. 18, 1940), 8; "Transition," *Newsweek*, 16 (Dec. 2, 1940), 6.

12. Walter Winchell, [Column], Philadelphia *Record* (Dec. 16, 1940).

13. [Photograph], *Harper's Bazaar*, 75 (Jan., 1941), 50–51.

14. Ruth Reynolds, "Love Collaborates with Hemingway," New York *Mirror* (Dec. 1, 1940).

15. "*Life* Goes Hunting . . .," 118.

16. "Talk of the Town," *New Yorker*, 16 (Dec. 28, 1940), 10.

17. "*Look* Examines Ernest Hemingway," 21.

18. "Ernest Hemingway Interviewed by Ralph Ingersoll," *PM* (June 9, 1941), 6–10.

19. "War Effort," *Time*, 40 (Sept. 28, 1942), 41.

20. Elsa Maxwell, "Party Line," New York *Post* (July 14, 1943).

21. Malcolm Cowley, "A Portrait of Mr. Papa," *Life*, 26 (Jan. 10, 1949), 87.

22. Earl Wilson, "This Is Ernest Hemingway—in Beard and Bare Feet," New York *Post* (May 2, 1944), 17.

23. Leonard Lyons, "The Lyons Den," New York *Post* (May 2, 1944), 18.

24. "People," *Time*, 43 (May 15, 1944), 32.

25. [Photograph], *PM* (May 21, 1944), 7.

26. "Transition," *Newsweek*, 22 (May 29, 1944), 6, 8.

27. Orrin Klapp, *Symbolic Leaders: Public Dreams and Public Men* (Chicago: Aldine, 1964), 216–217.

28. "People," *Life*, 16 (June 26, 1944), 37.

29. EH, "Voyage to Victory," *Collier's*, 114 (July 22, 1944), 13.

30. Ibid., 56.

31. Ibid., 57.

32. William Van Dusen, "Hemingway's Longest Day," *True*, 44 (Feb., 1963), 55, 62.

33. Leicester Hemingway, *My Brother, Ernest Hemingway* (New York: Fawcett, 1963), 219–220.

34. "Hemingway 'Captures Six,'" New York *Times* (Aug. 4, 1944), 3.

35. Harry T. Gorrell, "A Close Hemingway Call," Kansas City *Star* (Aug. 6, 1944), 6.

36. EH, "Battle for Paris," *Collier's*, 114 (Sept. 30, 1944), 84.

37. Ibid., 86.

38. EH, "How We Came to Paris," *Collier's*, 114 (Oct. 7, 1944), 67.

39. Quoted in S.L.A. Marshall, "How Papa Liberated Paris," *American Heritage*, 13 (April, 1962), 99.

40. Robert Capa, *Slightly Out of Focus* (New York: Henry Holt, 1947), 168–171. Malcolm Cowley, among others, told substantially the same story in "A Portrait of Mr. Papa," 88–89.

41. Marshall, 99–101.

42. John Groth, *Studio Europe* (New York: Vanguard, 1945), 204, 214.

43. Cowley, 88.

44. Groth, 205–209, 214.

45. EH, "The GI and the General," *Collier's*, 114 (Nov. 4, 1944), 46.

46. "War and Mr. Hemingway," New York *Times Book Review* (April 8, 1945), 23.

47. EH, "War in the Siegfried Line," *Collier's*, 114 (Nov. 18, 1944), 73.

CHAPTER 9

1. "People," *Time*, 47 (March 18, 1946), 46; 46 (Sept. 3, 1945), 49; 48 (Dec. 16, 1946), 45; 51 (March 8, 1948), 39; (Feb. 9, 1948), 40; 47 (April 15, 1946), 45.

2. Mary Harrington, "They Call Him Papa," New York *Post Weekend Magazine* (Dec. 28, 1946), 3.

3. "Bell Tolls for Three of Ernest's Wives," New York *Sunday Mirror Magazine* (Oct. 28, 1945), 20.

4. John A. Stone, "Hemingway Sets the Style," *American Weekly* (Sept. 8, 1946), 6–7.

5. Carlos Baker, *Ernest Hemingway: A Life Story* (New York: Scribners, 1969), 455.

6. Ibid., 464, 487, 491, 497.

7. EH, "The Great Blue River," *Holiday*, 6 (July, 1949), 60–62.

8. "The Hemingways in Cuba," *Harper's Bazaar*, 84 (March 1, 1950), 172–173.

9. "On the Scene in Cuba," *Vogue*, 116 (Nov. 15, 1950), 104–105.

10. "Roaring Charm," *Flair*, 1 (Feb., 1950), 110–111.

11. Earl Wilson, "It Happened Last Night," New York *Post* (Jan. 3, 1947), 44; New York *Post* (Feb. 26, 1948), 30; Philadelphia *Daily News* (Sept. 1, 1952), 22.

12. Leonard Lyons, "The Lyons Den," New York *Post* (Jan. 7, 1952), 22.

13. Mary Hemingway, "Life with Papa," *Flair*, 2 (Jan., 1951), 29, 116–117.

14. [Photograph], *Holiday*, 5 (Feb., 1949), 43; Leigh White, "Havana," *Saturday Evening Post*, 253 (March 31, 1951), 24.

15. EH, "The Shot," *True*, 28 (April, 1951), 25.

16. Ibid., 26–28.

17. "People," *Time*, 54 (Oct. 24, 1949), 44–45.

18. David Dempsey, "In and Out of Books," New York *Times Book Review* (Oct. 1, 1950), 8.

19. Maxwell Geismar, "To Have and To Have and To Have," *Saturday Review of Literature*, 33 (Sept. 9, 1950), 18–19; Chandler Brossard, "Everybody's Old Man," *New American Mercury*, 71 (Dec., 1950), 698–701.

20. Norman Cousins, "Hemingway and Steinbeck," *Saturday Review of Literature*, 33 (Oct. 28, 1950), 26.

21. Alfred Kazin, "The Indignant Flesh," *New Yorker*, 26 (Sept. 9, 1950), 117.

22. Isaac Rosenfeld, "A Farewell to Hemingway," *Kenyon Review*, 13 (Winter, 1951), 147–148, 154–155.

23. Ben Ray Redman, "The Champ and the Referees," *Saturday Review of Literature*, 33 (Oct. 28, 1950), 38.

24. John O'Hara, "The Author's Name is Hemingway," New York *Times Book Review* (Sept. 10, 1950), 1, 31.

25. "O'Hara on Hemingway," New York *Times Book Review* (Oct. 1, 1950), 37.

26. "Among the News That's Fit to Print," *Commonweal*, 52 (Sept. 22, 1950), 573–574.

27. "People," *Time*, 56 (Sept. 18, 1950), 48.

28. ". . . And New Champion," *Collier's*, 126 (Nov. 18, 1950), 86.

29. Evelyn Waugh, "The Case of Mr. Hemingway," *Commonweal*, 52 (Nov. 3, 1950), 97–98.

30. "People," *Time*, 56 (Oct. 30, 1950), 44.

31. William Faulkner, [Letter], *Time*, 56 (Nov. 13, 1950), 6.

32. EH, "'Hemingway Is Bitter about Nobody—But His Colonel Is,'" *Time*, 56 (Sept. 11, 1950), 110.

33. "For Your Information," *Newsweek*, 36 (Sept. 11, 1950), 13.

34. "The New Hemingway," *Newsweek*, 36 (Sept. 11, 1950), 94–95.

35. Harvey Breit, "Talk with Mr. Hemingway," New York *Times Book Review* (Sept. 17, 1950), 14.

36. "People," *Time*, 56 (Sept. 25, 1950), 42–43.

37. "Is Papa a Flopa?," *Night and Day*, 3 (March, 1951), 18–19.

38. Malcolm Cowley, "A Portrait of Mr. Papa," *Life*, 26 (Jan. 10, 1949), 86–101.

39. Baker, 470.

40. Denis Brian, "The Importance of Knowing Ernest," *Esquire*, 77 (Feb., 1972), 100.

41. Malcolm Cowley, *The Faulkner-Cowley File* (New York: Viking, 1966), 122, 125.

42. Cowley, "A Portrait of Mr. Papa," 87–89.

43. James Steel Smith, "*Life* Looks at Literature," *American Scholar*, 27 (Winter, 1957–1958), 36–37.

44. Cowley, *The Faulkner-Cowley File*, 121–122.

45. Brian, 100.

46. Lillian Ross, "Preface," *Portrait of Hemingway* (New York: Avon, 1965), 16.

47. Lillian Ross, "How Do You Like It Now, Gentlemen?," *New Yorker*, 25 (May 13, 1950), 36.

48. Ibid., 42.

49. Ross, *Portrait of Hemingway*, 16.

50. Ross, "How Do You Like It Now, Gentlemen?," 62.

51. Brian, 98.

52. A. E. Hotchner, *Papa Hemingway* (New York: Random House, 1966), 107–109; Phillip Young, *Ernest Hemingway: A Reconsideration* (College Park, Pa.: Pennsylvania State University Press, 1966), 14–15. Originally published as *Ernest Hemingway* (New York and Toronto: Rinehart, 1952).

53. Dwight Macdonald, *Against the American Grain* (New York: Random House, 1965), 172.

54. Morton Dauwen Zabel, "A Good Day for Mr. Tolstoy," *Nation*, 171 (Sept. 9, 1950), 230.

55. Joseph Warren Beach, "How Do You Like It Now, Gentlemen?," *Sewanee Review*, 59 (Spring, 1951), 311.

56. Ross, "How Do You Like It Now, Gentlemen?," 62.

57. EH, [Parker Pen Endorsement], *Life*, 24 (Jan. 26, 1948), inside cover; "People," *Time*, 51 (Feb. 9, 1948), 40, 43.

58. EH, "The Circus," *Ringling Brothers and Barnum & Bailey Circus Magazine and Program* (1953), 6–7.

59. EH, [Ballantine Ale Endorsement], *Life*, 33 (Sept. 8, 1952), 56–57.

60. EH, [Pan American Airlines Endorsement], *Holiday*, 19 (Feb., 1956), 60–61.

61. EH, "A Tribute to Mamma from Papa Hemingway," *Life*, 33 (Aug. 18, 1952), 92–93.

62. Young, 171.

63. Ibid., 8–11.

64. Ibid., 18–19.

65. "Giant of the Storytellers," *Coronet*, 25 (April, 1949), 16.

66. Young, 171.

67. EH, "African Journal," *Sports Illustrated*, 35 (Dec. 20, 1971), 59.

68. Arthur Calder-Marshall, [Review of *The Old Man and the Sea*], *Listener*, 48 (Sept. 18, 1952), 447.

69. Bennett Cerf, "Trade Winds," *Saturday Review of Literature*, 35 (Oct. 18, 1952), 6.

70. "A Great American Storyteller," *Life*, 33 (Sept. 1, 1952), 20.

CHAPTER 10

1. [Cover], *Look*, 18 (Jan. 26, 1954).

2. EH, "Safari," *Look*, 18 (Jan. 26, 1954), 28–29.

3. "Hemingway Going to Africa," Kansas City *Star* (June 16, 1953), 5; Leonard Lyons, "A Day in Town with Hemingway," New York *Post* (June 26, 1953), 26; "People," *Time*, 62 (July 13, 1953), 46.

4. "Dead or Alive," *New Yorker*, 29 (Feb. 6, 1954), 21–23.

5. "He's Down, He's Up," New York *Times* (Jan. 31, 1954), IV, 2.

6. "People," *Time*, 63 (Feb. 1, 1954), 31.

7. "Summer Fun with Ogden Nash," *Life*, 37 (July 12, 1954), 77.

8. "Only His Heroes Die," *Newsweek*, 43 (Feb. 1, 1954), 19.

9. Robert Ruark, [Column], Detroit *Free Press* (Jan. 30, 1954), 20.

10. Earl Wilson, "Fans Hail Hemingway as Invulnerable Papa," New York *Post* (Jan. 25, 1954), 3.

11. Ed Sullivan, [Column], Detroit *Free Press* (Jan. 28, 1954), 34.

12. Leonard Lyons, [Column], New York *Post* (Jan. 25, 1954), 20.

13. "Newsmakers," *Newsweek*, 43 (Feb. 15, 1954), 56.

14. John Barkham, "Trade Winds," *Saturday Review*, 38 (Feb. 13, 1954), 6.

15. EH, "The Christmas Gift: Part I," *Look*, 18 (April 20, 1954), 32.

16. Ibid., 37.

17. Harvey Breit, "The Sun Also Rises in Stockholm," New York *Times Book Review* (Nov. 7, 1954), 1.

18. Kurt Bernheim, *"McCall's* Visits Ernest Hemingway," *McCall's*, 83 (May, 1956), 10.

19. "Hemingway Is the Winner of Nobel Literature Prize," New York *Times* (Oct. 29, 1954), 1, 10.

20. "Nobel's Hemingway: The Rock," *Newsweek*, 44 (Nov. 8, 1954), 88.

21. "Heroes: Life with Papa," *Time*, 44 (Nov. 8, 1954), 27.

22. "The Old Man Lands Biggest Catch," *Life*, 37 (Nov. 8, 1954), 25–29.

23. Robert Ruark, [Column], Philadelphia *Daily News* (Aug. 28, 1952).

24. "Focus on Headlines and Headliners," *Focus*, 5 (Oct., 1955), 11.

25. John Owen, "Inside Hemingway: His Strange Search for Love and Death," *See*, 15 (May, 1956), 28–30.

26. "Last One of a Kind," *Picture Week*, 2 (Feb. 28, 1956), 12.

27. Sidney Franklin, Marlene Dietrich, Leonard Lyons, et al., "Who the Hell Is Hemingway?," *True*, 36 (Feb., 1956), 14–19, 25–31, 68.

28. Doug Kennedy, "The Editor Speaking," *True*, 36 (Feb., 1956), 6.

29. "Sportsman: Ernest Hemingway," *Sports Illustrated*, 1 (Oct. 4, 1954), 9–10.

30. Reginald Wells, "A Christmas Choice of Fair and Fancy Game," *Sports Illustrated*, 3 (Dec. 26, 1955), 40–42; Clementine Paddleford, "Cooking a la Hemingway," *This Week* (May 24, 1959), 30–33.

31. "Search: The Truly Big One," *Newsweek*, 47 (May 7, 1956), 53; [photograph], New York *Times* (May 24, 1956), 11.

32. "Hemingway and the Great Outdoors," *Wisdom*, 3 (June, 1956), 14–15.

33. Milt Machlin, "Hemingway Talking," *Argosy*, no vol., (Sept., 1958), 34.

34. *Look*, 19 (Nov. 15, 1955), 38–39; *Argosy*, 338 (June, 1954), 18–19, 62–72; *Fisherman*, 9 (Jan., 1958), 34–35, 78–82; *Field and Stream*, 59 (May, 1954), 45–48, 96–105.

35. A. E. Hotchner, "All-Star Bullfight," *This Week*, (Aug. 8, 1954), 8–9.

36. Marlene Dietrich, "The Most Fascinating Man I Know," *This Week* (Feb. 13, 1955), 8–9.

37. Eugene O. Fleming, "People Who Avoided the Ruts of Life," *Cosmopolitan*, 146 (Jan., 1959), 30–31.

38. Leo Gurko, *Heroes, Highbrows and the Popular Mind* (Indianapolis and New York: Bobbs-Merrill, 1962), 35.

39. "An American Storyteller," *Time*, 64 (Dec. 13, 1954), 70–71.

40. A. E. Hotchner, "Hemingway Talks to American Youth," *This Week* (Oct. 18, 1959), 10–11, 26.

41. "From the Wisdom of Ernest Hemingway," *Wisdom*, 3 (June, 1958), 18–20.

42. EH, "Hemingway Speaks His Mind," *Playboy*, 8 (Jan., 1961), 55, 95–97.

43. EH, "A Man's Credo," *Playboy*, 10 (Jan., 1963), 120, 124, 175; EH, "Advice to a Young Man," *Playboy*, 11 (Jan., 1964), 153, 225–227.

44. "The Old Man by the Sea," *Pageant*, 10 (March, 1955), 114–119.

45. Yousuf Karsh, "The Camera's Eye: Ernest Hemingway," *Atlantic*, 200 (Dec., 1957), 102–103.

46. Earl Wilson, [Column], New York *Post* (Nov. 9, 1955), 17.

47. T. F. James, "Hemingway at Work," *Cosmopolitan*, 143 (Aug., 1957), 52.
48. "Behind the Scenes," *Look*, 20 (Sept. 4, 1956), 20.
49. EH, "A Situation Report," *Look*, 20 (Sept. 4, 1956), 24.
50. Ibid., 26–31.
51. George Plimpton, "The Art of Fiction, XXI—Ernest Hemingway," *Paris Review*, 5 (Spring, 1958). 60–89.
52. Denis Brian, "The Importance of Knowing Ernest," *Esquire*, 77 (Feb., 1972), 165.
53. [Photographs], New York *Times* (May 21, 1959), 5; (July 19, 1959), 12; New York *Times Magazine* (Sept. 13, 1959), 54; *Newsweek*, 53 (June 8, 1959), 52; John Crosby, "The Son Rises," New York *Herald Tribune* (June 8, 1959), II, 1; John Crosby, "Afternoon with the Bulls," New York *Herald Tribune* (June 10, 1959), II, 1.
54. "Spain's Greatest Matadors . . . and Their New Deadly Duel," *Newsweek*, 54 (July 27, 1959), 87; "Stirring Drama in Spain," *Life*, 47 (Sept. 7, 1959), 28; Eric Sevareid, "Mano a Mano," *Esquire*, 52 (Nov., 1959), 42–43.
55. "Newsmakers," *Newsweek*, 44 (Sept. 21, 1959), 74–75.
56. EH, "The Dangerous Summer," *Life*, 49 (Sept. 5, 1960), 77–88, 91–92, 94, 96–100, 102, 104, 106, 109; (Sept. 12, 1960), 60–66, 68, 73, 75–76, 78–80, 82; (Sept. 19, 1960), 74–76, 78, 81–82, 84, 87–88, 90, 95–96.
57. Quoted in "Two Prideful Rivals and a Prideful *Life*," *Life*, 49 (Sept. 5, 1960), 2.
58. EH, "TDS" (Sept. 5, 1960), 78.
59. EH, "TDS" (Sept. 12, 1960), 73.
60. EH, "TDS" (Sept. 5, 1960), 86, 104, 106; (Sept. 12, 1960), 66; (Sept. 19, 1960), 81.
61. EH, "TDS" (Sept. 19, 1960), 78.
62. Quoted in Carlos Baker, *Ernest Hemingway: A Life Story* (New York: Scribners, 1969), 554.

CHAPTER 11

1. "A Giant Passes," New York *Times* (July 3, 1961), 14; quoted in "France Shocked Over Hemingway," New York *Times* (July 4, 1961), 9; "Ernest Hemingway and His World," New York *Herald Tribune* (July 3, 1961), 12.
2. "Mourned by Kennedy," New York *Times* (July 3, 1961), 6; "France Shocked Over Hemingway," New York *Times* (July 4, 1961), 9; "Ordonez Kills Two Bulls in Honor of Hemingway," New York *Times* (July 4, 1961), 9.
3. "The Bell Tolls for Hemingway and an Era," Louisville *Courier-Journal* (July 4, 1961), 10.
4. Peter Finchley, "Ernest Hemingway—The Bell Tolls for Thee," *Astrology: Your Daily Horoscope*, 98 (Oct., 1961), 18–20.
5. Leonard Lyons, [Column], Philadelphia *Inquirer* (July 5, 1961), 37; [Column], New York *Post* (July 23, 1961), M–7; Earl Wilson, [Column], Philadelphia *Daily News* (July 5, 1961), 58; [Column], Detroit *Free Press* (July 10, 1961), 11; Walter Winchell, [Column], Detroit *News* (July 7, 1961), 8.
6. Robert Ruark, "One Last Safari for the Old Man," Detroit *Free Press* (July 7, 1961), 9; Robert Cantwell, "The River That Will Flow Forever," *Sports Illustrated*, 15 (July 17, 1961), 52–59.
7. Robert Ruark, "Exploding the Myth of Hemingway," Detroit *Free Press* (Aug. 7, 1961), 9; "Papa Had No Use for Sham," *Field and Stream*, 66 (Oct., 1961), 8.

8. Ruark, "Papa Had No Use for Sham," 110.

9. Joseph Alsop, "Hemingway," New York *Herald Tribune* (July 5, 1961), 18. Also see "A Cuban Visit with Hemingway," New York *Herald Tribune* (March 9, 1960), 18.

10. "The Bell Tolls," *Newsweek*, 58 (July 10, 1961), 32; "The Hero of the Code," *Time*, 78 (July 14, 1961), 87; "Hemingway: Driving Force of a Great Artist," *Life*, 51 (July 14, 1961), 60–61.

11. Norman Mailer, "The Big Bite," *Esquire*, 58 (Nov., 1962), 34.

12. Irving Howe, "Hemingway: The Conquest of Panic," *New Republic*, 145 (July 24, 1961), 19–20; Alfred Kazin, "Young Man, Old Man," *Reporter*, 29 (Dec. 19, 1963), 36; Wright Morris, "One Law for the Lion," *Partisan Review*, 28 (Sept.–Nov., 1961), 541–551.

13. Dwight Macdonald, "Ernest Hemingway," *Encounter*, 18 (Jan., 1962), 115–118, 120–121.

14. Leslie Fiedler, "An Almost Imaginary Interview," *Partisan Review*, 29 (Summer, 1962), 395–405.

15. Megan Biesele, "An Interview with Leslie Fiedler," *Generation*, 18 (n.d.), 25.

16. "Hemingway: Driving Force of a Great Artist," *Life*, 51 (July 14, 1961), 59–68.

17. Ray Bradbury, "The Kilimanjaro Machine," *Life*, 58 (Jan. 22, 1965), 71–72, 74–76, 79.

18. Ibid., 69.

19. Alfred G. Aronowitz and Peter Hamill, *Ernest Hemingway: The Life and Death of a Man* (New York: Lancer, 1961), 84–97, 114–115, 124–129, 171–173, 92, 222.

20. Milt Machlin, *The Private Hell of Hemingway* (New York: Paperback Library, 1962), 14, 31, 8.

21. Kurt Singer, *Hemingway: Life and Death of a Giant* (Los Angeles: Holloway House, 1961), 94, 156, 174, 74, 88.

22. Quoted in ibid., 22.

23. Singer, 12.

24. Leo Lania, *Hemingway: A Pictorial Biography* (New York: Viking, 1961), 17, 102, 90, 76.

25. "The Giants: Ernest Hemingway," Philadelphia *Inquirer* (April 10–27, 1968).

26. Jed Kiley, "Ernest Hemingway: A Title Fight in Ten Rounds," *Playboy*, 3 (Sept., 1956), 19, 28, 34–38; (Oct., 1956), 55–56; (Nov., 1956), 67, 70, 84–86; (Dec., 1956), 61–62, 75; 4 (March, 1957), 51–52, 60, 66; (April, 1957), 63, 66; (Aug., 1957), 45–46, 50, 52, 60, 66–67; (Sept., 1957), 65–66.

27. Leicester Hemingway, "My Brother, Ernest Hemingway," *Playboy*, 8 (Dec., 1961), 48–78; 9 (Jan., 1962), 36–48, 136–145; 9 (Feb., 1962), 26–42; 9 (March, 1962), 32–42, 106–108; Patrick Hemingway, "My Papa, Papa," *Playboy*, 15 (Dec., 1968), 197–200, 263–268; Arnold Gingrich, "Horsing Them In with Hemingway," *Playboy*, 12 (Sept., 1965), 123, 256–258; Kenneth Tynan, "Papa and the Playwright," *Playboy*, 11 (May, 1964), 97, 138–141; William F. Dolan, "Papa's Planet," *Playboy*, 15 (April, 1968), 131, 182–183.

28. Sam Boal, "'The Hemingway I Know,'" *Gent*, 2 (Dec., 1957), 7–10, 55–57; John Nugent, "Pat Hemingway Tells 'The Truth About My Old Man,'" *Climax* (Aug., 1962), 9–13, 64; Jay Robert Nash, "A Last Hurrah for Hemingway,"

Swank, 13 (Jan., 1967), 12–15, 78–80; Jerry Hopkins, "The Glass Also Rises," *Rogue* [vol., date, page unknown]; Harrison Lane, "Hemingway's Shillelagh," *Sir*, 23 (Nov., 1966), 38–39, 66–67; Robert Bell Cranston, "Portrait of Ernest Hemingway as a Young Ambulance Driver," *Gent* [vol., date, page unknown]; Denis Zaphiro as told to Worth Bingham, "Hemingway's Last Safari," *Rogue*, 8 (Feb., 1963), 18–20, 87–88; Charles Miron, "Ernest Hemingway—The Truth," *Cavalcade*, 5 (Nov.–Dec., 1966), 8–10.

29. Jack Matthews, "The Man Who Looked Like Hemingway," *Dapper* (Dec., 1967), 10–12, 64–71.

30. Robert Emmett Gina, "Life in the Afternoon," *Esquire*, 57 (Feb., 1962), 104–106; Howard Nelson, "Hemingway without Tears," *Fact*, 2 (Jan.–Feb., 1965), 44–47.

31. John Dos Passos, "Old Hem Was a Sport," *Sports Illustrated*, 20 (June 29, 1964), 58–67.

32. Gingrich, 123.

33. Arnold Gingrich, "Scott, Ernest and Whoever," *Esquire*, 66 (Dec., 1966), 186–189, 322–325.

34. Kenneth Crawford, "Good Man in a Fight," *Newsweek*, 58 (July 17, 1961), 32.

35. William Van Dusen, "Hemingway's Longest Day," *True*, 44 (Feb., 1963), 54–55; S.L.A. Marshall, "How Papa Liberated Paris," *American Heritage*, 13 (April, 1962), 5–8, 92–101.

36. Robert Manning, "Hemingway in Cuba," *Atlantic*, 216 (Aug., 1965), 101–108.

37. Geoffrey Bocca, "Hemingway's Havana—Today," *This Week* (Aug. 6, 1967), 6–7; Sally Belfrage, "The Haunted House of Ernest Hemingway," *Esquire*, 59 (Feb., 1963), 66–67.

38. Zack Taylor, "The Special Outdoor World of Ernest Hemingway," *Sports Afield*, 148 (Dec., 1962), 52–55; Chuck Meyer, "Hemingway the Boatman," *Motor Boating*, 114 (July, 1964), 21–23.

39. Mary Hemingway, "Hemingway," *Look*, 25 (Sept. 12, 1961), 19–23; "A Sentimental Safari," *Life*, 54 (April 19, 1963), 88–99; "To Africa with Love," *Harper's Bazaar*, 97 (Jan., 1964), 110; "Havana," *Saturday Review*, 48 (Jan. 2, 1965), 40–41; "To Parajiso with Papa and Pilar," *Sports Illustrated*, 23 (July 12, 1965), 62–70; "Hemingway's Spain," *Saturday Review*, 50 (March 11, 1967), 48–49; "Harry's Bar in Venice," *Holiday*, 43 (June, 1968), 62–63; see also the interviews with Mrs. Hemingway by Helen Mackel, "A Look Back, A Look Ahead," *Good Housekeeping*, 156 (Feb., 1963), 32–34, 36–37; and by Oriana Fallaci, "My Husband, Ernest Hemingway," *Look*, 30 (Sept. 6, 1966), 62–68.

40. Mary Hemingway, "Hemingway," 23.

41. Mary Hemingway, *How It Was* (New York: Knopf, 1976).

42. Patrick Hemingway, 197–200; Nugent, 9–13.

43. Leicester Hemingway, *My Brother, Ernest Hemingway* (New York: Fawcett, 1963), 53–60, 85–92.

44. Ibid., 25, 32, 99–100.

45. Marcelline H. Sanford, *At the Hemingways* (Boston: Atlantic-Little Brown, 1962), 184.

46. "Mrs. Grace Hemingway Reveals . . . My Son, Ernest Hemingway," *National Insider* (Feb. 3, 1963), 10–11; quoted in William White, "The Hemingway Industry," *American Book Collector*, 14 (Nov., 1963), 8–10.

47. A. E. Hotchner, *Papa Hemingway* (New York: Random House, 1966), 3–18.

48. Ibid., 33–34, 46.

49. Ibid., 89.

50. Phillip Young, "On Dismembering Hemingway," *Atlantic*, 218 (Aug., 1966), 45–49.

51. Hotchner, 139.

52. Ibid., 86.

53. Ibid., 6.

54. John Tebbel, "Papa's Troubled Legacy," *Saturday Review*, 49 (April 9, 1966), 30–31, 91–92.

55. [Gertrude Stein], *The Autobiography of Alice B. Toklas* (New York: Harcourt Brace, 1933), 255–256.

56. George Plimpton, [Interview with EH], in *Writers at Work: The Paris Review Interviews, Second Series* (New York: Viking, 1965), 227.

57. Quoted in Carlos Baker, *Ernest Hemingway: A Life Story* (New York: Scribners, 1969), 539.

58. Mary Hemingway, "The Making of a Book: A Chronicle and a Memoir," New York *Times Book Review* (May 10, 1964), 27.

59. EH, "Paris," *Life*, 56 (April 10, 1964), 60–93.

INDEX